Shelley and Doug,

Hope you find
one or two recipes you
like in this book.
The chimichangas sound
good to me.

Have fun!

Mother + Dad

(I started to write Grandmother) Smile!

American Regional Cooking

for 8 or 50

George Karousos
Bradley J. Ware
Theodore H. Karousos

John Wiley & Sons, Inc.
New York   Chichester   Brisbane   Toronto   Singapore

Front cover photograph: Lobster Delnero; recipe on p. 33

Acknowledgments

Our belief is that good nutrition must be of paramount concern to professional chefs in the 1990s and beyond. It has been our pleasure to work with Dorothy DeLessio, MS, RD, who researched and compiled the nutritional data included throughout this book. Her experience and insight develop this belief to a practical application in preparation of food from each of the regions of America.

We also wish to thank Ron Manville, Louise R. Phaneuf, and Sheila Thompson-Ware for their efforts in making this book a reality.

Dedication

This book is dedicated to the many chefs of the United States, who, with hard work, created the most fascinating cuisine in the world today.

Publisher: Thomas Woll
Senior Editor: Claire Thompson
Managing Editor: Frank Grazioli
Editorial Production: Julie Sullivan / Editorial Services of New England, Inc.
Color Insert Photography: Ron Manville

This text is printed on acid-free paper.

Library of Congress Cataloging-in-Publication Data:
Karousos, George, 1944–
    American regional cooking for 8 or 50 / George Karousos, Bradley
Ware, Theodore Karousos.
        p.   cm.
    Includes bibliographical references (p. 282) and index.
    ISBN 0-471-57085-0
    1. Cookery, American.   I. Ware, Bradley J. (Bradley John), 1953–.
II. Karousos, Theodore.   III. Title.   IV. Title: American
regional cooking for eight or fifty.
TX715.K187   1993
641.5973—dc20   92-27316
                                                                          CIP

Printed in the United States of America

10   9   8   7   6   5   4   3   2   1

Contents

Preface

I magine Carnegie Hall moments before a performance. Feel the energy, the excitement in the air. Picture yourself listening to the cacophonous sounds of fifty tuning instruments; the violins, the trumpets, the piano. Suddenly, people scurry to their seats as the conductor taps the podium. Within seconds, as if by magic, those disconcerting sounds have now been transformed into a beautiful symphony—a medley of instruments, with each musician contributing the perfect notes.

Now picture the United States of America, 50 states—one country, one nation. Just as each musician contributes the right note in the symphony, so, too, each state provides a perfect ingredient to create the masterpiece we have come to call American regional cooking. Through hundreds of years of refinement, countless substitutions, and an endless array of experiments, American regional cooking has slowly been transformed into its present-day form. Immigrants from all corners of the world have married their diverse culinary traditions to indigenous ingredients and Native American cooking styles.

Yet for many, American regional cooking is amorphous or even nonexistent. Masked in a shroud of mystery and concealed by a pervasive intangibility, American regional cooking has always existed in the shadows of the world's great cuisines. For years, it has eluded explanation, circumventing the probes of curiosity. Is American cuisine elusive because the United States is so large a country that defining one all-encompassing cuisine would seem impossible? Is its elusiveness a result of American history? What happened in the past to prevent American regional cooking from taking its place in the forefront of world cuisines?

Perhaps the answers lie in the fact that before World War II the status of a chef in the United States was that of a blue collar worker, unlike today, where the position of the American chef has been elevated to that of a celebrity. Moreover, 30 years ago, in order to learn to be a chef, one had to study abroad or secure an apprenticeship in a European kitchen. Now Americans can earn degrees in the culinary arts at outstanding schools in America. There are over 350 culinary schools in the United States today.

Some examples of the larger schools are Johnson and Wales University in Rhode Island, the Culinary Institute of America in New York, and the Culinary Academy of San Francisco.

The time has come for American food critics and food trade and consumer magazines to shift their attention from the classical cuisines of Europe to American regional cooking. American culinary schools need to recognize the fact that 90 percent of their graduates will work in restaurants and institutions in the United States. These chefs will work in different regions of the country and will be expected to prepare the regional cuisine and to innovate new dishes using local ingredients.

The map of the United States can be divided into seven broad culinary regions. The seven regions are New England, the mid-Atlantic states, the deep South, Texas and the Southwest, the Midwest and mountain states, Pacific Northwest and Alaska, and California and Hawaii.

Each region has contributed to making American regional cooking great, and each region has contributed its own distinctive influences.

New England: The cuisine of Connecticut, Maine, Massachusetts, New Hampshire, Rhode Island, and Vermont derives from Yankee ingenuity and reflects the basic values of our earliest settlers.

Mid-Atlantic States: English, German, and Italian influences can be found in the cuisine of New York, New Jersey, Pennsylvania, Delaware, Maryland, and West Virginia.

The Deep South: Settlers from France, England, Scotland, and Ireland, as well as Native Americans and Africans have all contributed to the cuisine of Virginia, North and South Carolina, Tennessee, Georgia, Alabama, Mississippi, Florida, and Louisiana.

Texas and the Southwest: The cuisine of Texas, New Mexico, Nevada, Utah, and Arizona was greatly influenced by Native Americans and Spaniards.

Midwest and Mountain States: The 19 states that make up this region are often referred to as the heartland or breadbasket of America, and they provide the country with quality beef and grain. Native Americans, Spaniards, and the French have all influenced this hearty, no-nonsense cuisine. These states are Idaho, Montana, Wyoming, Colorado, North Dakota, South Dakota, Nebraska, Kansas, Oklahoma, Minnesota, Iowa, Wisconsin, Illinois, Missouri, Arkansas, Michigan, Indiana, Ohio, and Kentucky.

Pacific Northwest and Alaska: The Northwest is blessed with an abundance of seafood, fertile farmlands, dairylands, and orchards. The cornerstone of the cuisine of Alaska, Oregon, and Washington is freshness.

California and Hawaii: These states are the true melting pot of the United States. Virtually every race and nationality in the U.S. contributed to the development of the healthy cuisine of this region, which reflects a casual life-style.

The hypothesis that America is the center of gastronomy will be examined in Chapter 1. The history of American regional cooking is explored in Chapter 2. Also, because good food and good wine go hand in hand, we have included a chapter on the history of wines, and there is a wine suggestion with each entrée. Considering that many Americans are extremely health conscious, a book on American cooking would not be complete without a chapter on nutrition. After trying some of the recipes included here, we believe you too will be convinced that America is the center of gastronomy.

❦ A Note on Recipe Quantities

The recipes in this book are for 8 and 50. If one were to use the multiple of 6.25 (50 ÷ 8) to multiply the ingredients for 8 to get the ingredients for 50, the results would not be as accurate as the recipes now stand. Multiplying recipes looks good on paper, but, unfortunately, does not work as well in practice, especially when expanding the recipe to yield large quantities. Many ingredients do not work well when increased in quantity, and many times waste and overbalance of ingredients occurs within the recipe. Therefore, to cater for 100 people, it would be satisfactory to multiply one of our recipes for 50 by 2 as a starting point. However, the recipe will still need to be tested and readjusted for balance of ingredients.

The metric equivalents in the recipes are usually rounded off to the nearest tenth of a measurement. For example, 1.42 liters is rounded off to 1.4 liters.

CHAPTER 1

America: The Epicenter of Gastronomy

American regional cooking has its roots in the history of the original inhabitants, the first European settlers, and the immigrants who have dotted our shores, fished our seas, and sowed our fields. Its essence is unique; the culmination of many cultures and ideas, American regional cooking is only now receiving the attention it so justly deserves.

Like refined gold in the hands of a goldsmith, American regional cooking has become brilliant and radiant. After 200 years of evolution, it stands strong and tall and is able to challenge its international competitors in the arena of the culinary olympics. Over the past 20 years, American chefs have competed with European chefs and won countless awards. Perhaps surprisingly, American food prepared by American chefs has won more gold medals than any European cuisine. It is time to revere American regional cooking with the same enthusiasm so often held for European cuisine. Why should pilgrimages be made to Europe in search of the latest food trends when there is exceptional cuisine right here in the United States? The time has come to spotlight American cooking traditions, styles, and innovations.

So, just as we are proud of our nation, we should also be proud of our cuisine. American chefs should be commended for their freedom of expression, imagination and creativity, which has propelled their cooking into the forefront of the culinary world. It is this ingenuity that has shifted the center of gastronomy from Europe to the United States.

Although many of today's world-renowned chefs may disagree, the United States has become the center of gastronomy. Many historians and social scientists believe food and culture are inseparable. Throughout history, the center of culture has also been the center of gastronomy. Athens was first, followed by Rome. With the fall of the Roman Empire, the center shifted to the capital of the Byzantine empire. During the Renaissance, Constantinople gave way to Florence as the center of gastronomy. In time, Italy was replaced by France. Today, however, the United States has surpassed Europe and is the true center of gastronomy.

Many people believe that American regional cooking is a conglomerate of various ethnic cuisines. However, if cooking is an art, then American regional cooking can be described as a collage. America is a synthesis of nationalities and backgrounds, and each has participated in the development of the nation's cuisine. This same mosaic also existed in France. Centuries ago, the French adopted the world's best cooking styles—Algerienne from Algiers; Anglaise from England; Ardennoise from Belgium and Luxembourg; Catalano from Spain; Florentine from Italy; Gauloise from Germany, Switzerland, and Holland; Greque from Greece; Hongroise from Hungary; Indienne from India; Macedoine from Macedonia; Porto from Portugal; Turque from Turkey; Viennoise from Austria; and Zingara from the gypsies of the Byzantine empire—and refined them into what is known today as French cuisine.

It may be surprising to discover that foods assumed to have been created by the French actually are variations of ancient Greek dishes. Bouillabaisse is one example. In 600 BC, when the Phoenician Greeks founded Marseilles and Nice, they brought along their recipe for fish stew, called *kaccavia*. The French refined the recipe and changed its name. They also renovated Greek and Roman recipes to create pâté. However, the French did not stop there. They adopted the Greek approach to life, which philosophers would later term "gastronomy."

The ancient Greeks made countless cultural contributions to the world. Inadvertently they also provided a philosophical basis for good eating. Through the centuries, Greek cookery has lost its identity, but no one can deny its influence. Athenaeus wrote about the original seven sages of the kitchen in *The Deipnosophis*. Each sage established recipes and techniques still used today. Orion invented white sauce, brown sauce originated with Lampriades, Nereus made eel fit for the gods, Agres taught how to filet fish, Atlantus made the perfect cordial, Euthymus taught how to cook vegetables, and Amphicles revealed that culinary merit does not lie in extravagant trimmings. Gastronomy, the philosophical basis for good eating, was a way of life for these men.

What does gastronomy mean today? Is it where all the good chefs live or an area with good restaurants? Or is gastronomy something else? Brillat-Savarin provides an answer. In *The Physiology of Taste*, he says gastronomy is all that relates to nourishment. He believed that gastronomy rules our whole lives. Gastronomy is not a cluster of 20 good restaurants, but rather is a way of life, which can be seen in America today.

Interestingly, a Greek philosopher named Archestratus has influenced American chefs. Archestratus is known as the father of gastronomy and author of the world's first cookbook. He lived around 350 BC and was so curious about cooking that he travelled land and sea in search of the best foods and cooking methods. Archestratus stressed the use of fresh, seasonal ingredients and light sauces to enhance natural flavors. His methods included slow cooking, simmering, and testing. Archestratus believed that nature provided all the spices, herbs, and seasonings needed to create exceptional dishes. His ideas have influenced the cuisines of the world.

Today, Archestratus's influences can be found in American regional cooking. Most chefs, however, are unaware that they are disciples of Archestratus. When a chef cares about the well-being of customers and prepares nutritious meals with fresh products, natural flavors, and light sauces, the traditions of Archestratus are being continued.

Contrary to Archestratus's light cooking methods, other chefs throughout history have popularized the use of heavy spices and thick sauces. To understand this trend, picture a time when kitchens did not have electricity, refrigeration, ice machines, ventilation, or air conditioning. Food did not arrive daily in refrigerated trucks, it was delivered by horse-drawn wagons. When food reached the kitchen, it had already started to spoil. Chefs had little choice but to mask the bad smell and taste. With today's modernizations, there is no need to debase fresh food by over spicing it or covering it with heavy sauces. Escoffier made heavy sauces famous, but his creations came from the period of the late 1800s. If Escoffier were alive today, he would still be a revolutionary in the kitchen, but today he would be inventing lighter sauces.

Today Americans are setting the culinary pace for the rest of the world. Here are a few of the ways:

- Americans are eating well and are concerned with nutrition.
- American food products are accepted around the world.
- American manufacturers are producing state-of-the-art food processing equipment.
- American-based food companies invest millions of dollars each year in developing better ways to preserve food, renovate old recipes, and create new ones.
- Food scientists are working to develop food for the future—already astronauts are testing these foods.
- American farms not only feed people in this country, but also serve as a breadbasket for other nations.
- American eating habits have changed. Lighter fare is preferred nowadays. European eating habits, on the other hand, have remained virtually the same for generations.
- American chefs are preparing superb meals low in fat, cholesterol, sugar, and sodium.
- The toughest food standards and health regulations in the world are enforced in the United States.

American chefs are ahead of their European counterparts in healthful cooking. European chefs like cream and butter and care only about taste. For example, during a cooking demonstration given by a famous European chef, someone from the audience asked what he did to reduce cholesterol and fat in his cooking. The chef replied, "I am not a doctor. I am a chef." This attitude toward nutrition does not prevail with American chefs.

The United States is currently in the midst of a *food revolution.* There is a feeling of excitement and change in the air not witnessed since the days of the Enlightenment. Americans are experiencing a change of consciousness. They are increasingly concerned with fitness, health, and the importance of proper nutrition. The health craze is not a passing fad, but a way of life for many people. As a result, American regional cooking has developed an innovative style and character unlike any other. Already restaurants are updating their menus. Even fast food restaurants are offering healthier choices.

It is essential that American regional cooking continues to be developed. To do so, American chefs should emphasize their own local cuisine. Because the freshest ingredients taste the best, chefs should use ingredients grown in their own region. For example, New England has excellent seafood (Rhode Island is known as the "Ocean State") and at the Sea Fare Inn in Portsmouth, Rhode Island, different ways to prepare lobsters, swordfish, and haddock are always being developed.

American cooking schools should devote more time to teaching students about American regional cooking. Graduates will go on to cook in American institutions and will be expected to prepare this cuisine of tomorrow.

Moreover, American culinary schools should revise their curricula, emphasizing American regional cooking. The culinary world underwent a drastic change in 1973 when ten European chefs introduced nouvelle cuisine. Not only did these ten chefs affect eating habits in France, they changed eating habits all over the world. If ten chefs can have such a dramatic impact on the way we eat, why can't the 10,000 annual graduates of American cooking schools make an impact as well?

Although many people label the cuisines from our melting pot simply as "ethnic," in time they will recognize these creations for what they really are, American regional cooking.

Wave upon wave of settlers brought the seeds of their traditions and planted them in American soil. These settlers nurtured the seeds until they grew into a grand and beautiful tree—American regional cooking. Just as gardeners must tend to their lawns, so, too, must we cherish our culinary heritage. Always remember that today's cuisine will become tomorrow's traditional fare.

2

The History of American Regional Cooking

America is God's crucible, the great melting pot where all the races of Europe are melting and reforming.
The Melting Pot, Israel Zangwill

A merican cuisine, more than that of almost any other cuisine, has been shaped by the history of the country itself. For two hundred years, America has been seen as a bountiful land, rich in natural resources and full of opportunities.

❧ Native Americans

Full of thick forests and thriving streams, the land of the early Native Americans provided them with all they needed; wild game, fresh fish and fowl, wild berries, nuts and fruits. These were their ingredients and their cooking methods were equally simple. Meats were either boiled or roasted over an open flame. Native Americans knew the secret to steaming vegetables by using an open pit, hot coals, and wet leaves.

Sources of food varied throughout the seasons. If weather permitted, Native Americans had a bountiful harvest. Huge hunting campaigns would also increase food surplus. This bounty was not without a problem—lack of storage space. As a consequence, Native Americans learned the art of food preservation through smoking or drying. During buffalo-hunting season, villages were crowded with rafters full of meats, hanging like laundry, to dry in the sun. Freshly caught salmon, halibut, cod, and haddock were stretched across rooftops to dry.

Native Americans were not only excellent hunters and fishermen, they were also farmers, the first to cultivate what today comprises almost 50 percent of the world's foods: maize, beans, peanuts, potatoes, tapioca, squash, pumpkins, papayas, guavas, avocados, pineapples, tomatoes, chili peppers, cacao, and chicle, just to name a few. For the first European settlers the most important of these was corn, for corn would help them survive the harsh winters in the New World, giving rise to that wonderful holiday called Thanksgiving.

Just as varied as the climates in which native Americans lived, so, too, were their diets full of variety. In the Northeast and Southeast, thick woods were cleared and cultivated. Northern Native Americans used maple syrup, tree sap, and corn for sweeteners. In the Midwest, Native Americans searched the Great Lakes region and the plains for wild rice and buffalo. On either seaboard, abundant fish and shellfish provided the necessary staples in a well-rounded diet. Whether wild or cultivated, from the land or from the sea, these were the humble beginnings of one of the world's richest and most misunderstood cuisines—American regional cooking.

🦃 The Early European Settlers

Like a magnet, the New World drew thousands of settlers to its shores. The first colonists landed on America's shores with nothing more than a dream for a better life and the bare necessities. Facing many hardships and uncertain travails, these settlers all held one thing in common—the intrinsic need to survive.

Survival meant adaptation; to the land, to the climate, and perhaps most importantly, to the foods available in the New World. The settlers brought with them certain provisions: wheat, oatmeal, dried peas, vinegar, oil, salt, sugar, root vegetables, seeds, spices, poultry, and various types of farm animals. With knives and other tools, they grew orchards and planted carrots, turnips, parsnips, radishes, cabbages, spinach, green beans, and artichokes. Knowing only that which they had left behind, the first explorers often experimented with their traditional recipes, substituting and adapting certain ingredients for those indigenous to the New World.

In New England, the first colonists were dumbfounded by the abundance of game and fish. The colonists learned from the natives how to hunt. Birds could be captured by the hundreds. Passenger pigeons, once the most abundant of birds, were hunted to extinction. Wild turkeys, as numerous in the woods as rabbits are today, were already becoming scarce by 1700. Recipes from Europe were adapted to incorporate fresh game and native vegetables. Tough meats were made tender through slow cooking, boiling, and marinating.

Yet, long before the English settled at Jamestown and Plymouth, the Spanish had already established their influence in the southeastern half of the United States and in the vast territories of Florida and those just north of the Rio Grande. These sixteenth-century colonists were primarily soldiers and missionaries. Devout Catholics, they were in need of wine for the sacrament of Holy Communion, and were responsible for establishing the first Californian vineyards. Spanish influence also gave way to citrus fruit trees. Oranges, dates, and figs were brought from Spain, sweet potatoes and avocados were introduced to the region by the Spanish plunderers from Mexico. The Spanish also introduced sheep into their colonies in 1598.

In the mid-seventeenth century, during the struggle between England and Holland over supremacy in the colonial world, a tiny, Dutch trading post (New Amsterdam) at the mouth of the Hudson River became an English possession and was renamed New York. Although an English possession, New York remained distinctly Dutch in character.

The Dutch were excellent farmers and dairymen, long regarded as the best in Europe. They continued to be so in the New World. As early as 1625, farm animals were sent over from Holland in special ships equipped with clean, sanded stalls, the best oats, hay and straw, and plenty of water. The Hudson River supported such livestock, and provided the growing metropolis with a thriving fishing trade. Salmon and sturgeon swam in the Hudson, and New York harbor offered crabs, lobsters, and clams.

The middle colonies of Pennsylvania, New Jersey, and Delaware were a rich and diverse landscape of peoples and culture. In 1861, William Penn founded the colony of Pennsylvania. Pennsylvania offered a haven to the Quakers and others who wanted to live in a spirit of peace and brotherly love. Penn avidly advertised his new colony. As a result, he attracted many immigrants from all parts of the world.

In the colonized areas of New Jersey and the Delaware River valley the Dutch and Swedes created a farmer's paradise. Wheat and rye were produced in large quantities as cash crops. Apples, peaches, cranberries, beans, wheat, and flax were found in abundance; giving rise to New Jersey's nickname, the ''Garden State.''

In 1638, a group of Swedes settled what is now Wilmington on the Delaware River. With their traditions of hard work and husbandry, they introduced the log cabin to the New World.

Although English cooking was the predominant style in the middle colonies, it was certainly not the only one. In addition to the Dutch influence near the Hudson, there was the German or ''Deutsch'' influence. These German-speaking people were isolationist in nature. As a result of their differences in language and religion, and their fear of the unfamiliar, many settled in the woodlands alone or in small groups.

These pioneers brought along the things they had known. Many of their foods were straight from the old country; sauerbraten, dumplings, and noodles. They also kept their grand tradition of baking which was very important to them. The bread baking equipment were the first articles to be brought into a new kitchen or bakehouse. Every Friday was baking day. Thanks to the Pennsylvania Dutch, for example, we have such wonderful creations as noodles, coffee cake, pudding cake, and cheesecake.

The colony of Carolina, later known as North and South Carolina, attracted German, Swiss, and Scotch-Irish farmers, as well as expansionist English migrants from Virginia. On the coast, French refugees called Huguenots took root. The Huguenots were educated, able-bodied, and somewhat well off. Taking advantage of generous land terms, many Huguenots acquired huge plantations outside of Charleston, farming cash crops such as tobacco, cotton, and rice.

Rice became a source of wealth in South Carolina by accident. In 1694, a ship carrying rice from Madagascar to England was forced off course and stopped at Charleston for repairs. The colonists were so happy to see visitors that they willingly helped the captain and his crew. The very appreciative captain repaid the town's hospitality with a gift of some of his cargo—rice. The rice grew so well in the Carolina climate, that shortly thereafter it became a staple crop.

🐝 The Industrial Revolution

Closely linked to the birth of the nation was the advent of the Industrial Revolution, an exciting time to be part of the American scene. The United States grew from the 13 original colonies into a sprawling nation spanning the entire continent. Tying all this together was an incredible transportation network of canals, railroads, and stage coaches which made travel easier. Spawned by the Industrial Revolution, inventions such as the cotton gin, sewing machine, and telegraph set the stage for radical changes in the American life-style.

A direct product of the Industrial Revolution was "big city life" which changed American eating habits forever. Since colonial working people often worked within walking distance of their homes, they had their main meal at midday. After heads of families began to work far from their homes, it eventually became customary to serve the main meal in the evening.

As cities grew, so did the impact on American palates. There were wonderful fresh or imported items to buy in a city market—pineapples from the West Indies, oranges and lemons from Sicily, tinned delicacies from France, and fresh deep-sea fish caught just that morning. The large cities attracted both local and not-so-local farmers with their huge, open-air markets. These markets provided city dwellers with a variety of foods both from America and abroad. Philadelphia, for example, attracted people and foods from the middle colonies as well as from the Carolinas.

By the 1870s, the American food industry consisted of small, independent producers creating and marketing their products themselves. However, with the advent of westward expansion and the development of the railroad, Americans were able to incorporate a variety of food items from around the country into their diets. Consequently, the food industry became largely dependent upon the costs of transportation and storage. The railroads had opened the Great Plains, an ideal location for raising herds of cattle, and eventually a higher quality of corn-fed beef was being transported across the country. Refrigerated cars were transporting vegetables and fruits which would have otherwise perished, from the South to the northern states.

As with other industries that prospered during the Industrial Revolution, the food industry underwent a dramatic change. Americans began to be concerned with health and cleanliness and demanded safe, quality food products. Thus, the nation witnessed the birth of companies eager to gain market control with their processed foods. Innovators provided technological advances which ultimately altered eating habits all over the world. Battle Creek, Michigan, became the capital of convenient, ready-to-eat breakfast food. William R. Kellogg developed a highly processed grain called "Cornflakes," which was followed by Charles W. Post's "Grape Nuts."

Henry J. Heinz was another food giant, whose corporation mass-produced pickles and condiments and packaged them into glass jars using a new steam pressure method. Canning was also a popular trend. The Joseph Campbell Company made strides toward correcting the problem of storing these products with the invention of condensed soups packaged in smaller cans.

Most importantly, mass production enabled the food companies to sell to national markets. Inevitably, advertising and promotion became crucial elements of the food industry. Before long, advertisements in newspapers, magazines, on billboards along highways, and on the sides of trolley cars were persuading Americans to eat particular food products. Not surprisingly, by the beginning of the nineteenth century, the food-processing industry made up 20 percent of America's entire manufacturing industry. In the ensuing decades, however, new culinary influences began arriving on America's shores.

❦ The New Wave

Between 1820 and 1919, over 30 million people immigrated to the United States. Many left their homelands in search of religious or political freedom, yet the vast majority were driven to America by food shortages and poverty. Over eight million Germans and Austrians, four million Irish, three million Italians, two million English, two million Scandinavians, and other ethnic groups in smaller numbers, came to America in search of a better life. Each carried his or her own culinary heritage. Gradually, the immigrants settled all over the country, adapting to the American way of life, while, at the same time, incorporating their ethnic backgrounds into American culture. Before long, ethnic foods became a significant component of the American diet.

For example, Americans were greatly inspired by the recipes brought by German and Austrian immigrants. Some favorites include wiener schnitzel, German potato salad, and apple strudel. Yorkshire pudding came with immigrants from the British Isles; stews from Ireland; oatcakes from Scotland; and fruit bread from Wales. Italians provided pasta dishes and classics such as veal parmesan and chicken cacciatore. Because of their flavor and lack of expense, Italian recipes are, perhaps, the most widely used in the United States today. The Scandinavians easily reproduced their recipes with native ingredients and were able to preserve their culinary heritage, giving us Swedish meatballs, potato sausage, and Danish pastry.

Although fewer in number, the people who came to America from Central Europe, Poland, Russia, Greece, and Asia also had a dramatic impact on American regional cooking. The thousands of immigrants from Central Europe brought recipes for goulash, liver dumplings, and sweet rolls. Polish food traditions include kielbasa or Polish sausage, doughnuts filled with fruit, coffee cake, and a wide assortment of breads. Newcomers from Russia, Lithuania, Finland, Latvia, Estonia, Armenia, Georgia, and Ukraine brought such recipes as beef Stroganoff and chicken Kiev. The Greeks also influenced American regional cooking with their classic recipes for moussaka, souvlaki, and baklava. Moreover, Americans quickly developed an appreciation for Asian food. Chinese and Japanese restaurants serving sukiyaki, teriyaki, and chow mein, began opening across the country.

In addition to the ethnic groups mentioned, many more nationalities have played a role in the development of American regional cooking. Immigrants from Mexico, the West Indies, South America, Puerto Rico, Cuba, and, most recently Southeast Asia, have all poured their recipes into the proverbial melting pot.

CHAPTER 3

The Tradition of Wine and Food

The history of wine has been directly linked to the history of humankind since ancient times. No one knows when wine was first tasted, but wine was proffered to the Greek and Egyptian gods as a gift. The Greeks attributed the origin of wine to their god Dionysus while Egyptians attributed it to their god Osiris.

The earliest traces of wine come from Mesopotamia and the Caucasians. In Egypt and China, vineyards were being planted around 3000 BC. Greece was the first country in Europe to make wine, but the process was learned from Egyptian and Eastern sources. The delta of the Nile proved an ideal location for the production of wine.

The Greeks enjoyed their wines and often served them sweetened and diluted with water. The sweet grapes were crushed in huge vats of stone and later allowed to mature in earthenware crocks. Grapes from Greece were probably exported to other Greek colonies in Southern Italy and Sicily where the wine was similarly produced.

Like the Greeks, the Romans made amber, white, and red wines. Romans preferred sweet wines like the Greeks. When the Romans conquered an area, wine production soon followed. For example, in France, the Romans planted a hardy grape called "Picatum." By the end of the first century AD, wine was being exported to Rome from France.

In Christianized Europe, monasteries were furnished with vineyards through the philanthropy of the nobility. Throughout the Middle Ages, the Church was the major producer of wine.

By the 1850s, vineyards had been established in other countries such as Australia, South Africa, and America. When Leif Erikson discovered America, he found a country with thick wild green vines and gave it the name Vineland. The European settlers found that native vines grew well in the eastern part of the United States, but European vines did better in California.

The Spanish established vineyards in California and wine consumption soon became part of the daily routine there. But widespread wine consumption in the United States did not occur until the 1960s. There were a number of reasons for the slow growth of wine consumption. First, Americans traditionally drank whiskey, beer, and rum. During the colonial period when water was not always safe to drink, most people drank liquor out of necessity. Second, Prohibition in the United States in the 1920s halted production of all spirits except sacramental and medicinal wines for a period of 14 years.

Cider was one of the first alcoholic drinks produced in large quantities because of the abundance of apples in America. Cider was easily produced as part of the natural fermentation process. Rum also was popular because it was inexpensive and sweet and more potent than cider. Only the privileged and wealthy like Thomas Jefferson, John Adams, and George Washington could indulge in wine consumption.

From 1769 until the 1830s, wine production in California was successful on a small scale. The Franciscan monks were responsible for the modest success of Californian wines. It was not until Count Agoston Haraszthy de Mokesa arrived on the scene in 1839 that American wine gained real success. In 1862, Haraszthy, often referred to as the father of California viticulture, marketed his first zinfandel, an extremely popular table wine in the marketplace today.

While Haraszthy was active in California, New York wineries, mostly from the Finger Lakes region, were winning prizes in France for their sparkling wines. The Nicholas Longworth winery, in the Ohio Valley, also using American grape varieties, was noted for its sparkling wines too. However, California, known for the quality of its soil and its ideal climate, was the most successful wine-growing region. By 1875, California was producing nearly four million gallons of wine a year. During the next half century, phylloxera or grape louse, and Prohibition, would have a disastrous effect on wine production in America. Phylloxera is a vine disease caused by the aphid phylloxera vastatrix. Originating in Asia and introduced to Europe around 1860, it destroyed most European vineyards. Unfortunately, most of the world's finest vines, which use *vitis vinifera*, are particularly prone to it. As a result, many European wines are now grafted to the tougher American vine stocks.

During the Prohibition years of 1919 to 1933 many Californian vineyards went out of business or turned to the planting of table grapes. It was not until World War II that any headway was made in reviving the production of quality wines in America. By the 1950s, new hybrid grape varieties were being developed which made it possible to produce fine wines in geographic locations which had not been conducive to growing grapes. By the 1970s, the United States was producing wines that were comparable to European wines.

All fine wines are made from *vitis vinifera* grapes. Once the grape has been selected, the vintner goes through the cycle of planting, growing, pruning, waiting, and, finally, harvesting. The growing process of the vines is as complex as producing the wine itself.

Perhaps the most important element to growing wine is climate. Vines, in general, can withstand the winter months because they are dormant then. However, when spring arrives and budding begins, a small frost can destroy an entire crop. A large amount of rain is needed to water the soil. However, too much rain can cause mildew and rot. Climate weighs so heavily on the success of wine, that there are only a few areas in the world where excellent wine can be produced: California, Washington State, New York State, France, Spain, Italy, Germany, Australia, and New Zealand.

A vine may take five to seven years to produce good wine grapes. If the vine has had proper attention, it will produce for 25 to 45 years. The key to proper care of the vine is pruning and cultivation. If the vine is subjected to unnecessary pruning, the vine will become unproductive, while too little pruning will produce a diluted wine. Frost, infestation, and disease can destroy the vineyard. To ensure that the vine is receiving proper nourishment, the soil must be aerated, moist, and clean, and must be fertilized with precision. Too much fertilizer will cause the vine to overproduce.

The grapes must not be picked prematurely as they need to contain enough sugar to allow them to fully ferment. If the grapes are picked too late, the grapes will absorb too much dampness and will be unbalanced. Indeed the wine producer must be very skilled if the harvested grapes are to produce quality wine.

Below is a list of grapes used in the leading American wines:

Alicante Bouschet, used for blending, has a deep red color.

Barbera, originally from Italy, produces a fine delicate wine which improves with age.

Cabernet Sauvignon, the grape of Bordeaux. It produces the unequalled red variety in California today.

Carignane, used mainly for mixing generics and is a red grape produced in warm areas.

Charbono, holds up well, is a dark fruity grape.

Chardonnay, produces the best white wine in California. It is the grape used in the making of burgundies.

Chenin Blanc, slightly sweet and spirited.

Emerald Riesling, a hybrid grape that is tart and fruity.

Flora, a cross between Semillon and Gewürztraminer.

Folle Blanche, a sharp and acidic white grape used for blending.

French Colombard, produces somewhat sweet and cloudy wine if not cooled sufficiently. Used for blending and as a white varietal.

Fumé Blanc, produces a sharp fruity white wine.

Gamay, is the grape of French Beaujolais. In California, the wine produced from this grape is more varietal and potent in character.

Gamay Beaujolais, more closely related to Pinot Noir grapes than to Gamay, produces a light red wine.

Gewürztraminer, a seasoned white grape from Alsace, France, produces a flowery white.

Gray Riesling, despite its name, is not a Riesling but is an average white, popular in northern California.

Green Hungarian, produces a flat wine unlike Hungarian wines.

Grenache, a sweet grape used in rosé wines.

Johannisberg Riesling, is the grape of the Moselle and Rhine regions in Germany. This wine can be fruity, light to sweet.

Merlot, is an integral partner to Cabernet in Bordeaux, known for its softness as opposed to other sharp reds. It is becoming a varietal used for smooth, drinkable reds.

Muscat, has a distinct bouquet and hidden richness, used for a sweet dessert wine.

Petit Sirah, produces soft reds with a hint of character, also known as the Duriff.

Pinot Blanc, makes white wines that are full bodied.

Pinot Noir, the red grape of Burgundy. The California reds can sometimes lack the depth and complexity of the French Pinot Noir.

Pinot St. George, a colorful red grape used for blending.

Ruby Cabernet, a cross between Carignane and Cabernet grape varieties, a red that has a pleasant flavor.

Sauvignon Blanc, makes a white wine with strong fruitiness.

Scheurebe, from a cross of Riesling grapes, makes a fruity, white wine.

Semillon, produces a white wine, crisp and light.

Sirah, a warm, flavorful, very dark grape from the Rhône valley.

Sylvaner, a picnic wine grape used primarily for blending.

Zinfandel, a red grape widely grown in California. There are many types of zinfandel wines; the best are the lighter varietal wines.

Within the last 20 years, wine and food have undergone a revolution. No longer are two or three bottles of wine served with dinner. People are watching their calories and their alcohol consumption. Americans are experimenting with wine and food combinations as well. Gone are the days when tradition called for Bordeaux with lamb and burgundy with game. Americans today are questioning the European traditions and proudly recognizing their own wine and food. Today, in American restaurants, food and wine combinations are more relaxed.

The following chart suggests some possible food and wine combinations:

Food	*Wine*
Appetizers	White Champagne.
Salads	Chenin Blanc, Riesling, or blush wine.
Beef/Lamb	Pinot Noir, Cabernet Sauvignon.
Seafood	Sauvignon Blanc, Chenin Blanc, Gewürztraminer, Riesling.
Game	Gewürztraminer, Riesling, Pinot Noir, Zinfandel.
Poultry	Riesling, Gewürztraminer, Gamay Beaujolais, White Cabernets, Pinot Noir.
Desserts	Riesling, Gewürztraminer, sweet sherry, port, Madeira.

Each entrée throughout this book will have recommended American wines for your enjoyment.

CHAPTER 4

Nutrition

Americans are in the midst of a food revolution; they are changing the way they eat. For generations, butter, fat back, or lard was the first ingredient in many recipes. Americans relied on fat to give food flavor and to disguise less than optimal ingredients or preparation techniques. The more fat in a food, the more Americans were willing to pay for it. Premium ice creams, prime cuts of meat, any rich foods high in fat were held in high regard. This was the land of plenty and people ate plenty of fat.

Then a little more than a decade ago American eating habits began to change. The Surgeon General issued the *Healthy People Report* which gave Americans a look at their overall health. The public responded slowly at first, but that response has grown steadily ever since. Americans took up their forks to battle the American diet of sweet, rich, low fiber, processed foods that research shows contributes to heart disease, stroke, and cancer. Chefs across the country joined the battle, replacing heavy, fat-laden dishes with lighter fare made from fresh ingredients. A new American cuisine began to emerge. This new cuisine is maturing, but still has all the freshness and vibrancy of youth. Perhaps that is why Americans have taken to it with such gusto.

The Greek physician, Hippocrates, is credited with saying "Let food be your medicine and medicine be your food." Science and history have proven that the food people eat does affect their health, but food is not medicine. At least, it shouldn't taste like medicine. Food and dining are meant to be pleasurable. The kind of food we eat reminds us of who we are and where we come from. It is generally a part of celebrations and is often considered a reward or a treat. Julia Child sums it up very nicely "Food should be fun! People shouldn't be afraid of food. They should, however, balance what they eat." This is the challenge a growing number of Americans are presenting to today's chefs: Prepare the freshest foods in the most delightful and creative way, but help us make healthy choices! Chefs are responding with enthusiasm. Restaurants are offering new versions of traditional regional American dishes and introducing new combinations of flavors. Emphasis is shifting to quality ingredients and culinary skill in producing dishes that tantalize the senses and comply with current nutrition principles.

The principles of nutrition stressed in the United States have changed over time as the eating patterns of the American people have changed and as research has become more sophisticated. From the days of the early settlers to the early 1900s, the major concern of most Americans was getting enough food and nutrients. Deficiencies of vitamins, minerals, and protein were not uncommon. The development of agriculture, food technology, and transportation brought about a change. Food became more plentiful, and people became more prosperous. Many people moved from farms to cities, and eating habits began to change. There was a shift from centering the diet around grains, starches, fruits, and vegetables, to focusing on foods high in saturated fat and cholesterol. Specialty high-fat items such as cheese and sausage became a regular part of the diet. This shift to a high fat and high cholesterol, low complex carbohydrate diet brought with it a dramatic rise in obesity and chronic diseases; heart disease, cancer, stroke, and adult-onset diabetes. These remain the leading causes of death and cost billions of dollars in health care in the United States. Research confirmed the connection between diet and these diseases, and nutritional demands shifted from dealing with undernutrition to dealing with diseases of excess.

America's "new" nutrition policy was defined in 1980 when the Department of Agriculture and the Department of Health and Human Services jointly published *Nutrition and Your Health . . . Dietary Guidelines for Americans*, which was revised in 1985 and again in 1990. This report focused America's attention on dealing with diseases of excess rather than diseases of deficiency. In general it recommends variety, moderation, and balance.

- Eat a variety of foods daily. Refer to Nutritional Notes (p. 279) for suggested daily servings.
- Maintain a healthy weight.
- Choose a diet low in total fat, saturated fat, and low in cholesterol.
- Choose a diet with plenty of vegetables, fruits, and grain products.
- Use sugars only in moderation.
- Use salt and sodium in moderation.
- If you drink alcoholic beverages, do so in moderation.

Variety, balance, and moderation are the foundation upon which modern nutrition is built. But these ideas are firmly rooted in the past. In fact, research shows that the Mediterranean diet, very similar to that of ancient Greece, promotes health and well being. It contains plenty of grains and vegetables, moderate amounts of fish, lean meat, poultry, wine, and oil. When fat is used, it is usually in the form of olive oil.

👅 Revolutionary Menu Planning

It is obvious that not all items on a menu will meet, or need to meet, the *Dietary Guidelines* exactly. The objective when planning a nutritionally sound menu is to offer enough choices to make it possible to select a meal that helps to balance the diet. The following are some recommendations to that end. In general, to reduce fat and increase complex carbohydrates, build the menu, or the meal, around grains and vegetables.

Increase Fiber

To increase fiber, use brown rice, wild rice, bulgur, millet, barley, rye, or quenoa in place of white rice. Offer bean soups, vegetarian entrées or side dishes, more vegetables, and salads. Mix beans, nuts, or seeds with rice or pasta as a side dish but keep in mind that nuts are high in fat. Replace all or part of the white flour in recipes with whole wheat flour. Add wheat germ, bran, or oat bran to baked goods. Serve whole-grain or multi-grain breads in place of white breads and rolls. Offer more fruit-based desserts. Serve fruits and vegetables with skins whenever possible. Thicken soups and sauces with pureed legumes, vegetables, or fruit.

Modify Fat

To modify fat, offer a variety of portion sizes of meat and fish. For example, offer a regular eight oz (225 g) portion of steak and a petite serving. Enhance the smaller portion with grains or vegetables. Offer entrées with less meat (3 to 4 oz; 85 to 115 g), and larger portions of vegetables or grains, or perhaps fruit when appropriate. Offer entrées that are low in total fat, saturated fat, and cholesterol, such as fish, poultry, game, and vegetables.

Select recipes that can be modified. Recipes that rely on fat as a major ingredient cannot be adapted to be low in fat. For example, fat-free mayonnaise is very difficult to prepare in the kitchen. The same is true for high cholesterol items. Recipes that rely on egg yolks or organ meats as main ingredients cannot be made low in cholesterol.

When possible, simply reduce or eliminate fat. This requires experimentation to determine how much fat can be left out without destroying the recipe. To compensate use oils with a distinct flavor, such as extra virgin olive oil. Infuse oils with herbs for flavor. The more flavor in the oil, the less will be needed.

Change the cooking method. Roast, bake, broil, steam, cook *en papillote*, poach, or microwave instead of frying, deep-frying, or boiling. Roast and broil meat and poultry on a rack so that the fat will drain off. Stir-fry or sauté in a small amount of oil or use a nonstick or well-seasoned pan and omit the oil. Replace the oil with broth.

Trim visible fat from meat before cooking and remove the skin from poultry before serving. Remove all visible fat from soups, sauces, and gravies.

Thicken sauces, soups, and gravies with pureed, cooked legumes, roasted vegetables, cooked potatoes, or starches rather than fat and roux. To reduce saturated fat, use monounsaturated (canola, olive, and peanut) and polyunsaturated oils (most soft margarines are made with unsaturated oil) or reduced fat spreads. Limit the use of butter, coconut oil, palm oil, palm kernel oil, lard, beef tallow, bacon fat, hydrogenated fats, and hard margarines. Replace high fat ingredients completely or in part with lower fat items, such as those listed in Nutritional Notes (pp. 280–281).

Modify Sodium

To lower consumption of sodium, reduce the amount of salt or salty ingredients such as soy sauce, monosodium glutamate, Worcestershire sauce, pickled vegetables, and most processed foods and mixes. Lower salt varieties of these items are sometimes available, and make suitable alternatives. Herbs, spices, wine, or fruit juices can be used to compensate for the lack of salt.

Preserve Vitamins and Minerals

Careful selection of fruit and vegetables will ensure the presence of vitamins and minerals. Choose fresh, whole, seasonal produce or high quality frozen ingredients. Some frozen fruits and vegetables are higher in vitamins because they are picked ripe and quick frozen, while some "fresh" produce is picked unripe and held to change color and firmness. Cooking time, temperature, and the amount of water are critical factors. Short cooking time, moderate temperatures, and small amounts of water minimize loss of vitamins and minerals. Alkalis, such as baking soda, destroy many vitamins.

The principles of good nutrition are driving the food revolution taking place across the country. The objective is to establish a concept of wellness and well-being through balance, variety, and moderation. Reducing fat by half in a recipe while preserving the flavor and texture of the dish is a step in the right direction. While the end product is not fat free, it fits better into a balanced diet. Increasing fiber is second nature to today's chef. The vegetables and fruits used to replace fat add color, flavor, texture, and fiber. The herbs, spices, wines, and fruit juices used to replace fat and sodium not only create more nutritious meals but challenge the imagination of the chef and delight the palate of the consumer.

🍎 A Nutritional Sample of Regional Dishes

American cooking is like American people—dynamic, constantly changing, and diverse. The cooking of each region is based on the foods indigenous to the region. Modern communication, transportation, and technology have diminished the differences among the regions, but each retains its own unique character.

Americans are selecting and adapting dishes that enhance the quality of their lives. They enjoy traditional foods, but are not bound by tradition. They look for variety and choice, and are moving toward balance, moderation, and a healthier way of life. Americans are acquainting themselves with the gastronomical roots of early Native American culture. As Chef Maccioni of Le Cirque in New York puts it: "Nothing new is being invented. It's all there. It is simply a matter of how we use it."

The following is a sampling of recipes from the various regions of America. A nutritional analysis of each recipe is included. For a healthy diet, total fat intake should not exceed 30 percent of a person's caloric intake and saturated fat should be limited to one third of the fat intake. All food eaten should be combined and balanced to achieve that goal. The goal for fiber is to eat 20 to 35 g each day. Sodium should be limited to 3000 mg per day.

APPETIZERS

Roasted Peppers with Garlic

		U.S.	Metric
	Portions:	8	8
Bell peppers, yellow, red, medium		8	8
Virgin olive oil		½ cup	60 ml
Garlic cloves, peeled, sliced		36	36
Balsamic vinegar		½ cup	120 ml
Thyme sprigs, fresh, leaves only		4	4
Basil, fresh		½ cup	16 g
Black pepper, fresh ground			

1. Roast the bell peppers as close to the heat of a broiler as possible, until charred, turning over for 5 minutes.
2. Steam roasted peppers for 10 minutes, or until the skin can be scraped from the peppers easily. Remove the core, seeds, and ribs.
3. Cut the peppers lengthwise into strips.
4. Combine the olive oil with the peppers in a skillet. Cook over low heat, covered, until peppers are very tender, approximately seven minutes.
5. Uncover the pan, remove peppers, raise heat to moderate, add the garlic and sauté until golden brown.
6. Add the balsamic vinegar, thyme, and basil. Simmer for one minute and remove from heat.
7. Arrange the pepper strips on plates and spoon the caramelized garlic dressing over them.
8. Serve at room temperature with plenty of fresh ground black pepper.

Portion	Calories	Fiber	Sodium	Fat	Saturated Fat
1	104	2 g	6 mg	7 g	1 g

SOUPS

Seafood Gumbo

	Portions:	U.S. 8	Metric 8
Sweet paprika		1½ tsp	3 g
Salt			
Cayenne		1 tsp	2 g
White pepper, fresh ground		½ tsp	1 g
Black pepper, fresh ground		½ tsp	1 g
Thyme, fresh		½ tsp	500 mg
Oregano		½ tsp	300 mg
Bay leaves		2	2
Virgin olive oil		3 Tbsp	45 ml
Onion, large, chopped		1	1
Celery ribs, chopped		4	4
Red bell peppers, medium, seeded, chopped		2	2
Filé powder		3 Tbsp	18 g
Garlic cloves, minced		2	2
Hot pepper sauce		1½ tsp	7 ml
Tomato sauce		16 oz	454 g
Clam juice		8 oz	240 ml
Water		8 oz	240 ml
Seafood, any mixture of fish pieces and mussels		2½ lb	1.1 kg

1. Prepare the spice mixture by combining the paprika, salt, cayenne, white and black pepper, thyme, and oregano with bay leaves in a small bowl. Set aside.
2. In a large, heavy saucepan heat the oil over medium heat and add the onion, celery, and red bell peppers. Sauté, stirring constantly until onions are soft but not brown, approximately 5 minutes.
3. Increase the heat and stir in the filé powder, garlic, hot pepper sauce, and reserved spice mixture. Stirring constantly, cook until fragrant, approximately 5 minutes.
4. Add the tomato sauce, clam juice, and water to the onion/spice mixture. Bring to a boil, then reduce heat. Simmer until vegetables are tender and sauce is slightly thick, stirring occasionally. Cook for 35 to 40 minutes.
5. Stir in the seafood and simmer until fish is just cooked through and shellfish has opened; no longer than 4 to 5 minutes.
6. Remove from heat and serve immediately.

Portion	Calories	Fiber	Sodium	Fat	Saturated Fat
1	220	2 g	1232 mg	7 g	1 g

Yellow Pepper and Bean Soup with Fresh Sage

	U.S.	Metric
Portions:	8	8
Navy beans, cleaned	1 lb	450 g
Water, as needed		
Virgin olive oil	3 Tbsp	45 ml
Yellow bell peppers, seeded and cut into small pieces	3	3
Onion, medium, chopped	1	1
Garlic, large cloves, chopped	4	4
Italian tomatoes, peeled, seeded, chopped, with liquid	4 cups	900 g
Chicken stock	1½ cups	360 ml
Sage leaves, fresh	8	8
Salt		
Sugar	½ tsp	2 g
Heavy cream	6 Tbsp	90 ml
Balsamic vinegar	1 tsp	5 ml
White pepper, fresh ground		

1. Soak the beans overnight, ensuring that they are covered with water.
2. Drain the beans and place them in a medium saucepan, adding cold water to cover by 2 in. (5 cm). Bring to a boil; reduce heat to a simmer and cook until the beans are tender (*not mushy*) or approximately one hour. Drain and reserve the beans.
3. Using a large, heavy saucepan, combine the olive oil, peppers, onion, and garlic. Sauté over low heat, stirring occasionally, until the vegetables are soft but not brown.
4. Add the tomatoes with liquid, chicken stock, fresh sage, salt, sugar, and the reserved beans to the vegetables.
5. Simmer until soup begins to thicken and beans become soft, approximately 30 to 40 minutes.
6. To finish, stir in the cream and vinegar, and season with fresh ground pepper.

Note: The heavy cream can be omitted.

Portion	Calories	Fiber	Sodium	Fat	Saturated Fat
1	256	12 g	163 mg	7 g	2 g

SALADS

Fresh Tuna and Warm Salad Greens

	U.S.	Metric
Portions:	8	8
Salad greens, mixture of green leaf, oak leaf, red leaf, and frisée	32 oz	900 g
Tuna steak, fresh	2 lb	900 g
Rosemary, fresh leaves	½ cup	12 g
Virgin olive oil	4 tsp	20 ml
Lemon juice, to taste		
Salt		
Black pepper, fresh ground		
Pine nuts, for garnish	2 Tbsp	30 g

1. Arrange the salad greens on salad plates.
2. Season the tuna by rubbing with rosemary leaves.
3. In a heavy skillet, heat the olive oil and cook the tuna steak on all sides until brown outside and rare in the middle. Add lemon juice while tuna is cooking. Remove tuna from skillet and transfer to a cutting board. Reserve the cooking juices for the dressing.
4. Using a sharp knife, slice the tuna, seasoning to taste with salt and pepper.
5. Arrange the tuna over each salad and pour cooking juices over the greens.
6. Garnish with pine nuts and serve warm.

Portion	Calories	Fiber	Sodium	Fat	Saturated Fat
1	220	1 g	320 mg	10 g	2 g

ENTRÉES

Grilled Salmon with Hazelnut Vinaigrette

		U.S.	Metric
	Portions:	8	8
Balsamic vinegar		3 Tbsp	45 ml
Dijon mustard		2 Tbsp	30 g
Shallots, minced		2 tsp	27 g
Salt			
Hazelnut oil		3 Tbsp	45 ml
Parsley, fresh		3 Tbsp	7 g
Black pepper, fresh ground			
Salmon filets, fresh, 8 oz (225 g)		8	8

1. Preheat oven to 450°F (230°C).
2. In a bowl, combine the balsamic vinegar, mustard, shallots, and salt.
3. Add the hazelnut oil, whipping constantly until sauce thickens slightly.
4. Stir in the parsley and fresh ground pepper. This vinaigrette can hold for up to two days in the refrigerator.
5. Grill the salmon filets on a warm grill. Do not overcook—the centers should be rare.
6. Serve warm salmon filets with hazelnut vinaigrette.

Note: Those who are nutrition conscious may wish to consider a 4 oz portion of an entrée.

Portion	Calories	Fiber	Sodium	Fat	Saturated Fat
1 8 oz (225 g) serving	373	0 g	419 mg	20 g	3 g

Marinated Roast Pork

	U.S.	Metric
Portions:	8	8
Sugar	2 tsp	10 g
Coarse salt	1¼ tsp	6 g
Black pepper, fresh ground	1¼ tsp	3 g
Coriander	¾ tsp	2 g
Cloves, ground	¾ tsp	2 g
Pork tenderloin, trimmed of fat	2 lb	900 g
Virgin olive oil	1¼ tsp	7 ml
Maple syrup	1¼ tsp	7 ml

1. In a bowl, combine the sugar, salt, pepper, coriander, and cloves. Add the tenderloin, rubbing the spice mixture into the meat.
2. Cover and refrigerate overnight.
3. Preheat the oven to 375°F (190°C).
4. Arrange the tenderloin to form a roast of even thickness. Tie with kitchen string at 2 in. (5 cm) intervals and place on a rack in a roasting pan.
5. Brush tenderloin with the oil and roast for 20 minutes.
6. Remove from oven and brush with maple syrup. Return to oven and roast an additional 25 minutes, basting several times with pan juices.
7. Remove from oven about 6 to 8 minutes before desired doneness. Meat will continue to cook during this time.
8. Slice tenderloin and serve with pan juices.

Portion	Calories	Fiber	Sodium	Fat	Saturated Fat
1	262	0 g	406 mg	13 g	4 g

Wild Mushroom Ragout with Roasted Polenta

	U.S.	Metric
Portions:	8	8
Sun-dried tomatoes	8 halves	8 halves
Wild mushrooms, or morels, dried	1 oz	28 g
Boiling water	1 cup	240 ml
Wild mushrooms, fresh	2 lb	900 g
Virgin olive oil	1 Tbsp	15 ml
Onions, medium, chopped	4	4
Garlic cloves, quartered	6	6
Dry red wine	1 cup	240 ml
Thyme sprigs, fresh, leaves only	4	4
Italian tomatoes, peeled, seeded, chopped, with liquid	7 cups	1.5 kg
Sugar	1 tsp	5 g
Salt		
Black pepper, fresh ground		

1. In a small bowl, combine the sun-dried tomatoes with the dried mushrooms (or morels) and the boiling water. Cover and set aside to steep for 12 to 15 minutes.
2. Transfer the tomato/mushroom mixture to a strainer. Reserve soaking liquid. Rinse the tomato/mushroom mixture under cold water, pressing with the back of a spoon to squeeze out excess water.
3. Chop tomato/mushroom mixture coarsely and reserve.
4. Thoroughly wipe grit from fresh mushrooms and trim rough ends. Cut up any mushrooms that are larger than 1 in. (3 cm). Set aside.
5. In a saucepan, combine the olive oil, onions, and garlic. Sauté until onions are golden brown, approximately 5 minutes.
6. Without disturbing sediment in the bottom of reserved tomato/mushroom liquid, spoon about 10 tablespoons (150 ml) into saucepan. Add the red wine and thyme and bring to a boil.
7. Boil for 1 minute, then stir in the tomatoes with their liquid, the tomato/mushroom mixture, sugar, and salt.
8. Cover and simmer, stirring occasionally, until vegetables are tender and ragout has thickened, no more than 15 to 20 minutes. Season with pepper.
9. Serve with Roasted Polenta (recipe follows).

Note: This ragout can be made up to four days in advance and refrigerated. If the ragout is too thick, thin with red wine. If too thin, reduce by boiling.

Portion	Calories	Fiber	Sodium	Fat	Saturated Fat
1	320	8 g	834 mg	9 g	1 g

Roasted Polenta

		U.S.	Metric
	Portions:	8	8
Yellow cornmeal, coarsely milled		2 cups	454 g
Salt		2 tsp	10 g
Water		6 cups	1.4 l
Virgin olive oil		4 tsp	20 ml
Garlic cloves, sliced		4	4
Rosemary sprigs, fresh, leaves only		4	4
Salt			
White pepper, fresh ground			

1. In a heavy saucepan, combine the cornmeal, salt, and water, and boil over high heat, stirring constantly.
2. Reduce heat to moderate and cook for approximately 10 minutes, stirring constantly to avoid scorching. Polenta is cooked when it pulls away from the sides of the pan.
3. Preheat oven to 375°F (190°C).
4. Firm the polenta by refrigerating for at least 35 minutes.
5. In a small bowl, combine the oil and garlic. Set aside for 15 minutes.
6. Slice the polenta into eight equal squares and brush lightly with garlic oil.
7. Arrange the polenta on a heavy baking pan. Sprinkle sides and tops of polenta with rosemary and season with salt. Bake for at least 22 minutes.
8. Remove and season with pepper. Serve on a bed of wild mushroom ragout.

Note: The nutritional analysis for Roasted Polenta is included in the analysis given for Wild Mushroom Ragout with Roasted Polenta on page 25.

DESSERTS

Gratin of Fresh Raspberries

		U.S.	Metric
	Portions:	8	8
Raspberries, fresh		4 cups	900 g
Sour cream		2 cups	480 ml
Brown sugar, dark		¾ cup	170 g

1. Preheat broiler until hot.
2. Spread half the raspberries at the bottom of soufflé dishes.
3. Stir half the sour cream and spread over the raspberries, leaving a ring of uncovered raspberries around the edge.
4. Sprinkle half the brown sugar over the sour cream, then repeat the layers.
5. Place soufflé dish under broiler, 3 to 4 in. (8 to 10 cm) from heat, and broil until sugar bubbles. Do not burn. Remove and serve immediately.

Per Serving	Calories	Fiber	Sodium	Fat	Saturated Fat
Made with sour cream:	230	4 g	37 mg	12 g	8 g
Made with half and half:	189	4 g	31 mg	9 g	5 g
Made with 1 cup of sour cream and 1 cup of nonfat yogurt:	184	4 g	43 mg	7 g	4 g

CHAPTER 5

New England

I ngredients native to a region should be used whenever practical, as is done at the Sea Fare Inn, Portsmouth, Rhode Island. For example, New England has excellent seafood. Fish tends to be low in fat and the oil in fatty fish is considered healthy. New England grows pumpkin, winter squash, berries, beans, and corn in abundance, which provide fiber, vitamins, and minerals with little or no fat. Traditional cooking methods such as steaming and boiling are simple and low in fat. The New England boiled dinner, for example, can be low in fat if the fat is trimmed from the meat before cooking and the fat skimmed from the broth before serving.

Salt pork, often used for flavor, is high in salt and fat but can be replaced by Canadian bacon or lean ham. Though fat is reduced, the salt remains. Omitting additional salt in the recipe will lower the overall salt content of the dish. No book on American cuisine would be complete without mentioning New England salt pork. Although salt pork is not considered the healthiest of foods by today's standards, a recipe is included here because salt pork was the heart and soul of early colonial cooking. Salting was an efficient and safe way to preserve meats during long New England winters.

New England white chowders can be modified by using lower fat substitutes for cream, such as half and half or whole milk. Some chefs now are using low-fat milk and thickening the broth with pureed potatoes. New Englanders continue a tradition of using herbs and spices brought there centuries ago from the East. These spices, and the condiments made with them, can be used to compensate for the flavor of fat and salt in cooking.

High-fat cheeses and specialty meats were introduced to the region by Portuguese, Italian, and French Canadian immigrants. These foods should be used in moderation or replaced with lower fat varieties.

New England desserts often contain cream, which is rich in saturated fats, and today's New Englanders lead the country in the consumption of ice cream. In cooking, substituting half and half for whole cream can save 124 calories and 16 grams of fat for each quarter cup used. Blueberries and raspberries appear in many New England desserts and these are an excellent nutrient-dense food. Maple syrup and molasses also associated with desserts from this region pose no major health problems and add flavor and interest.

APPETIZERS

Asparagus with Vermont Ham in Puff Pastry

		U.S.		Metric	
Portions:		8	50	8	50
Asparagus spears		16–24 (1 pound)	100–120	454 g	2.7 kg
Virgin olive oil		½ Tbsp	3⅛ Tbsp	7.5 ml	47 ml
Puff pastry (fresh or frozen)		8 oz	50 oz	227 g	1.4 kg
Eggs, beaten		1	6	1	6
Cooked ham, thin slices, 4–5 oz (113–142 g) each		8	50	8	50
Lemon juice		1 lemon	6 lemons	1 lemon	6 lemons
Heavy cream		½ cup	3¼ cups	120 ml	780 ml
Salt					
White pepper, fresh ground					

1. Peel and trim the asparagus.
2. Bring salted water and oil to a boil. (The oil helps the asparagus stay green.)
3. Poach the asparagus for approximately 7 minutes. Time will depend on the size of the asparagus.
4. Preheat oven to 375°F (190°C).
5. Roll out the puff pastry to 14 in. × 12 in. (35 cm × 30 cm) rectangles. If using frozen puff pastry, defrost sheets before cutting. Cut rectangles in half lengthwise; stack the 2 halves.
6. Trim strips to 11 in. × 5¼ in. (28 cm × 13 cm); cut in four equal pieces, resulting in eight 2¾ in. × 5¼ in. (7 cm × 13 cm) rectangles.
7. Place rectangles on a baking sheet, separated from each other.
8. Chill for 10 minutes.
9. Brush the dough with beaten egg.
10. Make 4 light, slanting cuts across the center of each rectangle. Make the cuts ⅓ in. (1 cm) in from the edges.
11. Bake until they puff, approximately 15 minutes.
12. Using a shrimp knife, cut center out of each case and carefully remove. Discard excess or soft dough.
13. Cut off the top 3 in. (8 cm) of each asparagus spear. Reserve.
14. Cut off an additional 3 in. (8 cm). Reserve these pieces.
15. Take 2 or 3 of the asparagus tips and roll in a ham slice. Do this for each slice of ham.
16. Place inside the puff pastry case with the asparagus tip pointing out. Cover with centers removed in step 12.
17. Combine the reserved asparagus and the lemon juice in a food processor. Puree.
18. Whip the heavy cream and slowly fold into the asparagus puree. Season with salt and pepper.
19. Heat the asparagus-filled pastry at 350°F (180°C) for 5 minutes.
20. Remove and serve at room temperature.

Chicken Liver Mousse with Fresh Tomato Sauce

	U.S.		Metric	
Portions:	8	50	8	50
Chicken livers	11 oz	8½ cups	312 g	1.9 kg
Bread crumbs, fresh	2 cups	12½ cups	454 g	2.8 kg
Onion, small, finely chopped	1	6¼	1	6¼
Butter	9 Tbsp	3½ cups	135 g	844 g
Garlic cloves, finely chopped	7	44	7	44
Parsley, fresh, chopped	2 tsp	½ cup	1.5 g	9.3 g
Eggs, whole	3	20	3	20
Oregano, fresh, chopped	4 tsp	½ cup	3 g	17 g
Salt				
Pepper				
Heavy cream	¾ cup	4¾ cups	180 ml	1.1 l
Virgin olive oil	3 Tbsp	1⅛ cups	45 ml	281 ml
Flour	3 Tbsp	1⅓ cups	21 g	131 g
Italian plum tomatoes (small can), chopped, with juice	1	6¼	1	6¼

1. Preheat oven to 350°F (180°C).
2. In a food processor, combine the chicken liver, bread crumbs, half of the onion, butter, half the garlic, parsley, as well as eggs, and one fourth of the oregano.
3. Season with salt and pepper and mix until smooth.
4. Add the cream and mix for a few seconds.
5. Transfer the mixture into small, buttered soufflé dishes.
6. Place the soufflé dishes in a baking pan half filled with water. Bake for 30 to 35 minutes.
7. While the mousse is baking, to prepare the tomato sauce heat the olive oil.
8. Add the remaining garlic and onion and cook for 5 to 8 minutes at low heat.
9. Add the remainder of the oregano, the flour, and the chopped tomatoes with juice. Simmer for 5 to 8 minutes.
10. Puree, then strain the mixture. Season with salt and pepper.

To Serve:

11. Place the chicken liver mousse in the center of a plate.
12. Spoon fresh tomato sauce around mousse and garnish mousse and sauce with chopped parsley.

Lobster Delnero

		U.S.		Metric	
Portions:		8	50	8	50
Lobsters, cooked, approximately 1¼ lb (560 g) each		4	25	4	25
Fish stock, as needed					
Heavy cream		⅓ cup	2 cups	80 ml	480 ml
Salt					
White pepper, fresh ground					
Bechamel sauce, hot		1⅔ cups	10⅓ cups	400 ml	2.5 l
Curry powder, to taste					
Zucchini, large, thinly sliced		1	7	1	7
Parmesan cheese, as needed					

1. Split the lobsters lengthwise, discarding the intestines, stomach, and gills. Reserve coral and lobster shell. Remove the flesh from the tails and claws and cut into slices. Sauté lobster meat in a little fish stock. Remove and keep warm.
2. Add the heavy cream and the coral to the sauté pan. Season with salt and pepper.
3. When this has thickened, add the bechamel sauce, then strain. Return the lobster meat to the mixture.
4. Add curry powder to the mixture.
5. Fill the lobster shells with the lobster and bechamel mixture and decorate with slices of zucchini.
6. Lightly coat with Parmesan cheese and bake in a preheated 425°F (220°C) oven until warm.

Salmon Puff with Mushroom and Peas

	Portions:	U.S.		Metric	
		8	50	8	50
Filet of salmon		14 oz	5½ lb	396 g	2.5 kg
Cognac		1 Tbsp	6 Tbsp	15 ml	90 ml
Virgin olive oil		2 Tbsp	¾ cup	30 ml	180 ml
Mint leaves, fresh, chopped		5	31	5	31
Salt					
White pepper, fresh ground					
Mushrooms, white, sliced		5 oz	2 lb	142 g	900 g
Shallot, chopped		1	6	1	6
Parsley, fresh, chopped		1 Tbsp	6 Tbsp	2 g	14 g
Lemon juice		½ lemon	3 lemons	½ lemon	3 lemons
Peas, fresh		⅓ cup	2 cups	76 g	473 g
Puff pastry		1 lb	6¼ lb	450 g	2.8 kg
Egg, beaten		1	6	1	6
Egg, large, unbeaten		1	6	1	6
Heavy cream		⅓ cup	2 cups	80 ml	480 ml
Nutmeg, to taste					

1. Cut the salmon into 1 in. × 2 in. (3 cm × 5 cm) strips.
2. In a bowl marinate the salmon with cognac, half the olive oil, mint, salt, and pepper for about 30 minutes.
3. Heat the remainder of the olive oil in a skillet and sauté the mushrooms with the shallots and parsley for 5 minutes.
4. Add the lemon juice and allow to cool. Season to taste and add the peas. *Note:* Add the peas last so that they retain their color.
5. Roll out pastry dough to a ⅛ in. (3 mm) thickness on a floured surface.
6. Using half the pastry, line an 8 in. to 10 in. (20 cm to 25 cm) tart pan. Do not stretch the dough.
7. Combine the salmon marinade with mushroom mixture and fill shell.
8. Cover with the remaining dough. Push down edges over the filling to form a double edge.
9. Brush with the beaten egg and cut a ½ in. (12 mm) round hole in center. Make fish cutouts with excess dough and brush with beaten egg.
10. Chill pie uncovered for 20 minutes to relax the dough.
11. Bake for 15 minutes in a preheated 400°F (200°C) oven along with fish cutouts.
12. Beat egg lightly with cream, salt, pepper, and nutmeg.
13. Remove pie from oven. Reserve the fish designs.
14. Using a funnel, pour cream mixture into center of pie.
15. Return to oven and bake for an additional 14 to 16 minutes.
16. Remove from pan and place fish cutouts on crust.
17. Let rest for 8 minutes before cutting. Serve warm.

Shrimp Wrapped in Bacon

	Portions:	U.S.		Metric	
		8	50	8	50
Shrimp, medium		16	100	16	100
Salt					
Black pepper, fresh ground					
Lemon		½	3	½	3
Bacon strips		16	100	16	100
For Sauce:					
Tarragon, fresh, chopped		1 tsp	2 Tbsp	750 mg	5 g
Lemon juice, fresh		½ tsp	1 Tbsp	2.5 ml	16 ml
Heavy cream		½ cup	3¼ cups	120 ml	750 ml
Salt					
White pepper, fresh ground					

1. Clean and devein shrimp.
2. Season with salt, pepper, and lemon juice.
3. Wrap the bacon strips around the shrimp.
4. Place the wrapped shrimp on bamboo skewers and bake in a preheated 400°F (200°C) oven for 8 to 10 minutes, or until bacon is cooked.

For Sauce:

5. In a small saucepan, combine the tarragon, lemon juice, and cream. Bring to a simmer and season with salt and pepper.
6. Serve with shrimp in equal portions.

Steamed Clams

	U.S.		Metric	
Portions:	8	50	8	50
Soft-shell clams	1.5 qt	2 gal	1.4 l	7.6 l
Water	1 cup	5 cups	240 ml	1.2 l
Onion, chopped	1	4	1	4
Celery sticks, chopped	3	1	3	1
Garlic cloves, chopped	5	1 bulb	5	1 bulb
Bay leaves	5	16	5	16
Black peppercorns	1½ Tbsp	4½ Tbsp	9 g	27 g
Butter, unsalted	3 oz	1 lb	85 g	450 g
Lemon juice	1 lemon	5 lemons	1 lemon	5 lemons

1. Soak the clams in cold water while washing thoroughly.
2. Place the clams in a stock pot.
3. Add water.
4. Combine the onion, celery, garlic, bay leaves, and peppercorns. Cover and let simmer for 10 minutes, or until the clams open.
5. Remove clams. Reserve the liquid.
6. Add the butter and lemon juice to the reserved liquid, whipping thoroughly until the butter has melted.
7. Place equal portions of the clams on serving plates.
8. Add approximately 4 oz of broth per serving.
9. Garnish with lemon and serve hot.

SOUPS

New England Clam Chowder

	U.S.		Metric	
Portions:	8	50	8	50
Clams	1½ qt	3 gal	1.5 l	11.4 l
Potatoes, peeled, diced	12 oz	6 lb	340 g	2.7 kg
Salt pork	3 oz	1 lb	85 g	454 g
Celery, chopped	3 oz	1 lb	85 g	454 g
Onion, chopped	2 oz	1 lb	57 g	454 g
Clam juice	1 pt	1 gal	0.5 l	3.8 l
Salt				
White pepper, fresh ground				
Thyme leaves, fresh, minced	Pinch	1 Tbsp	Pinch	3 g
Bacon fat	1½ oz	8 oz	43 g	227 g
Flour	2 Tbsp	¾ cup	14 g	88 g
Half and half	2 cups	3 qt	480 ml	4 l
Parsley, chopped, as needed				

1. Thoroughly wash the clams and soak for 20 minutes in cold water.
2. Steam clams in pan with small amount of water until they open.
3. Remove neck and stomach and reserve with the liquid.
4. Cook the potatoes in boiling salted water.
5. Drain and reserve the potatoes.
6. In a heavy stock pot, sauté the salt pork over medium heat until golden.
7. Add the celery and onion. Cook 5 to 8 minutes, until brown.
8. Add the clam juice, clams, reserved liquid, potatoes, salt, pepper, and thyme.
9. Simmer for 5 minutes.
10. Combine the bacon fat with the flour in a small sauté pan. Whisk until smooth.
11. Add to the chowder. Add half and half. Simmer for an additional 5 to 10 minutes.
12. Sprinkle with parsley and serve.

Note: Crabmeat Chowder is prepared using the same method. Substitute crabmeat for clams.

Pumpkin Soup

	U.S.		Metric	
Portions:	8	50	8	50
Onion, chopped	½ oz	8 oz	14.2 g	227 g
Shallots, chopped	3	4 oz	3	113 g
Butter, unsalted	6 Tbsp	1½ cups	90 g	360 g
Pumpkin puree	8 cups	5 lb	360 g	2.3 kg
Flour	1 oz	8 oz	28 g	227 g
Chicken stock	2 cups	3 qt	½ l	3 l
Heavy cream	1 cup	6½ cups	240 ml	1½ l
Salt				
White pepper, fresh ground				
Cloves, ground, to taste				
Nutmeg, to taste				

1. In a stock pot, sauté the onions and shallots in the butter.
2. Add the pumpkin puree. Simmer for 5 minutes, stirring constantly.
3. Add the flour and whip until smooth. Cook for 5 minutes.
4. Add the chicken stock. Simmer for 10 minutes.
5. Add the cream and cook an additional 5 minutes.
6. Season with salt, pepper, cloves, and nutmeg.
7. Serve hot, garnished with dollops of whipped cream.

Seafood with Lime Consommé   COLOR PLATE 1

		U.S.		Metric	
Portions:	8	50	8	50
Limes, small	3	18 ³/₄	3	18 ³/₄
Lobsters, approximately 1¹/₂ lb (680 g) each, cooked and shelled	1¹/₂	9	1¹/₂	9
Clams, steamed	8	50	8	50
Mussels, steamed	16	100	16	100
Shrimp, raw, peeled and deveined	26	165	26	165
Carrots, julienne	1¹/₂	9¹/₃	1¹/₂	9¹/₃
Celery, julienne	1¹/₂ ribs	9¹/₃ ribs	1¹/₂ ribs	9¹/₃ ribs
Salt				
White pepper, fresh ground				
Tabasco, to taste				
Fish stock, clarified	1 qt	6 qt	1 l	6 l
Lime juice	¹/₄ cup	1¹/₂ cups	60 ml	360 ml

1. Remove zest from limes and cut into narrow strips. Blanch in boiling water for approximately 2 minutes. Remove, rinse, and set aside.
2. Cut lobster meat into chunks.
3. Combine lobster meat, clams, mussels, shrimp, carrots, celery, and lime zest in a stock pot. Season to taste with salt, pepper, and Tabasco.
4. Add the fish stock and bring to a slight boil. Lower the heat and simmer for 4 to 5 minutes.
5. Add lime juice and adjust seasonings as necessary. Serve hot.

ENTRÉES

American Crossribs of Beef Braised in Red Wine

🐦 AMERICAN WINE SUGGESTION
Sebastiani Sonoma Cabernet Sauvignon

		U.S.		Metric	
Portions:		8	50	8	50
Butter, unsalted		2 Tbsp	¾ cup	30 g	180 g
Cognac		1 Tbsp	6 Tbsp	15 ml	90 ml
Thyme sprigs, fresh		3	19	3	19
Black peppercorns		7	43	7	43
Salt					
Black pepper, fresh ground					
Bay leaves		1	6	1	6
Virgin olive oil		1 Tbsp	6 Tbsp	15 ml	90 ml
Crossrib roast, boneless, rolled tightly, 5–5½ lb (2.3–2.5 kg) each		1	7	1	7
Carrot, chopped		1	6	1	6
Onion, small, finely chopped		1	6	1	6
Garlic cloves, minced		3	19	3	19
Veal stock		2 cups	3 qt	480 ml	3 l
Cabernet sauvignon		1 l	7 l	1 l	7 l
For Garnish:					
Turnips		2	12	2	12
Carrots, small		4	24	4	24
Green beans, slender, young		8 oz	50 oz	227 g	1.4 kg
Fresh peas		10 oz	7 ¾ cups	284 g	1.7 kg

1. In a saucepan, melt the butter. Add the cognac, thyme, peppercorns, salt, ground pepper, and bay leaf.
2. Simmer for 6 to 7 minutes. Remove and reserve.
3. Preheat the oven to 350°F (180°C).
4. Using a cast-iron pan, heat the olive oil and brown the crossrib roast on all sides.
5. Add the carrot, onion, and garlic. Cook for an additional 5 minutes.
6. Add the reserved herb mixture, veal stock, and cabernet sauvignon.
7. Bring to a boil, cover, and transfer to oven. Bake for 3½ hours.

For Garnish:

8. Peel and quarter the turnips.
9. Peel the carrots and slice.
10. Wash and trim the green beans.
11. Cook the vegetables for 10 minutes in salted water.
12. Blanch the peas in boiling water for 1 minute. Drain.
13. Remove the meat from the pan. Skim the fat from juices and pour over the meat. Serve hot, surrounded by vegetables.

Baked Halibut Steak with Fine Herb Sauce

ᏬᎧ AMERICAN WINE SUGGESTION
Sterling Vineyards "Winery Lake" Chardonnay

	U.S.		Metric	
Portions:	8	50	8	50
Butter, as needed to butter baking pan				
Shallots, minced	¼ cup	1½ cups	53 g	360 g
Halibut steak, 6 oz (170 g) each	8	50	8	50
Salt				
Black pepper, fresh ground				
Butter, cut in pieces	¼ cup	1½ cups	60 g	360 g
Shiitake mushrooms	1 lb	6¼ lb	454 g	2.8 kg
Dry white wine	1⅓ cups	8⅓ cups	319 ml	2 l
For Sauce:				
Spinach leaves, fresh, young, 12 oz bunches (340 g) blanched, dried, and cooled	2	12	2	12
Tarragon, 4 in.–5 in. (10 cm–12 cm) sprigs	2	12	2	12
Dill sprigs, fresh	6	38	6	38
Basil sprigs, fresh	2	12	2	12
Thyme sprigs, fresh	2	12	2	12
Ice, crushed	¼ cup	1½ cups	60 ml	360 ml
Butter	2 Tbsp	¾ cup	30 g	180 g
Salt				
Black pepper, fresh ground				
Dill, as needed for garnish				

1. Preheat oven to 375°F (190°C).
2. Butter a baking pan; sprinkle with shallots.
3. Place the halibut steaks in pan and season with salt and pepper; butter the top of each steak.
4. Add the shiitake mushrooms, reserving a few for garnish, and sprinkle with the wine. Bake for 10 to 12 minutes.

For Sauce:

5. Strain the cooking juices into a saucepan. Reduce by half.
6. In a food processor, combine spinach and herbs, and puree. Add the ice a few minutes after to retain color.
7. Add melted butter to the puree and process.
8. Add puree to the fish juices. Season with salt and pepper. Warm but do not boil the sauce.
9. Serve fish on warm plates, garnished with dill and shiitake mushrooms, accompanied by the sauce.

Chicken Breast Stuffed with Three Cheeses, Wrapped in Phyllo, and Served in a Pear Sauce

🐚 AMERICAN WINE SUGGESTION
Sakonnet Vineyards Rhode Island Red

	U.S.		Metric	
Portions:	8	50	8	50
Chicken breast, boneless, skinned, about 5 oz (142 g) each	8	50	8	50
White pepper, fresh ground				
Stilton cheese, crumbled	4 oz	1½ lb	113 g	709 g
Parmesan cheese	⅓ cup	2⅓ cups	85 g	530 g
Gruyère, imported	½ cup	3⅛ cups	113 g	709 g
Flour, as needed, for dredging				
Butter	¼ cup	1½ cups	60 g	360 g
Butter, unsalted	¼ cup	1½ cups	60 g	360 g
Phyllo dough sheets, found in frozen food section of supermarket	16	100	16	100

For Sauce:

Pears, ripe, firm	4	25	4	25
Lemon, small	1	6	1	6
Chicken stock	2 cups	3 qt	480 ml	3 l
Semisweet white wine, such as sauvignon blanc	½ cup	3⅛ cups	120 ml	750 ml
Green peppercorns	½ tsp	3¼ tsp	2 g	12 g
Heavy cream	3 Tbsp	1¼ cups	45 ml	280 ml

1. Flatten boneless, skinless chicken breast.
2. Make an incision to middle of chicken breast. Sprinkle with pepper. Do not season with salt; cheese is salty enough.
3. Blend all cheese to form a paste. Divide cheese equally among portions of chicken. Fold chicken breast closed. Dredge with flour.
4. In a heavy skillet, melt the butter, sauté the chicken breast on all sides for 30 seconds per side. Remove and cool.
5. Preheat the oven to 375°F (190°C).
6. Cut phyllo sheets in half. Brush each sheet with melted butter and stack in sets of 8 or 50.
7. Place chicken breast in the center of a stack of phyllo sheets and wrap.
8. Place the wrapped chicken breast on buttered baking sheet. Refrigerate until ready to use.
9. Bake for 15 minutes at 350°F (180°C).

For Sauce:

10. Peel, seed, half, and core the pears, reserving the skin and the cores.
11. Rub the pears with lemon juice to preserve color.

12. In a saucepan, combine the pear, skins, and core. Add the chicken stock, wine, and green peppercorns. Bring to a boil, then simmer for 7 to 8 minutes.
13. Remove pear halves and keep warm.
14. Bring pear juice mixture to a boil and reduce to half.
15. Strain and add the cream. Heat mixture.
16. Pour sauce on warm plates. Place chicken on top of sauce, fan pear halves around the chicken and serve.

Chicken in Whiskey Cream Sauce

 AMERICAN WINE SUGGESTION
Columbia Crest Merlot

	U.S.		Metric	
Portions:	8	50	8	50
Chicken	8 lb	50 lb	3.6 kg	22.5 kg
Flour, as needed, for dredging				
Virgin olive oil	2 Tbsp	¾ cup	30 ml	180 ml
Butter	2 Tbsp	¾ cup	30 g	180 g
Shallots, chopped	4	25	4	25
Onions, small, chopped	2	12	2	12
Salt				
White pepper, fresh ground				
Bay leaves	2	12	2	12
Thyme, fresh, chopped	1 tsp	2 Tbsp	1 g	6 g
Chicken stock	1 cup	1½ qt	240 ml	1.5 l
Whiskey	½ cup	3⅛ cups	120 ml	750 ml
Heavy cream	2 cups	3 qt	480 ml	3 l

1. Preheat oven to 375°F (190°C).
2. Cut chicken into pieces. Dredge in flour.
3. Heat oil and butter in a heavy skillet and sauté chicken until golden brown.
4. Add the shallots and onion, and season with salt and pepper. Cook for 2 minutes.
5. Add bay leaves, thyme, and chicken stock. Transfer to oven and bake for 20 minutes.
6. Remove from oven.
7. Skim fat.
8. Pour the whiskey over the chicken and flambé.
9. When flame dies, add the cream, and cook for 3 or 4 minutes.
10. Season with salt and pepper to taste, and serve.

Baked Veal Chops with a Fine Herb Stuffing   COLOR PLATE 2

🦞 AMERICAN WINE SUGGESTION
Robert Sinsky Vineyards Pinot Noir

		U.S.		Metric	
Portions:		8	50	8	50
Onions, small, chopped		4	25	4	25
Shallots, chopped		2 Tbsp	¾ cup	27 g	167 g
Butter, unsalted		¼ cup	1½ cups	60 g	360 g
Cooked ham, chopped		6 Tbsp	2⅓ cups	90 g	565 g
Wild mushrooms, chopped		¼ cup	1½ cups	60 g	360 g
Swiss cheese, grated		6 Tbsp	2⅓ cups	90 g	565 g
Parsley, fresh, chopped		3 Tbsp	1¼ cups	7 g	44 g
Bread crumbs		1 cup	6¼ cups	227 g	1.4 kg
Thyme, fresh		2 Tbsp	¾ cup	6 g	38 g
Chives, chopped		3 Tbsp	1¼ cups	30 g	188 g
Marjoram		3 Tbsp	1¼ cups	36 g	225 g
Salt					
Black pepper, fresh ground					
Veal chops, 6 oz (170 g) each		8	50	8	50
Virgin olive oil		3 Tbsp	1¼ cups	45 ml	280 ml
For Sauce:					
White wine		6 Tbsp	2⅓ cups	90 ml	560 ml
Brown veal stock		1 cup	1½ qt	240 ml	1.5 l
Demi-glaze		½ cup	3½ cups	120 ml	840 ml

1. Preheat oven to 375°F (190°C).
2. Sauté the onions and shallots in half of the butter until they become soft, approximately 2 minutes.
3. Add the ham and mushrooms and cook for 2 to 5 minutes. Transfer to a bowl, add the Swiss cheese, parsley, bread crumbs, thyme, chives, and marjoram. Season with salt and pepper. Mix well.
4. Using a sharp knife, make an incision in the veal chops from the side, so as to make a pocket.
5. Stuff veal chops with the mixture.
6. Heat the olive oil and remaining butter in a heavy skillet. Brown veal chops for 3 minutes on each side.
7. Remove from skillet and place in a baking dish.

For Sauce:

8. Add the wine, veal stock, and demi-glaze. Cook until tender (less than 1 hour).
9. Remove from oven and serve on warm plates.
10. Strain sauce and serve warm over veal chops.

Filet of Sole Stuffed with Salmon and Basil

🐦 AMERICAN WINE SUGGESTION
Silverado Sauvignon Blanc

		U.S.		Metric	
Portions:		8	50	8	50
Sole filets, small		8	50	8	50
Salt					
White pepper, fresh ground					
Salmon filets, cut in thin slices		1 lb	6 lb	450 g	2.7 kg
Spinach leaves, large, fresh		8	50	8	50
Basil, fresh, chopped		2 Tbsp	¾ cup	4 g	25 g
Butter, unsalted		1 Tbsp	6 Tbsp	15 g	90 g
Shallots, minced		1 Tbsp	6 Tbsp	13 g	80 g
Shiitake mushrooms, diced		8 oz	50 oz	227 g	1.4 kg
Dry white wine		½ cup	3 cups	120 ml	720 ml
Tomatoes, large		8	50	8	50
For Sauce:					
Heavy cream		½ cup	3 cups	120 ml	720 ml
Butter, soft		1 tsp	2 Tbsp	5 g	30 g
Flour		1 Tbsp	6 Tbsp	7 g	42 g
Chives, chopped		1 Tbsp	6 Tbsp	10 g	60 g

1. Preheat oven to 375°F (190°C).
2. Lay sole filets flat on a workbench.
3. Season with salt and pepper. Place sliced salmon flat on top of sole.
4. Place spinach leaves and basil on top of salmon. Roll up the sole filets.
5. In a sauté pan, combine the butter, shallots, and mushrooms. Sauté for 5 minutes. Remove from pan.
6. In the same pan, add the rolled filets of sole. Add the wine. Bring to a boil and taste for seasoning.
7. Then bake filets for 5 minutes in the oven. Reserve contents of pan.
8. Peel tomatoes, cutting out tops. Hollow out tomatoes and season with salt and pepper.
9. Place tomatoes in a preheated serving dish.
10. Remove filets of sole from oven and place one filet in each tomato.
11. Bake for an additional 5 minutes.

For Sauce:

12. Add the heavy cream to the contents of the sauté pan and cook for 5 minutes.
13. Add the butter and flour, whisking until smooth.
14. Add the chives. Strain before serving.

Filet of Sole Stuffed with Wild Mushrooms and Fresh Artichoke

🐚 AMERICAN WINE SUGGESTION
Sakonnet Vineyards Gewürztraminer

	U.S.		Metric	
Portions:	8	50	8	50
Filets of sole, 6 in.–7 in. (15 cm–18 cm) each	16	100	16	100
Salt				
White pepper, fresh ground				
Butter	¼ cup	1½ cups	60 g	360 g
Shallots, chopped	2	12	2	12
Wild mushrooms, diced	8 oz	3 lb	227 g	1.4 kg
Tomatoes, peeled, seeded, chopped	2	12	2	12
Artichoke hearts, fresh, cooked	4	25	4	25
Parsley, fresh, chopped	2 Tbsp	¾ cup	5 g	30 g
Dry white wine	2 cups	3 qt	480 ml	3 l
Heavy cream	2 cups	3 qt	480 ml	3 l
Artichoke bottoms, diced for garnish	4	25	4	25
Tomato, chopped for garnish	½	3	½	3
Chives, fresh, chopped for garnish	2 Tbsp	¾ cup	20 g	120 g

1. Preheat oven to 375°F (190°C).
2. Season the filets of sole with salt and pepper.
3. Sauté the shallots in butter in a heavy skillet for 1 or 2 minutes.
4. Add the wild mushrooms, tomatoes, artichoke hearts, and parsley. Sauté for 2 or 3 minutes. Season lightly with salt and pepper.
5. Heap some of the vegetable mixture at the center of half of the filets. Cover with the remaining filets. Place in an ovenproof dish.
6. Dot the top filets with butter. Pour wine into dish. Cover fish with parchment paper and bake for 5 to 6 minutes.
7. Remove fish and reserve.
8. Pour cooking juices into a heavy skillet. Bring to a boil, add cream, simmer to desired consistency. Taste and season. Remove from heat.
9. Spoon some sauce onto warm plates. Place the filets on the sauce, and garnish filets with artichoke bottoms, tomato, and chives.

Finnan Haddie

🐦 AMERICAN WINE SUGGESTION
Swan Cellars Pinot Noir

		U.S.		Metric	
Portions:		8	50	8	50
Smoked haddock, boneless		2½ lb	12 lb	1.1 kg	5.4 kg
Salt		1½ tsp	8 tsp	8 g	40 g
White pepper, fresh ground		¼ tsp	2 tsp	600 mg	5 g
Butter, melted		1 Tbsp	½ cup	15 g	120 g
Lemon juice		½ lemon	2 lemons	½ lemon	2 lemons

1. Place the smoked haddock on a baking sheet.
2. Season with salt and pepper and cover with wax paper.
3. Cover haddock with a second baking sheet.
4. Steam for approximately 12 to 15 minutes.
5. Brush haddock with melted butter.
6. Squeeze lemon over fish and serve with a light sauce.

Note: If the smoked flavor of the fish is too strong, soak it in cold water for one hour prior to cooking.

Lemon Pot Roast

❧ AMERICAN WINE SUGGESTION
Inglenook Vineyards Zinfandel

		U.S.		Metric	
Portions:		8	50	8	50
Virgin olive oil		1 Tbsp	6 Tbsp	15 ml	90 ml
Butter, unsalted		1 Tbsp	6 Tbsp	15 g	90 g
Sirloin beef		5 lb	31¼ lb	2.3 kg	14.1 kg
Flour, as needed					
Lemon juice		½ cup	3 cups	120 ml	720 ml
Water		½ cup	3 cups	120 ml	720 ml
Onion, chopped		½	3	½	3
Garlic cloves, mashed		1	6	1	6
Thyme, fresh, chopped		1 tsp	2 Tbsp	1 g	6 g
Salt		1 tsp	2 Tbsp	5 g	30 g
Black pepper, fresh ground		½ tsp	1 Tbsp	1.2 g	8 g
Lemon zest, grated		1 lemon	6 lemons	1 lemon	6 lemons

1. Preheat oven to 300°F (150°C).
2. Heat the olive oil and butter in a baking pan.
3. Dredge the meat with flour. Brown the roast on all sides for about 10 minutes.
4. Combine the lemon juice, water, onion, garlic, thyme, salt, and pepper in a bowl. Spread well over the meat.
5. Cover and transfer to oven. Bake for 3½ to 4 hours, or until meat is tender.
6. Remove meat and transfer to platter. Skim juices.
7. Taste for salt and pepper. Serve sauce with roast.
8. Garnish roast with grated lemon zest.

Lobster Dijonnaise   COLOR PLATE 3

❦ AMERICAN WINE SUGGESTION
Fumé Blanc

		U.S.		Metric	
Portions:	8	50	8	50
Lobster tails, baked, cooked, and chilled	8	50	8	50
Mayonnaise	½ cup	3 cups	120 ml	720 ml
Dijon mustard	2 tsp	¼ cup	10 g	60 g
Lemon juice	2 tsp	¼ cup	10 ml	60 ml
Tarragon wine vinegar	2 tsp	¼ cup	10 ml	60 ml
Chives, finely minced	2 Tbsp	¾ cup	20 g	120 g
Parsley, fresh, chopped	2 Tbsp	¾ cup	5 g	30 g
Salt				
White pepper, fresh ground				
Corn, string beans, and carrots, cooked, as needed for garnish				

1. Remove lobster meat from tails. Reserve shells for serving.
2. Chop meat into small pieces and reserve.
3. Combine mayonnaise, mustard, lemon juice, vinegar, chives, parsley, salt, and pepper, and mix well.
4. Add lobster meat, toss, and refrigerate until needed.
5. Serve in shells garnished with corn, beans, and carrots.

New England Boiled Dinner   COLOR PLATE 4

❧   AMERICAN WINE SUGGESTION
Chappelet Chenin Blanc

	Portions:	U.S.		Metric	
		8	50	8	50
Corned Beef		3 lb	19 lb	1.4 kg	8.6 kg
Garlic, as needed					
Peppercorns, black, as needed					
Parsnips, small		3	20	3	20
Carrots		6	30	6	30
Yellow turnips, small, skinned		8	50	8	50
Pearl onions, whole		8	50	8	50
Potatoes, small, peeled		8	50	8	50
Cabbage		1 head	5 heads	1 head	5 heads

1. Put corned beef, water, garlic, and peppercorn in stockpot.
2. Simmer for 4 hours or until fork penetrates thickest part of the corned beef.
3. Remove the meat.
4. Add the parsnips, carrots, yellow turnips, onions, and potatoes to the stock. Cook for 10 to 15 minutes.
5. Quarter the cabbage and add to the stock. Boil for an additional 5 minutes.

Note: Variations of this old-fashioned dish include adding a bouquet garni containing bay leaves, whole black peppercorns, fresh thyme, mustard seeds, and cloves. For added modern flair, try some Dijon mustard or fresh horseradish mixed with sour cream as an accompaniment.

New England Clam Boil COLOR PLATE 5

❧ AMERICAN WINE SUGGESTION
Vintage Chardonnay

		U.S.		Metric	
Portions:		8	50	8	50
Lobsters, 1¼ lb (560 g) each		8	50	8	50
Little necks		24	150	24	150
Mussels		24	150	24	150
Steamers		24	150	24	150
Corn on the cob (ears)		8	50	8	50
New potatoes, small		8	50	8	50
Onions, small		8	50	8	50
For Court Bouillon:					
Water, as needed					
Celery ribs, chopped		3	19	3	19
Carrots, chopped		2	12½	2	12½
Salt					
White pepper, fresh ground					
Bay leaves		3	19	3	19
Peppercorns, black, whole		2 Tbsp	¾ cup	12 g	72 g
Onions, chopped		2	12½	2	12½
Seaweed, bunches		1	6	1	6

For Court Bouillon:

1. In a large pot combine the water, celery, carrots, salt, pepper, bay leaves, peppercorns, onions, and seaweed. Bring to a boil.

For the Entrée:

2. In individual cheesecloths, arrange one lobster with equal amounts of little necks, mussels, steamers, corn, potatoes, and onion. Tie at the top to form a bundle and cook in the court bouillon over high heat, covered, for 10 minutes.
3. Remove, crack lobster tails, and serve.

Pork Loin with Mustard and Sage Sauce

❧ AMERICAN WINE SUGGESTION
Arterberry Pinot Noir

		U.S.		Metric	
Portions:		8	50	8	50
Pork loin, 4–5 lb (1.8–2.3 kg) each		1	6	1	6
Salt					
White pepper, fresh ground					
Dijon mustard		1 Tbsp	6¼ Tbsp	15 g	94 g
Sage, fresh, chopped		1 tsp	6¼ tsp	1 g	6 g
White wine		1 Tbsp	6¼ Tbsp	15 ml	93 ml
Celery stalk, chopped		1	6	1	6
Carrot, chopped		1	6	1	6
Onion, chopped		1	6	1	6
Shallot, small, chopped		1	6	1	6
For Sauce:					
Chicken stock		1 cup	1½ qt	240 ml	1.5 l
Heavy cream		½ cup	3 cups	120 ml	720 ml

1. Preheat oven to 375°F (190°C).
2. Season the pork loin with salt and pepper.
3. Blend the mustard, sage, and wine, and brush over pork. Reserve balance of wine mixture.
4. Roast for 30 minutes. Add the celery, carrots, onions, shallots, and the remainder of the wine mixture. Bake for an additional hour, or until internal temperature reaches 155°F (68°C) on a meat thermometer.
5. Transfer the pork to a warm plate and reserve.

For Sauce:

6. Skim fat from meat juice.
7. Add chicken stock and bring to a boil over medium heat.
8. Simmer for 7 minutes or until reduced by half.
9. Add drippings from platter of pork loin.
10. Add cream. Cook until thick, whisking constantly.
11. Season with salt and pepper.
12. Cut the meat in equal portions.
13. Strain the sauce over the meat and serve.

Rack of Lamb

❦ AMERICAN WINE SUGGESTION
Markham Merlot

		U.S.		Metric	
Portions:	8	50	8	50
Racks of lamb	2	13	2	13
Salt				
Black pepper, fresh ground				
Lemon	1	6	1	6
Rosemary, fresh, chopped	2 Tbsp	¾ cup	6 g	36 g
Parsley, chopped	2 Tbsp	¾ cup	5 g	30 g
Thyme, fresh, chopped	1 Tbsp	6 Tbsp	3 g	18 g
Garlic cloves, chopped	2	12	2	12
Scallions, chopped	4	25	4	25
Bread crumbs, dry	1 cup	6 cups	227 g	1.4 kg
Butter	2 Tbsp	¾ cup	30 g	180 g
Water	1 cup	1½ qt	240 ml	1.5 l

1. Remove fat and rib bones from racks of lamb. Reserve bones.
2. Preheat oven to 400°F (200°C).
3. Season lamb with salt, pepper, and lemon juice.
4. Place lamb in a baking pan with rib bones. Cook for 15 minutes.
5. Combine rosemary, parsley, thyme, garlic, scallions, and bread crumbs in a bowl. Melt the butter and add to mixture. Mix thoroughly.
6. Remove the lamb and cover with herb mixture.
7. Return lamb to oven and cook an additional 15 minutes.
8. Remove lamb from oven and reserve. Skim the fat from the pan, add water, and heat, stirring with wooden spoon.
9. Season to taste. Cook for 2 minutes.
10. Strain before serving with lamb.

Roast Prime Rib of Beef

🐝 AMERICAN WINE SUGGESTION
Meridian Vineyards Pinot Noir

		U.S.		Metric	
Portions:	8	50	8	50
Prime rib of beef, 5–6 lb (2.3–2.7 kg) each	1	7	1	7
Salt				
Black pepper, fresh ground				
Dry mustard, to taste				
Onion, small, chopped	1	6	1	6
Carrot, chopped	1	6	1	6
Celery stalk, chopped	1	6	1	6
Bay leaves	1	6	1	6
Thyme sprigs	3	18	3	18
Italian parsley sprigs	4	25	4	25

1. Preheat oven to 450°F (230°C).
2. Season the rib with salt, pepper, and dry mustard.
3. Roast in oven for 15 minutes.
4. Reduce oven temperature to 325°F (160°C). Roast to desired doneness.
   Note: 20 minutes per lb (45 minutes per kg) for medium rare.
5. When meat is half cooked, add the onion, carrot, celery, bay leaf, thyme, and parsley.
6. When meat is cooked, remove and keep warm.

Au Jus:

7. Skim fat from roasting pan, cover vegetables with water. Simmer for 15 minutes. Strain. Season with salt and pepper.

Roast Tuna with Fresh Tomato and Peppers

❧ AMERICAN WINE SUGGESTION
Robert Pepi Sauvignon Blanc

		U.S.		Metric	
Portions:		8	50	8	50
Virgin olive oil		4 Tbsp	1½ cups	60 ml	360 ml
Tuna steaks, 6 oz (170 g) each		8	50	8	50
Salt					
Black pepper, fresh ground					
Onion, small, sliced		1	6	1	6
Green bell pepper, peeled, seeded, and shredded		1	6	1	6
Red bell pepper, peeled, seeded, and shredded		1	6	1	6
Yellow bell pepper, peeled, seeded, and shredded		1	6	1	6
Garlic cloves, chopped		8	50	8	50
Tomatoes, peeled, seeded, and quartered		4	25	4	25
Bay leaves		4	25	4	25
Thyme, fresh, chopped		1 tsp	2 Tbsp	1 g	6 g
Dill, fresh, chopped		1 tsp	2 Tbsp	1 g	5 g
Parsley, fresh, chopped		4 Tbsp	1½ cups	9 g	58 g
Parsley, fresh, chopped, for garnish		1 Tbsp	6 Tbsp	2 g	15 g
Balsamic vinegar		3 Tbsp	1¼ cups	45 ml	280 ml

1. Preheat oven to 350°F (180°C).
2. In a skillet, sauté the tuna steaks in olive oil for 1 minute on each side. Season with salt and pepper. Remove tuna from pan and reserve.
3. Add onions to pan and sauté for 3 to 4 minutes.
4. Add peppers, garlic, tomatoes, bay leaves, thyme, and dill. Season with salt and pepper to taste. Cook for 6 or 7 minutes. Sprinkle with parsley.
5. Place fish on top of vegetable mixture and sprinkle with vinegar.
6. Place skillet in oven. Cook for 7 or 8 minutes.
7. Remove and serve in equal portions, garnished with parsley.

Salmon with Black Olive Paste

❧ AMERICAN WINE SUGGESTION
La Crema Pinot Noir

		U.S.		Metric	
Portions:		8	50	8	50
Salmon filets, 4 oz (115 g) each		8	50	8	50
Virgin olive oil		¼ cup	1½ cups	60 ml	360 ml
Shallots, chopped		¼ cup	1½ cups	53 g	333 g
Black pepper, fresh ground					
Salt					
Dry white wine		2 cups	3 qt	480 ml	3 l
Scallions, all white, one-half green tops, chopped		4	25	4	25
Black olive paste		¼ cup	1½ cups	60 g	360 g
Tomatoes, peeled, seeded, and chopped		4	25	4	25
Butter		¼ cup	1½ cups	60 g	360 g
Italian parsley		¼ cup	1½ cups	9 g	58 g

For Black Olive Paste:

Yield: 1½ cups			
Imported black olives	1 lb		450g
Virgin olive oil	¼ cup		60 ml
Garlic cloves, minced	4		4
Capers	2 Tbsp		16 g
Thyme	½ tsp		500 mg
Oregano	½ tsp		300 mg
Black pepper, fresh ground			

For Black Olive Paste:

1. In a food processor, combine the olives, oil, garlic, capers, thyme, oregano, and pepper. Mix well. Reserve in jar and refrigerate.

For the Entrée:

2. Preheat oven to 375°F (190°C).
3. Combine the salmon, olive oil, shallots, salt and pepper to taste, and wine. Place in an ovenproof skillet. Bake for 5 minutes.
4. Remove salmon and keep warm.
5. Place skillet over high heat and add scallions, black olive paste, tomatoes, salt, and pepper. *Note:* Use salt sparingly, since olive paste is salty.
6. Bring mixture to a boil and whisk in butter.
7. Add Italian parsley.
8. Taste for seasoning and serve with salmon filet.

Sautéed Haddock

❧ AMERICAN WINE SUGGESTION
Sterling Sauvignon Blanc

		U.S.		Metric	
Portions:		8	50	8	50
Haddock filets		3 lb	18 lb	1.4 kg	8.1 kg
Flour		1/2 cup	3 cups	60 g	350 g
Milk		1 cup	6 cups	240 ml	1.5 l
Bread crumbs		1 1/2 cups	9 cups	340 g	2 kg
Salt					
Black pepper, fresh ground					
Butter, unsalted		1/4 cup	1 1/4 cups	60 g	300 g
Vegetable oil		1/4 cup	1 1/4 cups	60 ml	300 ml
Red wine vinegar		1 3/4 Tbsp	1/2 cup	26 ml	120 ml
Lemon wedges, as needed for garnish					
Parsley, fresh, chopped, as needed for garnish					

1. Preheat oven to 350°F to 375°F (180°C to 190°C).
2. Place flour, milk, and bread crumbs in three separate bowls.
3. Cut the haddock into equal portions. Season with salt and pepper.
4. Dredge each piece of fish individually with flour, dip into milk, and lightly coat with bread crumbs.
5. In a heavy skillet, heat the butter and oil.
6. Sauté the haddock on both sides for approximately 4 to 5 minutes per side, or until golden.
7. Remove from skillet and place on a baking sheet.
8. Sprinkle with red wine vinegar and bake in oven for 8 minutes or until fish is flaky.
9. Garnish with lemon wedges and sprinkle with parsley.

Note: This method of preparation is not limited to haddock. It also works well with filet of sole, halibut, striped bass, scrod, and cod.

Sea Fare's Beggar's Bundle   COLOR PLATE 6

🦃 AMERICAN WINE SUGGESTION
Rodney Strong "Chalk Hill" Chardonnay

		U.S.		Metric	
Portions:	8	50	8	50
Haddock	1½ lb	9⅓ lb	680 g	4.2 kg
Scallops	½ lb	3 lb	225 g	1.4 kg
Lobsters, approximately 1½ lb (680 g) each; cooked and shelled	2	12½	2	12½
Crab meat	½ lb	3⅛ lb	225 g	1.4 kg
Filet of sole	½ lb	3⅛ lb	225 g	1.4 kg
Tarragon, fresh, chopped	1 tsp	2 Tbsp	750 mg	4.5 kg
Salt				
White pepper, fresh ground				
Lemon juice, fresh	1 lemon	6¼ lemons	1 lemon	6¼ lemons
Phyllo dough	1 lb	6 lb	450 g	2.7 kg
Butter	8 tsp	1 cup	40 g	240 g
Zucchini, julienne, as needed for garnish				
Baby carrots, as needed for garnish				

For Red, Green, or Yellow Pepper Sauce:

Peppers, large, red, green, or yellow	2		2	
Butter	1 Tbsp		15 g	
Shallots, chopped	2		2	
Mushrooms, sliced	2		2	
White wine	½ cup		120 ml	
Heavy cream	1½ cups		360 ml	
Salt				
Cayenne pepper	⅛ tsp		300 mg	

For Sauce:

1. Thoroughly wash the peppers.
2. Split peppers in half, and remove stems and seeds.
3. Place peppers in a blender and puree. Reserve the puree.
4. In a small saucepan, melt the butter. Add chopped shallots and mushrooms. Sauté for 2 to 3 minutes.
5. Add the wine. Reduce to about one third.
6. Add the cream and the pepper puree.
7. Add salt and cayenne.
8. Simmer for a few minutes and strain. Keep warm.

For the Entrée:

9. In a large bowl, combine haddock, scallops, lobster meat, crab meat, and filet of sole.
10. Lay out 2½ sheets of phyllo dough. Place some of the fish mixture in the center of the dough. Make sure there is enough filling to make a plump bundle. Drizzle with some butter to keep moist.

11. Stand a wooden spoon or a knife in the center of the filling and gather the dough to the center, using your hands to form a bundle. Press the phyllo firmly so that it sticks together.
12. Tie each phyllo bundle with a strand of zucchini.
13. Bake the bundles in a preheated 350°F (180°C) oven until golden brown.
14. To serve, spoon sauce onto plates, place one bundle at the center of the sauce, and garnish with zucchini and baby carrots. Serve immediately.

Swordfish Vinaigrette COLOR PLATE 8

 AMERICAN WINE SUGGESTION
Pouilly Fumé

		U.S.		Metric	
Portions:		8	50	8	50
Swordfish steaks, 8 oz (225 g) each		8	50	8	50
Salt					
White pepper, fresh ground					
Zucchini, slices, 1 per steak		8	50	8	50
For Vinaigrette:					
Lemon juice, fresh		2½ lemons	16 lemons	2½ lemons	16 lemons
Virgin olive oil		2 cups	3 qt	480 ml	3 l
Tomatoes, peeled, seeded, and diced		4	25	4	25
Salt					
White pepper, fresh ground					
Italian parsley sprigs		8	50	8	50
Baby carrots, julienne		2	12½	2	12½
Baby zucchini, julienne		2	12½	2	12½
Basil sprig, minced		1	6¼	1	6¼
Tarragon sprig, minced		1	6¼	1	6¼
Capers		3 Tbsp	1⅛ cups	45 g	255 g
Green olives, diced		3 Tbsp	1⅛ cups	45 g	255 g

1. Season swordfish with salt and pepper.
2. Grill swordfish for 4 to 5 minutes per side, depending on thickness.
3. In boiling water, blanch the zucchini.

For Vinaigrette (can be prepared 2 hours in advance):

4. In a small bowl, combine the lemon juice, oil, tomatoes, salt, pepper, parsley, carrots, zucchini, basil, tarragon, capers, and olives. Mix well.
5. To serve, arrange zucchini slices in a circle. Place swordfish steaks on top of the zucchini and drizzle with vinaigrette.

Sea Fare's Chicken with Wild Mushrooms and Scallops

COLOR PLATE 7

🦃 AMERICAN WINE SUGGESTION
Adams Vineyards Chardonnay

		U.S.		Metric	
Portions:		8	50	8	50
Chicken breasts, skinned and trimmed		8	50	8	50
Clarified butter		¼ cup	1½ cups	60 ml	360 ml
Scallops, rinsed and drained		16	100	16	100
Wild mushrooms, cleaned and trimmed		2 cups	12½ cups	450 g	2.7 kg
Salt					
White pepper, fresh ground					
Chives, chopped		2 Tbsp	¾ cup	20 g	120 g
For Sauce:					
Shallots, finely chopped		½ cup	3 cups	115 g	675 g
Bay leaves		1	6	1	6
Clarified butter		3–4 Tbsp	1⅓ cups	45–60 g	330 g
Curry powder		1 tsp	2 Tbsp	2 g	12 g
Chicken stock		½ cup	3 cups	120 ml	720 ml
Heavy cream		1 cup	1½ qt	240 ml	1.5 l

For Sauce:

1. Sauté the shallots and bay leaf until golden in the butter.
2. Add curry powder and chicken stock. Stir well and simmer for 8 to 10 minutes, or until reduced to about one third and pasty.
3. Add the cream and simmer. If too thick, add more chicken stock. Pass through a fine sieve and reserve.

For the Entrée:

4. Preheat oven to 420°F (215°C).
5. Season the chicken breasts.
6. Warm a sauté pan and melt half the butter. Add the chicken breasts and brown on both sides. Make sure they do not stick. Place in the preheated oven.
7. In a pan, sauté the scallops in the remaining butter. Make sure they are cooked through, but still juicy. Remove and keep warm.
8. Add the mushrooms to the pan. Season with salt and pepper and sauté gently. Drain off butter and keep warm.
9. After 5 to 6 minutes, remove the chicken from the oven. Breasts should be cooked through but still juicy.
10. Place chicken on warm plates, golden side up.
11. Accompany with mushrooms and scallops and cover with curry sauce. Sprinkle with fresh chives and serve.

Shellfish in Cream Sauce

❧ AMERICAN WINE SUGGESTION
Silverado Chardonnay

		U.S.		Metric	
Portions:		8	50	8	50
Mussels		24	150	24	150
Lobsters, live, 1½ lb (675 g) each		3	20	3	20
Dry white wine		¾ cup	4¾ cups	180 ml	1.1 l
Scallops		1½ lb	9½ lb	675 g	4.2 kg
Maine shrimp		2 lb	12½ lb	1 kg	5.6 kg
For Sauce:					
Butter, unsalted		½ cup	3⅛ cups	120 g	750 g
Flour		¼ cup	1½ cups	28 g	175 g
Garlic cloves, peeled, minced		4	25	4	25
Clam juice		1 cup	1½ qt	240 ml	1.5 l
Heavy cream		1 cup	1½ qt	240 ml	1.5 l
Dry white wine		1 cup	1½ qt	240 ml	1.5 l
White pepper, fresh ground					
Cayenne pepper, to taste					
Fennel, minced		2 Tbsp	¾ cup	28 g	168 g
Bay leaves		1	6	1	6
Dill, fresh, chopped, as needed for garnish					

1. Preheat oven to 400°F (200°C).
2. Thoroughly wash the mussels and steam open. Drain.
3. In a large stockpot, heat enough water and wine to boil the lobsters.
4. Once water is boiling, place the lobsters in the pot and cover. Simmer for 12 minutes.
5. Remove lobsters from the shell and cut into two-in. pieces. Set aside.
6. Ready scallops and shrimp in an ovenproof casserole. Set aside.

For Sauce:

7. In a heavy saucepan, melt the butter.
8. Add the flour and garlic and sauté over low heat, stirring constantly for 2 minutes.
9. Remove from heat. Add the clam juice, cream, and wine.
10. Return to heat, stirring sauce until thickened.
11. Add white pepper, cayenne, fennel, and bay leaf. Stir well.
12. Pour the sauce over the scallops and shrimp. Bake for 20 minutes.
13. Add the mussels and lobster and bake for an additional 5 minutes.
14. Garnish with chopped dill and serve.

Stuffed Turkey

🦃 AMERICAN WINE SUGGESTION
Beaulieu Vineyards "Los Carneros" Pinot Noir

	U.S.		Metric	
Portions:	8	50	8	50
Turkey, fresh, 10–12 lb (4.5–5.4 kg), for 50: 18–20 lb (8–9 kg) each	1	2	1	2
Salt				
Butter	1 oz	4 oz	28 g	114 g
Baked dressing	1½ lb	6 lb	675 g	2.7 kg
For Dressing:				
Onion	3 oz	16 oz	85 g	454 g
Drippings, from bird	3 oz	16 oz	85 g	454 g
Celery, chopped	3 oz	16 oz	85 g	454 g
Soft bread	¾ lb	4 lb	338 g	1.8 kg
Chicken stock	1½ cups	2⅓ qt	360 ml	2.3 l
Thyme, fresh, chopped	½ tsp	4 tsp	500 mg	4 g
Sage, fresh, chopped	½ tsp	4 tsp	500 mg	4 g
Salt	2 tsp	2 Tbsp	10 g	30 g
Black pepper, fresh ground	⅓ tsp	2½ tsp	1 g	5 g
For Giblet Gravy:				
Giblets, cooked				
Chicken fat	3 Tbsp	1 cup	45 ml	240 ml
Flour	3 Tbsp	1 cup	21 g	130 g
Chicken stock	1½ pt	3 qt	720 ml	2.9 l
Salt				
Black pepper, fresh ground				

1. Preheat the oven to 350°F (180°C).
2. Rinse and salt the cavity of the bird.
3. In a roasting pan, place turkey breast down, browning one side in butter.
4. Turn the bird, add giblets, and brown the other side.
5. Add 1 quart water per bird, and roast 3 to 4 hours, or until the flesh is tender.

For Dressing:

6. In a pan, sauté the onions in the drippings. Add the celery.
7. In a baking pan, break the bread into 1 in. pieces.
8. Add the sautéed onions and celery to the bread.
9. Add chicken stock, thyme, sage, salt, and pepper. Mix well.
10. Cover with paper to prevent a crust and bake at 350°F (180°C) for 30 minutes.

For Giblet Gravy:

11. Remove the giblets from the roasting pan. Chop finely.
12. Add the giblets, chicken fat, and flour to the pan in which the turkey was roasted. Brown lightly.

13. Add the chicken stock, whipping until smooth, approximately 10 minutes. Allow to thicken to desired consistency.
14. Season with salt and pepper. Strain.

Notes: *Chestnut Dressing:* Follow same method but add chestnuts cooked in deep fat at 360°F (180°C) until shells break and peel. 8 oz (225 g) for 8 people, or 2½ lb (1 kg) for 50 people.
Oyster Dressing: Follow the same method, but add chopped oysters. 6 oz (170 g) for 8 people, or 2 pt (1 kg) for 50 people.
Yield: Turkey yields 33 percent net cooked meat.
Frozen Turkey: If frozen turkey must be used, thaw before roasting. Do not soak in water.

Yankee Pot Roast

 AMERICAN WINE SUGGESTION
Charles Krug Zinfandel

	Portions:	U.S.		Metric	
		8	50	8	50
Boneless round or chuck roast		3 lb	20 lb	1.4 kg	9 kg
Butter		½ cup	1 lb	120 g	450 g
Beef stock		1 cup	2 qt	240 ml	2 l
Celery sticks		3 oz	1 lb	85 g	454 g
Baby carrots		8	50	8	50
Pearl onions		8	50	8	50
Potatoes, small		8	50	8	50
Parsnips, small		8	50	8	50
Salt					
Black pepper, fresh ground					
Bay leaves		1	3	1	3
Allspice, ground		Pinch	1 tsp	Pinch	1 g
Parsley, chopped, as needed					
Flour		2 Tbsp	½ cup	14 g	56 g

1. Preheat oven to 350°F to 375°F (180°C to 190°C).
2. Place the pot roast in a roasting pan with a small amount of butter and beef stock.
3. Cover with aluminum foil and cook for 1 hour.
4. Remove from oven and surround the roast with the vegetables. Add the remaining stock and butter.
5. Season with salt, pepper, bay leaf, and allspice. Cook an additional hour, until the meat and vegetables are tender.
6. Remove the pot roast. Slice the meat. Garnish with cooked vegetables. Sprinkle with parsley and serve.

For Sauce:

7. Heat the juice in the pan and strain.
8. Add the flour. Whip until smooth. Season with salt and pepper and serve on the side.

ACCOMPANIMENTS

Boston Baked Beans

		U.S.		Metric	
Portions:	8	50	8	50	
Dried Navy beans	1 lb	8 lb	450 g	3.6 kg	
Onion, large, chopped	1	5	1	5	
Dark brown sugar	2 Tbsp	1 cup	28 g	226 g	
Molasses	1/2 cup	2 cups	120 ml	480 ml	
Dry mustard	1 Tbsp	1/2 cup	6 g	48 g	
Rum, dark	1/2 cup	1 1/4 cups	120 ml	300 ml	
Water, to cover					
Tomato puree	2 oz	16 oz	57 g	454 g	
Salt pork	4 oz	1 1/2 lb	113 g	680 g	
Salt					
Black pepper, fresh ground					

1. Wash beans, soak at least 8 hours, and drain.
2. Combine beans, onion, sugar, molasses, mustard, rum, water, and tomato puree in clay baking pot. Mix thoroughly.
3. Cut salt pork into equal strips and place in bean mixture. Season with salt and pepper.
4. Cover and bake in preheated 300°F (150°C) oven for 3 to 4 hours. Reduce the heat to 250°F (120°C). Cook until the beans are tender, adding water as necessary.

Boston Brown Bread

		U.S.		Metric	
Portions:	8	50	8	50	
Bread flour	1/2 cup	3 cups	113 g	680 g	
Rye flour	1/2 cup	3 cups	113 g	680 g	
Graham flour	1/2 cup	3 cups	113 g	680 g	
Corn meal	1/2 cup	3 cups	113 g	680 g	
Baking soda	1 tsp	2 Tbsp	3 g	18 g	
Milk	1 cup	6 cups	240 ml	1.4 l	
Molasses	1/3 cup	2 cups	80 ml	480 ml	
Salt	1/2 tsp	1 Tbsp	2 g	18 g	
Eggs	1	6	1	6	
Raisins	1/3 lb	2 lb	150 g	900 g	

1. In a large bowl, mix together the bread flour, rye flour, graham flour, and corn meal.
2. Dissolve the baking soda in a small amount of milk. Combine remaining milk, molasses, salt, egg, and mix well. Add raisins if desired. Add the dissolved baking soda.
3. Combine the flours and the liquid to make a well-mixed dough.
4. Butter baking tin and fill three-quarters. Cover. Steam for 3 hours.

New England Salt Pork

		U.S.	Metric
	Portions:	8	8
Lean salt pork		4 lb	1.8 kg
Flour		8 Tbsp	56 g
Lard		4 Tbsp	60 g
For Gravy:			
Salt pork drippings		½ cup	120 ml
Flour		6 Tbsp	42 g
Milk		4½ cups	1.1 l

1. Cut salt pork into ½ in. (1 cm) slices.
2. Cover salt pork slices in warm water. Soak for 4 hours. Change water 3 or 4 times. Pat dry.
3. Grease heavy skillet with lard. Flour each slice of pork and sauté until a rich, crusty brown texture is achieved. Remove pork and reserve.

For Gravy:

4. Stir ¾ of the flour into the salt pork drippings. Blend thoroughly.
5. Add a little milk, stirring until smooth.
6. Add a little more milk. Mix well.
7. Gradually stir in remaining milk. Cook over low heat, stirring constantly.
8. Stir until thick. Remove from heat.

Old-Fashioned Potato Salad

		U.S.		Metric	
Portions:		8	50	8	50
Potatoes		1½ lb	10 lb	680 g	4.5 kg
Onion, minced		½	3	½	3
Green bell pepper, chopped		1½ oz	9 oz	42 g	255 g
Celery, chopped		2½ oz	1 cup	70 g	450 g
Red wine vinegar		1 Tbsp	½ cup	15 ml	120 ml
Shallot, minced		1	5	1	5
Sugar		1 tsp	2 Tbsp	5 g	30 g
Eggs, hard-boiled		1	8	1	8
Mayonnaise		4 oz	3 cups	60 ml	720 ml
Parsley		¼ oz	2 oz	7 g	57 g
Pimento		½ oz	4 oz	14 g	114 g
Salt					
Black pepper, fresh ground					

1. Boil potatoes for 20 to 25 minutes, or until soft. Drain, peel, and slice. Keep warm.
2. Combine onions, green pepper, celery, vinegar, shallots, and sugar. Add to the potatoes.
3. Thinly slice hard-boiled eggs. Add to potatoes.
4. Add the mayonnaise, parsley, pimento, salt, and pepper. Mix well.

Note: To prevent browning of potatoes, do not mix potato salad in metal container. For best results, mix less than 10 pounds of potatoes at a time.

Red Corn Beef Hash

	Portions:	U.S.		Metric	
		8	50	8	50
Corn beef, cooked, chopped		2 cups	3 qt	454 g	2.8 kg
Potatoes, cooked, chopped		1½ qt	9 qt	1.4 kg	8.5 kg
Onions, finely chopped		1½ cups	9 cups	340 g	2.1 kg
Beets, chopped		2 cups	3 qt	454 g	2.8 kg
Salt					
Black pepper, fresh ground					
Worcestershire sauce		1½ tsp	3 Tbsp	8 ml	45 ml
Light cream		½ cup	3 cups	120 ml	720 ml
Bacon drippings or butter		¼ cup	1½ cups	60 ml	360 ml

1. In a bowl, combine the corn beef, potatoes, onions, beets, salt, pepper, Worcestershire sauce, and cream. Mix well.
2. Using a skillet, heat the bacon drippings or butter. Add the mixture. Cook at low heat, stirring occasionally.
3. Remove from heat and serve.

Note: This dish is a perfect example of Puritan thriftiness, for it utilizes leftovers from New England boiled dinner.

Spaghetti Squash with Red and Yellow Peppers and Garlic Sauce

	U.S.		Metric	
Portions:	8	50	8	50
Spaghetti squash	2	12½	2	12½
Salt				
White pepper, fresh ground				
Virgin olive oil	6 Tbsp	2⅓ cups	90 ml	500 ml
Garlic cloves	2	12½	2	12½
Red bell pepper, julienne	½	3½	½	3½
Yellow bell pepper, julienne	½	3½	½	3½
Scallions, chopped	8	50	8	50
Oregano, fresh, chopped	1 tsp	6¼ tsp	600 mg	4 g
Basil, fresh, chopped, reserve some leaves for garnish	2 Tbsp	¾ cup	4 g	25 g

1. Preheat oven to 350°F (180°C).
2. Cut the squash in half lengthwise and wrap each half in foil.
3. Bake for 35 to 40 minutes.
4. Remove squash from foil, discard seeds, and shred into a bowl. Season with salt and pepper.
5. Cover and reserve.
6. Heat the oil in a heavy skillet.
7. Sauté the garlic. Add the red and yellow peppers and scallions. Sprinkle with oregano, salt, and white pepper. Sauté for 1 to 2 minutes.
8. Add the spaghetti squash. Mix well.
9. Serve on warm plates and garnish with chopped basil and basil leaves.

Succotash

	Portions:	U.S.		Metric	
		8	50	8	50
Lima beans, fresh		2 cups	3 qt	454 g	2.8 kg
Corn kernels		2 cups	3 qt	454 g	2.8 kg
Butter		2½ Tbsp	1 cup	38 g	240 g
Lean bacon, cut into pieces		4	25	4	25
Whipped cream		½ cup	3 cups	120 ml	720 ml
Salt					
White pepper, fresh ground					
Parsley, fresh, chopped, as needed					

1. In a small saucepan, boil lightly salted water.
2. Add the lima beans and cook 5 or 6 minutes.
3. Add the corn kernels. Cook until vegetables are tender. Drain.
4. In a skillet, melt the butter and add the bacon. Cook 5 to 6 minutes.
5. Add the vegetables and remaining ingredients. Sauté until hot.
6. Serve as a side dish.

Note: This dish was created by the Narragansett Indians and was introduced to the Pilgrims at the first Thanksgiving.

DESSERTS

Apples Baked in Maple Syrup

	U.S.		Metric	
Portions:	8	50	8	50
Apples, red or green, large	8	50	8	50
Walnuts, chopped	8 tsp	1 cup	38 g	227 g
Raisins	8 tsp	1 cup	38 g	227 g
Maple syrup	½ cup	3 cups	120 ml	720 ml
Butter, sweet	½ cup	3 cups	120 ml	720 ml
Cinnamon, ground, to taste				
Nutmeg, ground, to taste				
Heavy cream	1½ cups	9 cups	360 ml	2.1 l

1. Preheat oven to 375°F (190°C).
2. Core apples, taking care not to cut through the bottom. Place in baking dish.
3. Fill each apple with 1 tsp of walnut and 1 tsp of raisins. Pour in 1 Tbsp of maple syrup and 1 Tbsp of sweet butter.
4. Sprinkle with cinnamon and nutmeg.
5. Add ½ in. (1 cm) of water to baking dish and bake for 20 to 25 minutes.
6. To serve, transfer to serving dishes and drizzle with cream.

Note: The Algonquin Indians taught the colonists how to collect maple sap by cutting a slash in tree trunks.

Indian Pudding

	U.S.		Metric	
Portions:	8	50	8	50
Milk, cold	3 cups	5 qt	720 ml	5 l
Yellow corn meal	½ cup	1½ lb	113 g	680 g
Sugar	¼ cup	1 lb	57 g	450 g
Molasses	½ cup	2½ pt	120 ml	1.1 l
Lemon rind	1	3	1	3
Eggs, lightly beaten	2	12	2	12

1. Preheat oven to 400°F (200°C).
2. Bring the milk to a boil in a double boiler or steam kettle.
3. Add the corn meal. Cook slowly until mixture becomes mush.
4. Remove from heat and add sugar, molasses, lemon rinds, and beaten egg.
5. Pour mixture into pudding dishes or pan.
6. Place in bain-marie and bake until brown.
7. Serve hot with whipped cream.

Pumpkin Pie

	U.S.	Metric
Portions:	8	8

For Pie Crust:

Flour	2 cups	225 g
Salt	1/4 tsp	1.3 g
Butter, unsalted, cut in pieces	2/3 cup	160 g
Ice water	3–4 Tbsp	45–60 ml

For Pie:

Pumpkin, fresh cooked or canned	2 cups	450 g
Eggs, whole, beaten	2	2
Brown sugar	3/4 cup	90 g
Half and half	1 cup	240 ml
Milk	1/2 cup	120 ml
Brandy	1 Tbsp	15 ml
Corn starch	1 Tbsp	11 g
Ginger	1 tsp	10 g
Cinnamon	3/4 tsp	1.5 g
Salt	1/2 tsp	2.5 g
Vanilla	1 tsp	5 ml
Molasses	1 Tbsp	15 ml
Egg whites	2	2

For Pie Crust:

1. Sift together flour and salt in a mixing bowl.
2. Add butter and rub into flour until mixture is like a coarse meal, then mix in enough water to make dough sticky.
3. Knead briefly, using hands, until smooth.
4. Gather dough and wrap in plastic wrap.
5. Refrigerate 1 to 2 hours before using.

For Pie:

6. Preheat oven to 425°F (220°C).
7. Mix together pumpkin and eggs.
8. Stir in brown sugar, half and half, milk, and brandy.
9. Add corn starch, ginger, cinnamon, salt, vanilla, molasses, and egg whites. Stir well.
10. Remove pie dough from refrigerator and roll out to a circle large enough to line 9 in. (20 cm) pie plate. Line plate with dough, pressing on bottom and sides.
11. Spoon pumpkin filling into pie shell, spreading evenly.
12. Bake for 15 minutes.
13. Reduce temperature to 350°F (180°C). Bake for 20 to 25 minutes, or until a thin knife blade comes out clean when inserted in pie.
14. Let pie cool before serving.
15. Serve with whipped cream.

Lemon Soufflé Torte

	U.S.		Metric	
Portions:	8	50	8	50
For Pastry Shell:				
Flour	1¼ cups	7½ cups	135 g	844 g
Sugar	1 Tbsp	6 Tbsp	15 g	90 g
Butter, chilled and cut into small pieces	½ cup	3½ lb	120 g	750 g
Vanilla extract, to taste				
Cold water	2 Tbsp	¾ cup	30 ml	180 ml
For Lemon Paste:				
Lemons	5	30	5	30
Lemon juice	⅓ cup	2 cups	80 ml	480 ml
Sugar	½ Tbsp	3¼ Tbsp	7.5 g	49 g
Bottled water, unflavored	⅓ cup	2 cups	80 ml	480 ml
For the Soufflé:				
Sweet pastry shell	1	6	1	6
Eggs, large, separated	4	25	4	25
Granulated sugar	½ cup	3 cups	120 g	720 g
Lemon paste	1 tsp	2 Tbsp	5 g	28 g
Lemon juice, fresh	½ cup	3 cups	120 ml	720 ml
Heavy cream	¼ cup	1½ cups	60 ml	360 ml
Corn starch	½ tsp	3 tsp	2 g	11 g

For Pastry Shell:

1. Preheat oven to 350°F (180°C).
2. Using a food processor, combine the flour, sugar, butter, and vanilla. Mix well until evenly blended.
3. Add the water while blending, turning the machine on/off until a dough forms.
4. Immediately roll the dough between 2 sheets of plastic wrap. Roll into an 11 in. (28 cm) circle.
5. Peel top layer of plastic wrap and reverse dough onto 9 in. (20 cm) tart pan with removable base.
6. Using thumbs and forefingers, extend dough slightly over the rim.
7. Using a fork, prick the bottom of shell. Chill for 10 minutes before baking.
8. Bake without filling for 5 minutes. Check for and deflate air bubbles during baking.
9. Continue to bake until crisp and pale golden. Add filling.

For Lemon Paste:

10. Using a vegetable peeler, peel lemons, taking only the colored part of the skin.
11. Combine the lemon peel, lemon juice, sugar, and water. Bring to a boil and simmer for 20 minutes, or until all the liquid has evaporated.

12. Transfer to a food processor, and blend until smooth. Add cold water and scrape sides of processor as needed. Consistency should be between that of a paste and a puree. Store in refrigerator until needed.

For the Soufflé:

13. Reduce oven heat to 325°F (160°C).
14. In a metal bowl, place egg yolks, ¾ of the sugar and beat until pale in color.
15. Add the lemon paste, lemon juice, and cream. With the bowl over a pan of simmering water, whisk the mixture for 6 to 7 minutes, or until it thickens slightly.
16. In a separate bowl, whisk egg whites until they hold shape.
17. Add the remainder of sugar and the corn starch to the egg white.
18. Beat until the meringue is stiff and shiny.
19. Fold into egg yolk mixture.
20. Place mixture into the prepared shell and bake for 12 minutes. Dust with confectioner's sugar and serve at room temperature.

CHAPTER **6**

Mid-Atlantic States

O wner Sirio Maccioni of Le Cirque restaurant in New York City describes his modern approach to cooking in the following way: "Good cooking is simplicity. If the chef uses fresh ingredients, there is no need to cover them up with heavy sauces." This "simple classical" cooking is the phoenix born from the ashes of one of the most diverse and sophisticated cuisines in the country, the cuisine of the mid-Atlantic states (Pennsylvania, Maryland, New York, New Jersey, Delaware, and West Virginia).

The mid-Atlantic states are the true melting pot of America. Nearly every immigrant group has passed through this region, leaving its mark on food and custom. New York City, for example, originally settled by the Dutch and the British, is currently home to more than 100 different nationalities. These varied ethnic groups endeavor to keep their national cooking alive and contribute exotic ingredients to the regional fare.

Healthful, low-fat, high carbohydrate dishes from China and the Mediterranean are contrasted with rich desserts and sauces from France and other parts of Europe. When selecting from among this medley of cuisines, the chef should keep the general guidelines for healthy eating in mind. The kind of fat, as well as the amount used, must be considered. Chinese dishes, for example, are generally low in fat (about 20 percent of the calories) and generous in vegetables and starch. Mediterranean food is low in fat (about 25 percent of the calories) and the kind of fat used is often monounsaturated olive oil. The possibilities for creative cooking are as boundless as the number of cultures that inhabit this region and the variety of nutritious ingredients that abound here. The rich farmlands provide fresh fruits and vegetables and the ocean offers a variety of seafood.

The only truly regional cuisine of the mid-Atlantic states is that of the Pennsylvania Dutch. Many Pennsylvania Dutch dishes, such as scrapple, sausages, and pies, tend to be high in fat. Pennsylvania Dutch cooking is also well seasoned, so fat can be reduced with minimal effect on flavor. Lean pork dishes can be complemented by dandelion salads with reduced fat dressings. Desserts should stress fresh fruits while

75

minimizing pastry and cream sauces. The pickles, preserves, and relishes for which this area is famous make appetizing, low-fat accompaniments. These are, however, high in salt and should not be over-stressed. Apple butter and jams are excellent butter substitutes on toast, muffins, and breakfast or dinner rolls.

APPETIZERS

Cold Snapper in a Caper Cream Sauce

	U.S.		Metric	
Portions:	8	50	8	50
Dry white wine	1 qt	6 qt	1 l	6 l
Garlic cloves, peeled, crushed	1¼	7½	1¼	7½
Lemon wedges	1½ lemons	9 lemons	1½ lemons	9 lemons
Carrots, peeled, sliced	1½	9	1½	9
Celery stalks	1½	9	1½	9
Parsley sprigs, leaves only	5¼	32	5¼	32
Black peppercorns	11	68	11	68
Snapper filet, fresh, cleaned, skinned	8 lb	50 lb	3.6 kg	22.5 kg
For Sauce:				
Garlic cloves, peeled, crushed	3	18	3	18
Capers, drained	¼ cup	1½ cups	32 g	200 g
Egg yolk, hard boiled	5	31	5	31
Salt				
White pepper, fresh ground				
Scallions, green only, chopped	2½	15	2½	15
Parsley, coarsely chopped	1 cup	6 cups	37 g	225 g
Virgin olive oil	1 cup	1½ qt	240 ml	1.5 l
Vinegar, white wine	⅓ cup	2 cups	80 ml	480 ml
Heavy cream	1¼ cups	7½ cups	300 ml	1.8 l

1. Place wine in a fish poacher and add enough water to fill pan halfway.
2. Add the garlic, lemon, carrot, celery, parsley, and peppercorns. Bring to a boil.
3. Simmer for 10 to 12 minutes.
4. Poach fish in liquid for 10 to 15 minutes, depending on thickness.
5. Remove and cover with a damp towel. Refrigerate for 4 hours.

For Sauce:

6. Combine the garlic, capers, egg yolk, salt, pepper, scallions, and parsley in food processor. Puree for several seconds, until smooth.
7. Add oil and vinegar, while continuing processing with pulsing action.
8. In a separate bowl, whip heavy cream until soft peaks form.
9. Fold sauce into cream and let set. Chill for 25 minutes.
10. Remove snapper and serve on a bed of chilled sauce.

Duck Liver with Madeira

		U.S.		Metric	
Portions:	8	50	8	50
Duck liver, trimmed	¾ lb	4½ lb	340 g	2 kg
Butter	2½ Tbsp	1 cup	38 g	240 g
Onion, chopped	1–2	10–12	1–2	10–12
Salt				
Black pepper, fresh ground				
Madeira	¾ cup	4½ cups	180 ml	1.1 l
Walnuts, chopped	1¾ cups	10½ cups	400 g	2.4 kg
Butter	½ cup	3½ cups	135 g	840 g
Nutmeg	½ tsp	1 Tbsp	1 g	6 g
Thyme	¾ tsp	4½ tsp	750 mg	4.5 g
Fennel, powdered	Pinch	To taste	Pinch	To taste
Walnut halves, unbroken	8	50	8	50
Toast, cut into strips as needed				

1. Preheat broiler.
2. Cut liver into pieces and place on broiler. Sprinkle with butter, add onions, and season with salt and pepper.
3. Broil close to heat for about 1 or 2 minutes per side. Remove and reserve.
4. Pour ½ of the Madeira in a food processor or blender and puree, adding a few walnuts at a time until all have been added. Puree until smooth.
5. Add the remainder of the Madeira and the liver. Puree until smooth. Stop the machine occasionally and scrape the sides.
6. Add the butter, nutmeg, thyme, and fennel. Mix thoroughly.
7. Place mixture into ramekins, topping with walnut halves, and chill in a refrigerator for a minimum of 12 hours or, preferably, overnight.
8. Serve with toast.

Ham Mousse

		U.S.		Metric	
	Portions:	8	50	8	50
Butter		¼ cup	1½ cups	60 g	360 g
Flour		¼ cup	1½ cups	28 g	169 g
Milk, heated		1 cup	1½ qt	240 ml	1.4 l
Dijon mustard		1 Tbsp	6 Tbsp	15 g	90 g
Sage		¼ tsp	1½ tsp	250 mg	1.5 g
Cayenne					
Madeira		¼ cup	1½ cups	60 ml	360 ml
Egg yolks		2	12	2	12
Heavy cream		½ cup	3 cups	120 ml	720 ml
Gelatin		2 Tbsp	¾ cup	30 g	180 g
Chicken stock		½ cup	3 cups	120 ml	720 ml
Cooked ham, skinned, trimmed, cut into chunks		1 lb	450 g	6 lb	2.7 kg
Watercress for garnish					

1. In a heavy pan, heat the butter and stir in flour. Cook over low heat for 2 minutes.
2. Slowly add the hot milk, stirring well. Cook until thick, stirring well.
3. Add the mustard, sage, cayenne, and Madeira. Blend well.
4. In a bowl, combine the egg yolks with the cream, whisking constantly.
5. Stir a small amount of hot white sauce into the egg mixture.
6. Add egg mixture to hot white sauce, continuing to cook over low heat. Stir until thick.
7. In a separate bowl, soften the gelatin in the chicken stock for several minutes; stir into the hot white sauce.
8. In a food processor, finely chop the ham. Stir into hot white sauce.
9. Pour into a 1 qt (1 l) mold and chill for at least 8 hours.
10. Garnish with watercress before unmolding.

Leek and Wild Mushroom Quiche

		U.S.		Metric	
Portions:		*8*	*50*	*8*	*50*
Wild mushrooms, dried		2 oz	12½ oz	57 g	354 g
Pie shell		1	5	1	5
Leeks, white only		4	25	4	25
Butter		¼ cup	1½ cups	60 g	360 g
Eggs, large		5	31	5	31
Light cream		1½ cups	9 cups	360 ml	2.1 l
Mixed herbs, dried, as needed					
Salt					
White pepper, fresh ground					
Gruyère cheese, grated		¾ cup	4½ cups	170 g	1 kg

For Pie Shell Pastry: Yields 2 pie shells

Flour		2 cups		225 g	
Salt		¼ tsp		1 g	
Vegetable shortening		¾ cup		170 g	
Water		¼ cup		60 ml	

For Pie Shells:

1. Combine flour and salt in a bowl.
2. Cut in shortening with pastry cutter until coarse. Stir well with a spoon.
3. Gradually add the water until dough has formed.
4. Wrap dough in plastic wrap and chill for at least 45 minutes before using.

For Custard:

5. Preheat oven to 425°F (220°C).
6. Soak the mushrooms for 35 minutes in enough warm water to cover them. Clean and chop.
7. Roll out pastry to ⅛ in. (3 mm) thick on a floured surface. Line a 12 in. (30 cm) pie plate or quiche dish with pastry.
8. Cover pastry with wax paper and bake for 10 to 12 minutes or until golden brown. Remove and cool. Reduce oven temperature to 350°F (180°C).
9. In a medium skillet, sauté the leeks in butter for 2 minutes.
10. Add the mushrooms and cook for an additional 2 minutes. Transfer to a bowl and reserve.
11. In a separate bowl, break and beat the eggs.
12. Add the light cream, herbs, salt, and pepper. Mix well and add to the leek mixture, stirring well.
13. Pour mixture into pie shell and sprinkle with cheese.
14. Bake for 40 to 50 minutes or until top is golden.

Shrimp and Artichoke au Gratin

		U.S.		Metric	
Portions:		8	50	8	50
Butter		3 Tbsp	1⅛ cups	45 g	280 g
Onion, small, finely chopped		1	6	1	6
Scallions, small, finely chopped		2	12	2	12
Artichoke hearts		8	50	8	50
Flour		3 Tbsp	1⅛ cups	20 g	130 g
Butter		2 Tbsp	¾ cup	30 g	180 g
Light cream		1 cup	1½ qt	240 ml	1.5 l
Madeira		½ cup	3 cups	120 ml	720 ml
Salt					
White pepper, fresh ground					
Tarragon, chopped		1 tsp	2 Tbsp	750 mg	4.5 g
Dry mustard		4 Tbsp	1½ cups	24 g	150 g
Parmesan cheese, grated		1½ cups	9 cups	340 g	2 kg
Shrimp, peeled, deveined, chopped		2½ lb	15½ lb	1.1 kg	7 kg

1. In a heavy skillet, heat the butter. Sauté onions and scallions for 3 or 4 minutes.
2. Add the artichoke hearts and sauté for an additional 2 minutes.
3. In another pan, combine the flour with the butter. Cook, whisking constantly, for about 2 or 3 minutes.
4. Continue to whisk. Add light cream, slowly add the Madeira.
5. Season to taste with salt and pepper. Add the tarragon and simmer over low heat until the sauce thickens.
6. Once thickened, remove from heat. Add the dry mustard and grated cheese, mixing constantly.
7. Divide the artichoke mixture equally.
8. Add the shrimp and equal portions of the sauce.
9. Sprinkle with more grated Parmesan cheese and bake in 375°F (190°C) preheated oven for 20 to 28 minutes.

Smoked Salmon Tartare with Asparagus Mayonnaise

COLOR PLATE 9

		U.S.		Metric	
Portions:		8	50	8	50
Smoked salmon, chopped		1½ lb	9 lb	675 g	4.1 kg
Shallots, very finely chopped		½ cup	3 cups	100 g	640 g
Chives, chopped		½ cup	3 cups	80 g	480 g
Capers, chopped		3 Tbsp	1⅛ cups	24 g	150 g
Dijon mustard		2½ Tbsp	1 cup	38 g	238 g
White pepper, fresh ground					
For Garnish:					
Cucumbers		4	25	4	25
Egg yolks, hard-boiled		3	18	3	18
Sour cream		3½ cups	5 qt	840 ml	5 l
Capers, whole		⅓ cup	2 cups	40 g	240 g
Shallots, chopped		⅓ cup	2 cups	68 g	428 g
Lemon wedges		1 lemon	6 lemons	1 lemon	6 lemons
Chives, as needed					
Toast points, as needed					
For Mayonnaise:					
Egg yolks		3		3	
Asparagus, cooked, chopped		⅓ bunch		⅓ bunch	
Lemon juice		3 oz		90 ml	
Virgin olive oil		1 cup		240 ml	
Salt					
White pepper, fresh ground					

1. In a mixing bowl, combine the smoked salmon, shallots, chives, capers, mustard, and white pepper. Mix thoroughly and chill. When cold, form salmon patties.
2. Thinly slice the cucumbers and overlap them in a circle slightly larger than a salmon patty.
3. Center the salmon patties on top of the cucumbers.
4. Garnish with chopped egg yolks, sour cream, capers, shallots, chives, and lemon wedges.
5. Serve with toast points.

For Mayonnaise:

6. In a food processor or blender, blend the egg yolks, asparagus, and lemon juice.
7. With machine running, add the olive oil.
8. Season with salt and pepper to taste.
9. Serve salmon tartare with mayonnaise on the side.

SOUPS

Black Bean Soup

	U.S.		Metric	
Portions:	8	50	8	50
Dry black beans	1½ cups	9 cups	340 g	2 kg
Water	9 cups	3½ gallons	2.2 l	13.5 l
Butter	2 Tbsp	¾ cup	30 g	180 g
Smoked bacon, cut into small pieces	⅓ lb	2 lb	150 g	900 g
Onions, small, diced	1½	9	1½	9
Celery stalk, finely chopped	1	6	1	6
Beef stock	1½ qt	9 qt	1.4 l	9 l
Water	2 cups	3 qt	480 ml	3 l
Garlic, fresh, chopped	1 Tbsp	6 Tbsp	10 g	60 g
Parsley, fresh, chopped	1½ Tbsp	9 Tbsp	4 g	21 g
Bay leaves	1	6	1	6
Salt				
Black pepper, fresh ground				
Wine, Madeira or sherry	¼ cup	1½ cups	60 ml	360 ml
Eggs, hard-boiled, finely chopped	2	12	2	12
Lemon, sliced and diced	1	7	1	7

1. Soak the beans in water for 12 hours before preparing the soup.
2. Drain well before cooking.
3. In a stock pot, heat the butter; add the bacon, onion, and celery. Sauté for 4 or 5 minutes.
4. Add the black beans, beef stock, 2 cups (480 ml) of water for 8 servings [3 qt (3 l) for 50 servings], garlic, parsley, bay leaf, salt, and pepper. Bring to a boil.
5. Reduce heat and simmer for 2 to 2½ hours. Add more water as needed. The beans should always be covered with water.
6. Once the beans are cooked, transfer in batches to a blender and puree.
7. Return pureed beans to stock pot. Add the wine. Taste for seasoning.
8. Cook over low heat.
9. Gently mix in chopped egg. Ladle into hot bowls. Serve warm with lemon slices.

Note: This recipe is from the Coach House Restaurant, the New York City landmark owned and operated by Leon Lianides.

Garlic Soup

		U.S.		Metric	
Portions:		8	50	8	50
Virgin olive oil		6 Tbsp	2⅓ cups	90 ml	560 ml
French bread, thin slices		7	44	7	44
Garlic cloves, large, chopped		5	31	5	31
Beef consommé, hot		1½ qt	9 qt	1.5 l	9 l
Cumin		½ tsp	1 Tbsp	1 g	6 g
Salt					
Eggs		8	50	8	50

1. Preheat oven to 400°F (200°C).
2. In a large skillet, heat half the oil. Fry bread on both sides until golden. Drain on paper towels and reserve.
3. Pour oil from skillet, balance of olive oil, and garlic into a saucepan. Sauté over low heat.
4. Add reserved bread slices to saucepan.
5. Add the consommé, cumin, and salt to taste.
6. Bring to a low simmer and cook for 12 to 14 minutes.
7. Pour soup into soup bowls.
8. Crack eggs and add one to each bowl of soup.
9. Place in oven and cook until eggs are done, 7 to 9 minutes.

Scallop Soup

		U.S.		Metric	
Portions:		8	50	8	50
Sea scallops, chopped		1 lb	6 lb	450 g	2.7 kg
Butter		5 Tbsp	2 cups	75 g	480 g
Potatoes, medium, peeled, diced		6	38	6	38
Onions, chopped		2	12	2	12
Leeks, white only		2	12	2	12
Water		2 qt	3 gal	2 l	12 l
Fish stock		3 cups	1 gal	720 ml	4 l
Dry sherry		½ cup	3 cups	120 ml	720 ml
Heavy cream		½ cup	3 cups	120 ml	720 ml
Salt					
White pepper, fresh ground					
Chives, chopped, for garnish					

1. In a large skillet, sauté the scallops in ⅔ of the butter over low heat for several minutes. Remove and keep warm.
2. In a saucepan, heat the remaining butter and cook the potatoes, onions, and leeks until leeks have softened.
3. Add water, fish stock, and sherry. Bring to a boil. Lower heat, cover, and simmer for about 15 to 18 minutes.
4. Pour contents of pan into food processor, in several batches if necessary. Puree.
5. Add scallops and continue to puree.
6. Add the cream. Mix well.
7. Return soup to saucepan and season with salt and pepper.
8. Heat thoroughly. Serve garnished with chopped chives.

Vichyssoise

Portions:	U.S.		Metric	
	8	50	8	50
Chicken broth	2 qt	3 gal	2 l	12 l
Potatoes, medium, peeled and cut into 1 in. (3 cm) pieces	4	25	4	25
Leeks, trimmed, thoroughly washed, and cut into ½ in. (1 cm) slices	4	25	4	25
Whipping cream	1½ cups	9½ cups	360 ml	2.3 l
Salt	1½ tsp	9½ tsp	8 g	48 g
White pepper, fresh ground	¾ tsp	4½ tsp	2 g	11 g
Allspice, ground	¼ tsp	1½ tsp	200 mg	1.3 g

1. In a saucepan, combine the broth, potatoes, and leeks.
2. Bring to a boil over high heat. Reduce heat and simmer for 20 minutes, or until potatoes are tender.
3. Remove from heat and puree broth and vegetables in a food processor for approximately 1 minute.
4. Add cream and seasonings. Chill in refrigerator for 2 to 3 hours.

Note: Although vichyssoise is served cold, it can be served hot. Heat mixture for 3 to 5 minutes over a moderate heat. Vichyssoise was invented by accident in 1910 in the fabled kitchens of New York City's Ritz Carlton when cold cream fell into the chef's leek soup just before serving. Upon tasting, it was declared a complete success.

Wild Mushroom Soup

		U.S.		Metric	
Portions:		*8*	*50*	*8*	*50*
Butter, unsalted		½ cup	3 cups	120 g	720 g
Shallots, minced		3½	21	3½	21
Wild mushrooms, chopped		3 oz	18 oz	85 g	510 g
Flour		⅓ cup	2 cups	38 g	225 g
Chicken stock		7 cups	11 qt	1.7 l	10.5 l
Salt					
White pepper, fresh ground					
Egg yolks		3	18	3	18
Heavy cream		⅔ cup	5½ cups	160 ml	1.3 l

1. Heat the butter in a stockpot. Add the shallots and cook for 5 or 6 minutes. Add mushrooms and cook for 3 or 4 minutes.
2. Add the flour and continue to cook for 2 or 3 minutes, stirring constantly.
3. Add the chicken stock, and season with salt and pepper. Simmer for 30 to 40 minutes.
4. Combine egg yolks and heavy cream in a bowl. Mix well.
5. Lower heat under stock and add egg yolk–cream mixture, stirring constantly. Do not allow to boil. Simmer for 1 minute.

SALADS

Crabmeat Salad

	U.S.		Metric	
Portions:	8	50	8	50
Alaskan king crabmeat, cooked, shelled	1½ lb	9 lb	675 g	4.1 kg
Tomatoes, small, seeded, cut into strips	2	12	2	12
Celery stalks, julienne	2	12	2	12
Shallots, chopped	2	12	2	12
Coconut, fresh, grated	½ cup	3 cups	120 g	720 g
Chives, chopped	1 Tbsp	6 Tbsp	10 g	60 g
Salt				
White pepper, fresh ground				
Mixed greens	24 oz	9 lb	680 g	4 kg
Walnut oil dressing	1 cup	1½ qt	240 ml	1.5 l

For Walnut Oil Dressing:

	For 1 Cup		For 240 ml	
Sherry vinegar	½ cup		120 ml	
Shallots, minced	1		1	
Walnut oil	¾ cup		180 ml	
Chives, chopped	½ tsp		1.5 g	
Lemon juice	½ tsp		2.5 ml	
Salt				
White pepper, fresh ground				

For Walnut Oil Dressing:

1. Combine the vinegar and shallots in a saucepan. Bring to a boil and reduce by half. Remove and cool.
2. In a small bowl, slowly whisk walnut oil into the vinegar mixture, drop by drop.
3. Add the chives, lemon juice, salt, and pepper, stirring well to mix.
4. Refrigerate until needed.

For Salad:

5. Combine crabmeat, tomato strips, celery, shallots, and fresh coconut in a mixing bowl.
6. Add chives and season with salt and pepper. Mix well.
7. Add the mixed greens and salad dressing and toss, mixing well.

Waldorf Salad

	U.S.		Metric	
Portions:	8	50	8	50
Tart apples, cored, diced, but not peeled	4	25	4	25
Celery, chopped	2 cups	12½ cups	454 g	2.8 kg
Walnuts, chopped	½ cup	3 cups	115 g	680 g
Raisins	3 Tbsp	1 cup	45 g	240 g
Lemon juice	3 Tbsp	1 cup	45 ml	240 ml
Mayonnaise	¾ cup	4½ cups	180 ml	1 l
Salt				
Black pepper, fresh ground				
Romaine lettuce head	1	6	1	6

1. Combine apples, celery, walnuts, and raisins in a mixing bowl.
2. Add the lemon juice, mayonnaise, salt, and pepper.
3. Stir well until blended.
4. Line a large salad bowl with lettuce leaves.
5. Add salad to bowl and serve chilled.

ENTRÉES

Chicken Breast Stuffed with Goat Cheese

🐦 AMERICAN WINE SUGGESTION
Chateau Ste. Michelle Dry Riesling

	U.S.		Metric	
Portions:	8	50	8	50
Butter	¾ cup	4½ cups	180 g	1.1 kg
Goat cheese	⅔ lb	4 lb	300 g	1.8 kg
Mint leaves, fresh, chopped	½ cup	3 cups	16 g	96 g
Thyme, fresh	1 Tbsp	6 Tbsp	3 g	18 g
Shallots, chopped	⅓ cup	2 cups	75 g	425 g
Black pepper, fresh ground				
Chicken breasts, skinless, boneless	8	50	8	50
Salt				
Flour for dredging, as needed				
Clarified butter	¼ cup	1½ cups	60 ml	360 ml
Mint, fresh, as needed for garnish				

1. Preheat oven to 400°F (200°C).
2. In a mixing bowl, combine the butter, goat cheese, mint, thyme, shallots, and black pepper. Mix well and reserve at room temperature.
3. Make an incision in chicken breasts to form a pocket. Season with salt and pepper and stuff with cheese mixture.
4. Dredge the chicken breasts in flour.
5. In a skillet, heat the clarified butter and brown the chicken on all sides.
6. Transfer chicken breasts to a baking sheet. Bake for 22 to 25 minutes or until cooked. Baste 3 or 4 times during cooking.
7. Remove and let rest for 5 to 7 minutes. Slice and serve, garnished with fresh mint leaves.

Chicken with Apple-Curry Sauce

🐚 AMERICAN WINE SUGGESTION
Adams Vineyards Chardonnay

	U.S.		Metric	
Portions:	8	50	8	50
Chicken, cut in pieces, 2–2½ lb (0.9–1 kg) each	2	15	2	15
Clarified butter	⅔ cup	1 qt	160 ml	1 l
Butter	6 Tbsp	2⅓ cups	90 g	560 g
Onions, chopped	1 cup	6 cups	240 g	1.4 kg
Shallots, chopped	2 tsp	3 Tbsp	6 g	40 g
Garlic cloves, minced	3	18	3	18
Tart apples, peeled, cored, finely chopped	1½ cups	9 cups	360 g	2 kg
Flour	3½ Tbsp	1⅓ cups	24 g	150 g
Curry powder	1½ Tbsp	9 Tbsp	9 g	54 g
Cardamom, ground	⅔ tsp	4 tsp	5 g	30 g
Coriander, ground	1¼ tsp	2½ Tbsp	1.25 g	15 g
Salt				
Black pepper, fresh ground				
Chicken stock	3½ cups	5½ qt	840 ml	5 l
Lime rind, grated	2½ tsp	5 Tbsp	12 g	75 g
Lime juice	1¼ Tbsp	½ cup	18 ml	120 ml
Mango chutney, finely chopped	⅔ cup	1 qt	160 g	1 kg

1. Preheat oven to 300°F (150°C).
2. In a heavy skillet, sauté the chicken pieces in clarified butter until golden brown. Remove pan from heat and reserve pan drippings in skillet.
3. Transfer chicken to a baking pan. Cover with foil and bake for 20 minutes.
4. Using the same skillet, add butter to pan drippings and sauté onion, shallots, and garlic for 4 or 5 minutes.
5. Add the apples and sprinkle with flour, curry powder, cardamom, coriander, salt, and pepper. Mix well.
6. Add the chicken stock, lime rind, lime juice, and chutney. Bring to a boil.
7. Reduce heat and simmer for 5 to 8 minutes, until sauce reaches a thick consistency.
8. Pour around chicken and serve hot.

Crab Cakes Maryland-Style COLOR PLATE 10

🍷 AMERICAN WINE SUGGESTION
Simi Vineyards Sauvignon Blanc

	U.S.		Metric	
Portions:	8	50	8	50
Butter, unsalted	5 Tbsp	2 cups	75 g	480 g
Onion, large, finely chopped	1	6	1	6
Bread crumbs	1½ cups	9 cups	340 g	2 kg
Crab meat, flaked and cleaned	2 lb	12½ lb	0.9 kg	5.6 kg
Eggs, beaten	5	30	5	30
Salt				
White pepper, fresh ground				
Dry mustard	1½ tsp	3 Tbsp	3 g	18 g
Worcestershire sauce	1½ tsp	3 Tbsp	8 ml	45 ml
Light cream	3 Tbsp	1⅛ cups	45 ml	270 ml
Flour	⅓ cup	2 cups	38 g	225 g
Oil, vegetable, for frying, as needed				
Lemon wedges for garnish, as needed				

For Warm Tartar Sauce:

Mayonnaise	4 oz	1 qt	120 ml	1 l
Cream sauce	1 cup	2 qt	240 ml	2 l
Tarragon vinegar	¼ oz	2 oz	8 ml	60 ml
Sour pickles, chopped	½ oz	4 oz	14 g	113 g
Green olives, chopped	½ oz	4 oz	14 g	113 g
Parsley, chopped	1 tsp	5 tsp	700 mg	4 g

For Traditional Tartar Sauce:

Mayonnaise	8 oz	2 qt	240 ml	2 l
Sour pickles, chopped	2 oz	2 cups	57 g	454 g
Parsley, finely chopped	1 tsp	2 Tbsp	700 mg	5 g
Onion, small, finely chopped	¼	1	¼	1
Green olives, finely chopped	2 oz	1 lb	57 g	450 g
Tarragon vinegar	2 Tbsp	1 cup	30 ml	240 ml

1. In a pan, sauté the onions in butter until soft and golden in color. Remove from the heat.
2. Add the bread crumbs and the crab meat. Mix well.
3. In a large bowl, combine the eggs, salt, pepper, mustard, and Worcestershire sauce. Mix well. Add the crab meat mixture and the light cream. Again mix well.
4. Cut into small crab cakes. Dust with flour.
5. In a large skillet, add approximately 1 in. (3 cm) of vegetable oil and fry the floured crab cakes golden brown on both sides.
6. Serve with lemon wedges and warm tartar sauce or traditional tartar sauce.

For Warm Tartar Sauce:

7. Combine the mayonnaise and cream sauce.
8. Add the tarragon vinegar, sour pickles, olives, and parsley. Mix well.
9. Heat and serve warm.

For Traditional Tartar Sauce:

10. Combine mayonnaise, pickles, parsley, onions, olives, and tarragon vinegar.
11. Mix well.
12. Chill in refrigerator for at least 3 hours.

Duck Breast in Three-Peppercorn Sauce

🦃 AMERICAN WINE SUGGESTION
Beaulieu Vineyards "Rutherford" Cabernet Sauvignon

	U.S.		Metric	
Portions:	8	50	8	50
Duck breasts, trimmed	8	50	8	50
Salt				
Black pepper, fresh ground				
Clarified butter	¼ cup	1½ cups	60 ml	360 ml
For Sauce:				
Red wine vinegar	¾ cup	4½ cups	180 ml	1.1 l
Shallots, minced	⅓ cup	2 cups	70 g	438 g
Chicken stock	⅔ cup	1 qt	160 ml	1 l
Black peppercorns, whole	1 tsp	2 Tbsp	2 g	12 g
Red peppercorns	1 tsp	2 Tbsp	2 g	12 g
Green peppercorns	1 tsp	2 Tbsp	2 g	12 g
Butter, unsalted	¾ cup	4½ cups	180 g	1.1 kg
Salt				
White pepper, fresh ground				
Parsley, minced	¼ cup	1½ cups	9 g	56 g

1. Preheat oven to 375°F (190°C).
2. Season the duck breasts with salt and pepper.
3. Heat the butter in a heavy skillet and brown duck breasts on all sides.
4. Place skillet with duck in oven, and cook for 6 or 7 minutes.

For Sauce:

5. In a saucepan, combine the vinegar and shallots. Reduce mixture over high heat to approximately 2 Tbsp (30 ml) for 8 servings; ¾ cup (180 ml) for 50 servings.
6. Add the chicken stock and bring to a boil.
7. Add the peppercorns. Reduce the heat to moderate.
8. Add the butter, stirring constantly.
9. Taste and season with salt and pepper.
10. Add parsley.
11. Slice the duck breast and serve with sauce.

Duck Casserole

❧ AMERICAN WINE SUGGESTION
Rodney Strong Cabernet Sauvignon

	U.S.		Metric	
Portions:	8	50	8	50
Bacon strips, halved	1/3 lb	2 lb	150 g	0.9 kg
Ducks, trimmed of all fat, cut into pieces	2½	15½	2½	15½
Salt				
Black pepper, fresh ground				
Sausage, lean	2½ lb	15½ lb	1.1 kg	7 kg
Onion, minced	1 cup	6 cups	240 g	1.4 kg
Shallots, chopped	¼ cup	1½ cups	50 g	300 g
Garlic, minced	¼ cup	1½ cups	40 g	250 g
Chicken stock	3½ cups	5½ qt	840 ml	5 l
Red wine	1/3 cup	2 cups	80 ml	480 ml
Tomato paste	2 Tbsp	¾ cup	30 g	180 g
Thyme sprigs, leaves only	3	18	3	18
Bay leaves	2	12	2	12
Celery stalks	1½	9	1½	9
Parsley sprigs	4	25	4	25
Parsley, chopped, as needed for garnish				

1. Preheat oven to 375°F (190°C).
2. In a heavy skillet, sauté the bacon. Transfer bacon to a side plate. Pat dry and keep warm.
3. Season duck with salt and pepper. Using the same skillet as for bacon, brown duck on all sides. Remove and transfer to a casserole. Reserve skillet with drippings.
4. Using same skillet, sauté the sausage until brown. Transfer to casserole.
5. Using a clean sauté pan, add some of the sausage drippings, and sauté onions, shallots, and garlic for approximately 5 minutes. Add to casserole.
6. Add chicken stock, wine, and tomato paste to the casserole. Bring to a boil, skimming fat as necessary.
7. Add thyme, bay leaf, celery, and parsley sprigs.
8. Place reserved bacon on top and bake for about 1½ hours or until done.
9. Garnish with chopped parsley.

Eggs Benedict

🦃 AMERICAN WINE SUGGESTION
S. Anderson Brut Champagne

		U.S.		Metric	
Portions:		8	50	8	50
English muffins, split		8	50	8	50
Butter, as needed					
Baked ham slices		16	100	16	100
Water		3 qt	4½ gal	3 l	18 l
Salt					
Vinegar		2 Tbsp	¾ cup	30 ml	180 ml
Eggs		16	100	16	100
For Hollandaise Sauce:					
Vinegar		2 Tbsp	¾ cup	30 ml	180 ml
Water		5 Tbsp	2 cups	75 ml	480 ml
Salt					
Egg yolks		5	31	5	31
Butter, unsalted, soft		1 lb	6 lb	450 g	2.7 kg
Lemon juice, as needed					
White pepper, fresh ground					

1. Split and lightly toast the English muffins. Spread with butter.
2. Melt additional butter in a skillet. Sauté ham.
3. Place ham on English muffins. Keep warm.
4. In a saucepan, combine the water, salt, and vinegar. Bring to a boil and poach the eggs for 5 minutes.
5. Remove eggs and place on top of ham.
6. Cover with Hollandaise sauce.

For Hollandaise Sauce:

7. In a pan combine the vinegar with ⅘ of the water and a pinch of salt. Reduce by ⅔ and transfer pan to bain-marie.
8. Add the remaining water and the egg yolks to the reduction, whisking gently over low heat, while gradually adding the butter.
9. Do not let sauce get too hot or it will separate. Add water to ensure the sauce remains light.
10. Check for seasoning. Add a few drops of lemon juice.
11. Pass through a fine strainer. Keep at lukewarm temperature.

Note: Do not use an aluminum pan, which may cause Hollandaise to discolor. Mr. and Mrs. LeGrand Benedict were regular patrons of Delmonico's restaurant in New York City. The chef created this dish in 1920 when the Benedicts complained that there were no new items on the menu.

Grilled Lobster and Fresh Herbs

❧ AMERICAN WINE SUGGESTION
Fox Mountain Reserve Chardonnay

		U.S.		Metric	
Portions:		8	50	8	50
Lobsters, live, 1–1¼ lb (450–560 g) each		8	50	8	50
Garlic cloves, peeled, crushed		3	18	3	18
Salt					
Butter, unsalted		½ lb	3 lb	240 kg	1.4 kg
Oregano, fresh, finely chopped		¾ cup	4½ cups	24 g	145 g
Rosemary, fresh		¾ cup	4½ cups	36 g	216 g

1. Preheat grill until glowing hot.
2. In a bowl, combine garlic and salt.
3. Add melted butter, oregano, and rosemary. Set aside for 5 to 8 minutes.
4. Split lobsters in half.
5. Place lobster, flesh up, on the hot grill.
6. Rub the flesh with herb-butter mixture and grill for 10 minutes. Brush the lobster flesh as needed with herb-butter mixture.
7. Turn lobsters over and grill for an additional 3 to 4 minutes, or until meat is cooked.
8. Serve with herb butter spooned over the lobsters, or serve the sauce on the side.

Lamb Stew

❦ AMERICAN WINE SUGGESTION
Sterling Vineyards Merlot

		U.S.		Metric	
Portions:	8	50	8	50
Butter	9 Tbsp	3½ cups	135 g	840 g
Onions, small, chopped	3	18	3	18
Garlic cloves, minced	3	18	3	18
Shallots, minced	2	12	2	12
Virgin olive oil	1 Tbsp	6 Tbsp	15 ml	90 ml
Lamb, boneless, cut into cubes	2½ lb	15½ lb	1.1 kg	7 kg
Salt				
Black pepper, fresh ground				
Bay leaves, small	3	18	3	18
Cinnamon stick, small	1	6	1	6
Cloves, whole	4	25	4	25
Tomato sauce, canned	8 oz	50 oz	227 g	1.4 kg
Tomatoes, whole, 16 oz (450 g) can, with liquid	1	6	1	6
White wine	1½ cups	9 cups	360 ml	2.1 l

1. In a large, heavy skillet, combine ½ the butter with onion, garlic, and shallots. Sauté over low heat until golden.
2. Add the remaining butter and the oil. Continue to cook for 1 minute.
3. Add the lamb. Season with salt and pepper, and sauté for 6 minutes, stirring constantly.
4. Add the bay leaves, cinnamon sticks, cloves, tomato sauce, and whole tomatoes.
5. Add the white wine and mix well. Bring mixture to a boil. Cover and reduce heat. Simmer for 1 hour, or until lamb is tender. Add water if necessary.
6. Serve over pasta or rice.

Leg of Lamb

🐚 AMERICAN WINE SUGGESTION
Markham Vineyards Merlot

		U.S.		Metric	
Portions:		8	50	8	50
Leg of lamb 6–7 lb (2.7–3.2 kg) each		1	6	1	6
Lemon juice		1 lemon	6 lemons	1 lemon	6 lemons
Salt					
Black pepper, fresh ground					
Garlic cloves, peeled		3–4	25	3–4	25
Butter, melted		¼ lb	1½ lb	120 g	720 g
Water		1 cup	1½ qt	240 ml	1.5 l

1. Preheat oven to 400°F (200°C).
2. Rub the leg of lamb with lemon juice on all sides.
3. Season with salt and pepper.
4. Slice incisions in the leg of lamb and insert the garlic cloves.
5. Place in baking pan, pour the butter over the lamb. Add the water to the pan.
6. Bake for 2 hours or until cooked to taste.
7. Remove from oven, slice, and serve with pan juices.

Lobster Newburg COLOR PLATE 11

🐦 AMERICAN WINE SUGGESTION
Souverain Vineyards Chardonnay

		U.S.		Metric	
Portions:		8	50	8	50
Lobster meat, boiled, cold		4 lb	25 lb	1.8 kg	11 kg
Butter		½ cup	3⅛ cups	120 g	800 g
Salt					
White pepper, fresh ground					
Cayenne, to taste					
Paprika		1 tsp	2 Tbsp	2 g	14 g
Heavy cream		2 cups	3 qt	480 ml	3 l
Dry sherry		½ cup	3 cups	120 ml	720 ml
Egg yolks		3	18	3	18

1. Melt butter in a heavy skillet and sauté lobster meat.
2. Season with salt, pepper, cayenne, and paprika. Cook for several minutes.
3. Remove lobster meat and keep warm.
4. In the same pan, add the cream and sherry. Bring to a boil.
5. In a bowl, whip the egg yolks. Add to the saucepan, stirring constantly.
6. Return lobster meat to the cream mixture. Keep at low heat. Do not boil. Stir until thick.
7. Serve warm over rice or in puff pastry.

Note: In the 1890s at New York City's Delmonico's Restaurant, Mr. Delmonico honored one of his best customers, Ben Wenberg, by naming this dish Lobster Wenberg. After a quarrel between the two, the dish became known as Lobster Newburg.

London Broil with Madeira

🐄 AMERICAN WINE SUGGESTION
Lytton Springs Zinfandel

	U.S.		Metric	
Portions:	8	50	8	50
Butter, unsalted, melted	3½ Tbsp	1⅓ cups	53 g	323 g
Dijon mustard	¼ cup	1½ cups	60 g	360 g
Curry powder	1 Tbsp	6 Tbsp	6 g	36 g
Worcestershire sauce	2 Tbsp	¾ cup	30 ml	180 ml
London broil	2 lb	12½ lb	0.9 kg	5.6 kg
Salt				
Black pepper, fresh ground				
Madeira	1 cup	1½ qt	240 ml	1.5 l
Soy sauce	1 cup	1½ qt	240 ml	1.5 l
For Sauce:				
Butter, unsalted	2 Tbsp	¾ cup	30 g	180 g
Shallots, chopped	2 Tbsp	¾ cup	25 g	150 g
Garlic cloves, minced	1	6	1	6
Sour cream	1 cup	1½ qt	240 ml	1.5 l
Heavy cream	1 cup	1½ qt	240 ml	1.5 l

To Marinate Meat:

1. Combine butter, mustard, curry powder, Worcestershire sauce, salt, and pepper.
2. Season the London broil with mixture on both sides. Place on baking sheet.
3. Pour the Madeira and soy sauce over the meat. Refrigerate for at least 10 hours.
4. Preheat broiler on high.
5. Remove London broil from marinade. Reserve the marinade.
6. Broil the meat on high for 3 or 4 minutes per side.

For Sauce:

7. Melt the butter in a skillet. Add the shallots and garlic. Sauté lightly. Do not brown.
8. Add the sour cream, the reserved marinade, and the heavy cream. Taste for salt and pepper.
9. Bring to a boil. Simmer until thick.
10. Slice London broil into even portions and serve with Madeira sauce.

Maryland Fried Chicken

❧ AMERICAN WINE SUGGESTION
Beaulieu Vineyards Dry Sauvignon Blanc

	U.S.		Metric	
Portions:	8	50	8	50
Bacon, slices	12	75	12	75
Virgin olive oil, as needed for frying				
Flour	1½ cups	9½ cups	170 g	1 kg
Salt				
Black pepper, fresh ground	½ tsp	1 Tbsp	1 g	7 g
Frying chicken 3–3½ lb (1.4–1.6 kg) each, cut into serving pieces	2	12	2	12
For Gravy:				
Flour	¼ cup	1½ cups	28 g	170 g
Milk	2 cups	3 qt	480 ml	3 l
Heavy cream	2 cups	3 qt	480 ml	3 l
Salt				
White pepper, fresh ground				

1. In a large, heavy skillet, fry the bacon until brown. Remove bacon and drain on paper towels.
2. Add enough oil to bacon drippings to make 1 in. (3 cm).
3. Combine flour, salt, and pepper in a plastic bag. Shake well.
4. Coat each chicken piece with the flour mixture by placing it in the bag, sealing it, and shaking well. Repeat process until all pieces are well coated.
5. Heat oil in skillet. When bubbling, add chicken pieces and fry, turning occasionally, until nicely browned on all sides.
6. When brown, reduce heat and cover skillet. Cook over low heat for 25 minutes, or until tender. Remove chicken and keep warm.

For Gravy:

7. Drain excess fat from skillet, leaving enough to make gravy [about ½ cup (120 ml) for 8 servings; 3 cups (720 ml) for 50 servings].
8. Stir flour into pan drippings and cook for about 3 minutes.
9. Add milk and cream to skillet. Continue to cook, stirring occasionally until gravy is thick and smooth.
10. Add salt and pepper to taste.
11. Pour gravy over hot chicken and garnish with the reserved bacon strips.

Roast Chicken Breast with Honey-Mustard Sauce

COLOR PLATE 12

🍎 AMERICAN WINE SUGGESTION
Sierra Vista Fumé Blanc

	U.S.		Metric	
Portions:	8	50	8	50
Chicken breasts, 8–10 oz (225–280 g) each	8	50	8	50
Salt				
White pepper, fresh ground				
Zucchini, julienne	3	18	3	18
Carrots, julienne	3	18	3	18
For Sauce:				
Shallots, minced	3	18 ¾	3	18 ¾
Mushrooms, minced	2	12½	2	12½
Butter	2 Tbsp	¾ cup	30 g	180 g
White wine	½ cup	3 cups	120 ml	720 ml
Heavy cream	2 cups	3 qt	240 ml	3 l
Salt				
White pepper, fresh ground				
Dijon mustard	1 Tbsp	6¼ Tbsp	15 g	90 g
Whole-grain mustard	3 Tbsp	1⅛ cups	45 g	270 g
Honey, high quality	3 Tbsp	1⅛ cups	45 ml	280 ml

For Sauce:

1. Sauté the shallots and mushrooms in butter.
2. Add the wine, reduce by half, add heavy cream, and season with salt and pepper.
3. Add Dijon mustard. Strain through a fine sieve.
4. Add the whole-grain mustard and honey. Mix well and keep warm.

---

5. Season chicken breasts with salt and pepper.
6. Grill chicken until done. Remove from heat and thinly slice. Place on a bed of honey-mustard sauce and garnish with julienne vegetables.

Roast Goose

🦢 AMERICAN WINE SUGGESTION
Foppiano Petite Syrah

	U.S.		Metric	
Portions:	8	50	8	50
Goose, approximately 10 lb (5 kg)	1	6	1	6
Salt				
Pepper				
Butter	2 Tbsp	¾ cup	30 g	180 g
Onion	1	6	1	6
Chestnuts, cooked, chopped	3 cups	4½ qt	720 g	4.4 kg
Apples, peeled, sliced	3 cups	4½ qt	720 g	4.4 kg
Thyme	1½ tsp	3 Tbsp	150 mg	9 g
Soft bread crumbs	1½ cups	9 cups	360 g	2 kg
Eggs	1	6	1	6
Brandy	½ cup	3 cups	120 ml	720 ml
Cayenne, to taste				
Beef stock	2¼ cups	3½ qt	540 ml	3.5 l
Dry white wine	2¼ cups	3½ qt	540 ml	3.5 l
For Sauce:				
Butter, unsalted	4½ Tbsp	1¾ cups	68 g	420 g
Flour	⅓ cup	2 cups	38 g	225 g
Roasting juices, as needed				
Port wine	⅓ cup	2 cups	80 ml	480 ml
Salt				
White pepper, fresh ground				

1. Preheat oven to 450°F (230°C).
2. Wash goose thoroughly; pat dry. Season with salt and pepper, and set aside.
3. Sauté the onions in butter until soft. Add the chestnuts, apples, thyme, bread crumbs, eggs, brandy, cayenne, salt, and pepper. Cook slightly and remove from heat.
4. Stuff mixture into the cavity of the goose and close by tying the legs and wings together. Prick skin with a sharp fork before cooking.
5. Roast for 20 to 30 minutes, or until golden brown.
6. Heat beef stock and wine in a saucepan and add to the roasting pan.
7. Reduce oven temperature to 325°F (160°C) and roast for 1 hour and 45 minutes, or until done. Baste 4 or 5 times during roasting.

For Sauce:

8. Melt butter and add flour in a heavy saucepan. Cook for about 1 minute. Remove from heat.
9. Add roasting juices and bring to a boil, stirring constantly.
10. Finish with port wine, season to taste with salt and pepper.

Salmon Stuffed with Sole Mousse

🦃 AMERICAN WINE SUGGESTION
Silverado Chardonnay

		U.S.		Metric	
Portions:		8	50	8	50
For Poaching:					
Dry white wine		2 cups	3 qt	480 ml	3 l
Garlic cloves, peeled, mashed		2	12	2	12
Black peppercorns		1 Tbsp	6 Tbsp	6 g	36 g
Onion, quartered		1	6	1	6
Celery stalks		1	6	1	6
Lemons, halved		1	6	1	6
For Sole Mousse:					
Filet of sole		1½ lb	9 lb	675 g	4 kg
Egg whites		3	18	3	18
Heavy cream		1½ cups	9 cups	360 ml	2 l
Salt					
White pepper, fresh ground					
Dry sherry		¼ cup	1½ cups	60 ml	360 ml
Lemon juice		1 lemon	6 lemons	1 lemon	6 lemons
Cayenne		⅛ tsp	½ tsp	300 mg	1 g
Chives, chopped		¼ cup	1½ cups	40 g	250 g
Salmon filet		2½–3 lb	15½–18½ lb	1–1.5 kg	7–8 kg
For Sauce:					
Watercress, tightly packed		2 cups	3 qt	480 g	3 kg
Parsley, chopped		2 cups	3 qt	75 g	470 g
Scallions, green only, sliced		½ cup	3 cups	120 g	720 g
Mayonnaise		2 cups	3 qt	480 ml	3 l
Lemon juice		2 Tbsp	¾ cup	30 ml	180 ml
Salt					
White pepper, fresh ground					

1. In a large fish poacher, combine the wine, garlic, peppercorns, onion, celery, and lemon, with enough water to fill ¾ of the pan.
2. Bring to a boil and simmer for approximately 90 minutes. While liquid is simmering, prepare the mousse.
3. Using a food processor, combine sole, egg whites, cream, salt, pepper, sherry, lemon juice, and cayenne. Puree until smooth. Add the chives and reserve.
4. Place the salmon filet in cheesecloth.
5. Cut a pocket, lengthwise, in the salmon. Do not cut through filet.
6. Fill salmon pocket with mousse. Wrap the salmon pocket with the cheesecloth and secure it.

7. Poach salmon in liquid for approximately 10 minutes, depending on thickness of filet.
8. Remove salmon roll and wrap tightly with foil to maintain shape. Refrigerate for at least 6 to 8 hours to firm.

For Sauce:

9. Puree the watercress, parsley, and scallions in a food processor. Ensure puree is smooth.
10. Add mayonnaise and lemon juice, and salt and pepper to taste. Blend.
11. Unwrap the salmon. Cut into ½ in. (1.5 cm) slices and serve on a bed of sauce.

Roast Pork Loin with Horseradish-Apple Sauce

✍ AMERICAN WINE SUGGESTION
Sebastiani Reserve Chardonnay

	U.S.		Metric	
Portions:	8	50	8	50
Pork loin 4–5 lb (1.8–2.3 kg) each	1	6	1	6
Garlic cloves, peeled, mashed	3	18	3	18
Salt				
Black pepper, fresh ground				
Thyme	1 Tbsp	6 Tbsp	3 g	18 g
Dijon mustard	¼ cup	1½ cups	60 g	360 g
For Sauce:				
Horseradish, peeled, cut into small pieces	⅔ cup	4 cups	155 g	960 g
Heavy cream	½ cup	3 cups	240 ml	720 ml
Sour cream	1¼ cups	2 qt	300 ml	1.8 l
Scallions, minced	½ cup	3 cups	113 g	680 g
Salt				
Black pepper, fresh ground				
Cayenne, to taste				
Butter	¼ cup	1½ lb	60 g	360 g
Apples, peeled, cored, and cut into eighths	3–4	18–25	3–4	18–25

1. Preheat oven to 400°F (200°C).
2. Season loin with garlic, salt, pepper, thyme, and Dijon mustard.
3. Place in baking dish and roast for 1½ hours. Remove and let sit for 10 to 15 minutes.

For Sauce:

4. Using a food processor, puree the horseradish.
5. In a saucepan, heat the pork loin drippings and add the pureed horseradish.
6. Add the cream, sour cream, scallions, salt, pepper, and cayenne to taste.
7. Bring to a boil. Simmer for 5 to 8 minutes.
8. In a skillet, combine the butter with the apples and sauté for 5 or 6 minutes over medium heat.
9. Slice the pork loin. Serve with sauce, garnished with apples.

Sautéed Filet of Sole on a Tomato Coulis Vinaigrette

COLOR PLATE 13

❧ AMERICAN WINE SUGGESTION
Groth Vineyards Sauvignon Blanc

		U.S.		Metric	
Portions:	8	50	8	50
Filets of sole	16	100	16	100
Salt				
White pepper, fresh ground				
Lemon juice, fresh	1 lemon	6 lemons	1 lemon	6 lemons
Flour, as needed for dredging				
Oil	½ cup	3 cups	120 ml	720 ml
For Tomato Coulis:				
Walnut oil	3 Tbsp	1⅛ cups	45 ml	280 ml
Shallots, finely chopped	3	18¾	3	18¾
Garlic cloves, chopped	2	12½	2	12½
Tomatoes, pureed	8	50	8	50
Tomato paste	1 tsp	2 Tbsp	5 ml	30 ml
Dry white wine	½ cup	3 cups	120 ml	720 ml
White wine vinegar	3 Tbsp	1⅛ cups	45 ml	280 ml
Bay leaves	1	6	1	6
For Vinaigrette:				
Lemon juice, fresh	2½ lemons	16 lemons	2½ lemons	16 lemons
Virgin olive oil	2 cups	3 qt	480 ml	3 l
Tomatoes, peeled, seeded, and diced	4	25	4	25
Salt				
White pepper, fresh ground				
Parsley, chopped	1½ Tbsp	9 Tbsp	3.5 g	20 g
Basil, fresh	1 Tbsp	¾ cup	4 g	24 g
Tarragon, fresh	⅔ tsp	4 tsp	500 mg	3 g
Capers	2 Tbsp	¾ cup	30 g	180 g
Olives, green	¼ cup	1½ cups	60 g	360 g

For Vinaigrette (can be prepared 2 hours in advance):

1. In a small bowl, combine the lemon juice, oil, tomatoes, salt, pepper, parsley, basil, tarragon, capers, and olives. Mix well.

For Tomato Coulis:

2. Heat oil in a saucepan. Add shallots and garlic and cook for 1 minute.
3. Add the tomato puree, tomato paste, white wine, vinegar, and bay leaf. Simmer over medium heat for 20 minutes.

For the Fish:

4. Season the fish with salt, pepper, and lemon juice. Dredge in flour.
5. Heat oil in a heavy skillet and sauté for 3 to 4 minutes on each side.
6. Serve on a bed of tomato coulis drizzled with vinaigrette.

Sautéed Scallops with a Light Tomato Sauce COLOR PLATE 14

ᐓ AMERICAN WINE SUGGESTION
Meridian Chardonnay "Edna Valley"

	U.S.		Metric	
Portions:	8	50	8	50
Scallops, large, cleaned	20	125	20	125
Salt				
White pepper, fresh ground				
Zucchini, medium	3	18 ¾	3	18 ¾
Snow peas, stems and veins removed, julienne	1 lb	6¼ lb	450 g	2.8 kg
Butter	3 Tbsp	1⅛ cups	45 g	280 g
Tomatoes, ripe, peeled, seeded, and diced	2	13	2	13
Thyme, as needed for garnish				
Italian parsley, as needed for garnish				
For Sauce:				
Shallots, chopped	2 Tbsp	¾ cup	25 g	150 g
Butter, unsalted	½ lb	3 lb	240 g	1.4 kg
Tomatoes, peeled and seeded	8	50	8	50
Dry vermouth	1 cup	1½ qt	240 ml	1.5 l
Fish stock or clam juice	1 cup	1½ qt	240 ml	1.5 l
Salt				
White pepper, fresh ground				

For Sauce:

1. Sauté the shallots in ⅛ of the butter for 2 to 3 minutes.
2. Add the tomatoes and cook over low heat for 3 to 4 minutes.
3. Add the vermouth and fish stock. Raise the heat. Reduce by half.
4. Add the remaining butter. Season with salt and pepper.

For the Scallops:

5. Season the scallops with salt and pepper. Set aside.
6. Cut the zucchini into ⅛ in. (1 mm) slices along the diameter. Blanch the slices in boiling, salted water until tender.
7. Shock the zucchini slices in cold water to stop cooking. Drain and set aside.
8. Blanch the snow peas.
9. In a pan, sauté the scallops until golden. Remove scallops and add the zucchini slices to heat. Remove.
10. Cut scallops in half and arrange in a circle on a plate with the zucchini.
11. Make a nest with the snow peas and place in the center of each plate.
12. Surround with sauce. Garnish with chopped tomatoes, thyme, and Italian parsley leaves.

Scallops in Tomato and Garlic Cream Sauce

❧ AMERICAN WINE SUGGESTION
Fisher Vineyards "Coach" Chardonnay

	U.S.		Metric	
Portions:	8	50	8	50
Butter	5 Tbsp	1 lb	75 g	480 g
Garlic cloves	4	25	4	25
Heavy cream	2 cups	3 qt	480 ml	3 l
Plum tomatoes, fresh, diced	5	30	5	30
Salt				
White pepper, fresh ground				
Scallops, fresh	2 ¾ lb	17 lb	1.2 kg	7.7 kg
Flour	¾ cup	4½ cups	80 g	500 g
Butter	5 Tbsp	1 lb	75 g	480 g
Watercress, fresh, chopped, as needed for garnish				

For Sauce:

1. Sauté the garlic in butter over low heat. Do not brown.
2. Add the cream, tomatoes, salt, and pepper to taste. Simmer until sauce thickens, approximately 5 minutes. Remove and reserve.

For the Scallops:

3. Wash scallops well, and season with salt and pepper. Coat with flour.
4. Using a separate heavy skillet, melt the butter and sauté the scallops in batches for 2 minutes, stirring once or twice. Do not crowd the skillet or overcook scallops.
5. Remove scallops and transfer to tomato sauce. Heat until warm and serve immediately, garnished with watercress.

Sea Trout with Tomato-Basil Sauce

🦃 AMERICAN WINE SUGGESTION
Monterey Vineyards Sauvignon Blanc

	U.S.		Metric	
Portions:	8	50	8	50
Sea trout filets, cut into 8 oz (225 g) pieces	4 lb	25 lb	1.8 kg	11.3 kg
Virgin olive oil	¾ cup	4½ cups	180 ml	1 l
Basil, chopped	1¼ cups	7½ cups	40 g	240 g
Salt				
Black pepper, fresh ground				
For Sauce:				
Parsley, fresh, chopped	2½ cups	4 qt	47 g	294 g
Basil, fresh, chopped	½ cup	3 cups	16 g	100 g
Oregano, fresh, chopped	½ cup	3 cups	16 g	96 g
Garlic cloves, chopped	4	25	4	25
Salt				
Black pepper, fresh ground				
Cayenne, to taste				
Virgin olive oil	2½ Tbsp	1 cup	40 ml	240 ml
Red wine vinegar	2 Tbsp	¾ cup	30 ml	180 ml
Plum tomatoes, fresh, finely chopped	2½ cups	1 gal	570 g	3.5 kg

1. Preheat oven to 375°F (190°C).
2. Sprinkle half the oil on a baking casserole large enough to hold fish without crowding.
3. Spread the basil evenly over the olive oil.
4. Season fish with salt and pepper. Place fish over basil.
5. Bake for 12 minutes, or until fish is no longer opaque and flakes easily. Remove and keep warm.

For Sauce:

6. In a food processor, combine parsley, basil, oregano, garlic, salt, pepper, cayenne, olive oil, and vinegar. Puree.
7. Transfer mixture to a saucepan. Add tomatoes and heat. Do not boil; it will cause the sauce to lose its color and taste.
8. Serve hot over fish.

Shrimp Sauté   COLOR PLATE 15

❧ AMERICAN WINE SUGGESTION
Sierra Vista Fumé Blanc

	U.S.		Metric	
Portions:	*8*	*50*	*8*	*50*
Shrimp, medium	32	150	32	150
For Garnish:				
Parisian potatoes, as needed				
Spinach, boiled in salted water	3 lb	18 ¾ lb	1.4 kg	8.4 kg
Pearl onions, as needed				
For Sauté:				
Butter, clarified	1 cup	6¼ cups	240 g	1.4 kg
Salt				
White pepper, fresh ground				
Oregano	½ tsp	1 Tbsp	330 mg	2 g
Garlic	½ tsp	1 Tbsp	2 g	10 g
Lemon juice, fresh	1 lemon	6 lemons	1 lemon	6 lemons
Wine	½ cup	3 cups	120 ml	720 ml

1. Combine butter, salt, pepper, oregano, garlic, lemon juice, and wine in a sauté pan.
2. Add the shrimp and sauté for 2 to 3 minutes per side or until done.
3. In a little butter, sauté the spinach to warm it.
4. Garnish shrimp sauté with potatoes, onions, and spinach, and serve.

Veal with Pumpkin Sauce

🐃 AMERICAN WINE SUGGESTION
Henry Estate Chardonnay

	U.S.		Metric	
Portions:	8	50	8	50
Pumpkin, fresh, peeled, cleaned, cut in large pieces	2 lb	12½ lb	1 kg	6 kg
Salt				
White pepper, fresh ground				
Butter	3 Tbsp	1⅛ cups	45 g	280 g
Butter	¼ cup	1½ cups	60 g	360 g
Shallots, minced	2	12	2	12
Garlic cloves, minced	2	12	2	12
Veal cutlets, medium-sized	8	50	8	50
Heavy cream	⅔ cup	1 qt	160 ml	1 l

1. Preheat oven to 375°F (190°C).
2. Place pumpkin in a large baking dish. Bake for 1½ hours. Remove from oven. Season with salt, pepper, and butter before cooling.
3. In a food processor, puree the pumpkin and reserve.
4. In a skillet, heat the butter and sauté shallots and garlic for 2 or 3 minutes.
5. Add the veal cutlets to the skillet and sauté for 2 or 3 minutes per side.
6. Transfer veal cutlets to warm plates.
7. Mix the pumpkin puree and cream in sauté pan used for veal cutlets. Season with salt and pepper to taste.
8. Bring mixture to a boil. Reduce heat and simmer for 3 minutes.
9. Pour sauce over warm veal cutlets and serve.

Seafood with Lime Consommé   *p. 39*

Baked Veal Chops with a Fine Herb Stuffing *p. 44*

Lobster Dijonnaise *p. 49*

New England Boiled Dinner   *p. 50*

New England Clam Boil   *p. 51*

Sea Fare's Beggar's Bundle   *p. 58*

**Sea Fare's Chicken with
Wild Mushrooms and Scallops** *p. 60*

Swordfish Vinaigrette *p. 59*

**Smoked Salmon Tartare with
Asparagus Mayonnaise** *p. 82*

Crab Cakes Maryland-Style   *p. 92*

Lobster Newburg   *p. 99*

**Roast Chicken Breast with
Honey-Mustard Sauce**   *p. 102*

**Sautéed Filet of Sole on a
Tomato Coulis Vinaigrette** *p. 107*

Sautéed Scallops with a Light Tomato Sauce *p. 108*

Shrimp Sauté   *p. 111*

Sautéed Haddock with White Bean Salad   *p. 113*

Sautéed Haddock with White Bean Salad   COLOR PLATE 16

 AMERICAN WINE SUGGESTION
Pouilly Fuissé

Portions:	U.S.		Metric	
	8	50	8	50
For Salad:				
White beans, fresh	1 lb	6¼ lb	450 g	2.8 kg
Leek, white only, julienne	1	6¼	1	6¼
Carrots, julienne	1	6¼	1	6¼
Red onion, julienne	1	6¼	1	6¼
Salt				
White pepper, fresh ground				
Virgin olive oil	½ cup	3 cups	120 ml	720 ml
Wine vinegar	3 Tbsp	1⅛ cups	45 ml	280 ml
Garlic cloves, small	1	6	1	6
Italian parsley, small bunches, chopped	1	6	1	6
For the Fish:				
Haddock, pieces, approximately 8 oz (225 g)	8	50	8	50
Salt				
White pepper, fresh ground				
Lemon juice, fresh	1 lemon	6 lemons	1 lemon	6 lemons
Flour, as needed for dredging				
Vegetable oil	1 cup	6 cups	240 ml	1.4 l

1. Boil the beans in salted water until cooked. Drain and place in a large bowl.
2. Add the leeks, carrots, onions, salt, pepper, vinegar, garlic, oil, and parsley.
3. Season the haddock with salt, pepper, and lemon.
4. Dredge haddock in flour.
5. In a heavy skillet, warm the vegetable oil and sauté the haddock for 4 to 5 minutes per side, or until golden.
6. To serve, place haddock at the center of a bed of white beans on a serving plate.

Venison in Black Pepper Sauce

🐦 AMERICAN WINE SUGGESTION
William Hill Reserve Cabernet Sauvignon

		U.S.		Metric	
Portions:		8	50	8	50
Saddle of venison		7 lb	44 lb	3 kg	20 kg
Game marinade, as needed					
Garlic cloves, chopped		3	18	3	18
Butter		2½ Tbsp	1 cup	38 g	240 g
Thyme, fresh		1½ tsp	3 Tbsp	1.5 g	9 g
Salt					
Black pepper, fresh ground					
Black pepper sauce		2 cups	3 qt	480 ml	3 l

For Game Marinade:

Dry red wine		2 qt	3 gal	2 l	12 l
Red wine vinegar		¼ cup	1½ cups	60 ml	360 ml
Vegetable oil		½ cup	3 cups	120 ml	720 ml
Onions, medium, sliced		2	12	2	12
Carrots, sliced		2	12	2	12
Garlic cloves, crushed		2	12	2	12
Bay leaves, small		2	12	2	12
Thyme, fresh		1½ tsp	3 Tbsp	1.5 g	9 g
Marjoram, fresh		1½ tsp	3 Tbsp	6 g	36 g
Juniper berries		8	50	8	50
Salt					
Black pepper. fresh ground					

For Black Pepper Sauce: Yields 2 cups (720 ml) for 8; 3 qt (3 l) for 50

Onions, small, chopped		1	6	1	6
Shallots, chopped		1	6	1	6
Carrots, small, chopped		1	6	1	6
Butter		¼ cup	1½ cups	60 g	360 g
Parsley sprigs, chopped		3	18	3	18
Bay leaves		1	6	1	6
Red wine vinegar		¼ cup	1½ cups	60 ml	360 ml
Beef stock		3 cups	4½ qt	720 ml	4.4 l
Tomato paste		2 Tbsp	¾ cup	30 g	180 g
Black peppercorns		½ tsp	1 Tbsp	1 g	6 g
Red wine		½ cup	3 cups	120 ml	720 ml

For Game Marinade:

1. Combine all ingredients for game marinade in a large bowl. Mix well.
2. Marinate venison overnight.

For Black Pepper Sauce:

3. In a heavy skillet, sauté the onion, shallots, and carrots in butter over low heat.
4. Add the parsley, bay leaf, and wine vinegar. Increase heat and reduce mixture by half.
5. Add the stock and tomato paste. Bring to a boil. Lower heat and simmer for 1 hour.
6. During the last 5 minutes of cooking, add the peppercorns. Strain the sauce into another saucepan. Simmer 8 to 10 minutes.
7. Add the wine and reserve.

For the Venison:

8. Preheat oven to 500°F (260°C).
9. Remove venison from marinade. Rub venison thoroughly with garlic, butter, thyme, and pepper.
10. Place venison in shallow roasting pan and roast for 25 to 30 minutes, basting frequently.
11. Reduce heat to 325°F (160°C) and continue to roast to an internal temperature of 125°F (52°C).
12. Remove from oven, salt to taste, and let stand on a hot plate for 20 minutes.
13. Carve venison and serve with black pepper sauce.

ACCOMPANIMENTS

Hash Brown Potatoes

	U.S.		Metric	
Portions:	8	50	8	50
Potatoes, well scrubbed, cut into large pieces	3 lb	19 lb	1.4 kg	8.6 kg
Onions, medium-sized, finely chopped	1¼	8	1¼	8
Salt	1¼ tsp	8 tsp	8 g	40 g
Black pepper, fresh ground	1 tsp	2 Tbsp	2 g	14 g
Bacon drippings (or butter)	¼ cup	1½ cups	60 ml	360 ml
Virgin olive oil	2 Tbsp	¾ cup	30 ml	180 ml

1. Place potato pieces in a saucepan filled with cold water.
2. Bring to a boil over high heat. Reduce to moderate heat. Cook potatoes for approximately 10 minutes.
3. Drain and rinse well under cold water until cool enough to handle.
4. Grate potatoes coarsely into a mixing bowl. Toss with onion, salt, and pepper. Set aside.
5. In a heavy skillet, combine half the bacon drippings and half the olive oil. Heat over a moderate heat.
6. When skillet is hot, add the potato mixture, pressing down to form a thick cake. Fry for approximately 5 minutes, or until brown and crisp.
7. Turn cake over using a large spatula, add the remaining bacon drippings and olive oil. Make sure bacon drippings and olive oil are distributed around skillet, and then fry other side until brown, approximately 5 minutes longer.

Philadelphia Cinnamon Buns

	U.S.	Metric
	For 24 Breakfast Buns	For 24 Breakfast Buns
Flour	8 cups	900 g
Baking powder	10 tsp	27 g
Salt	1 Tbsp	15 g
Butter, unsalted	1½ cups	360 g
Eggs	4	4
Whipping cream	1⅓ cups	320 ml
Brown sugar, firmly packed	2 cups	480 g
Cinnamon, ground	2 tsp	4 g
Walnuts, finely chopped	1 cup	128 g
Raisins	1 cup	225 g

1. Preheat oven to 400°F (200°C).
2. In a large bowl, combine the flour, baking powder, and salt.
3. Cut in the butter until flour forms coarse crumbs.
4. In a separate bowl, beat the eggs and add one cup cream. Add this to the flour mixture and stir well.
5. On a floured surface, roll out the dough.
6. Form into a square approximately ½ in. (1 cm) thick.
7. In a separate bowl, mix together brown sugar, cinnamon, chopped walnuts, and raisins. Spread evenly over the dough.
8. Roll dough and pinch closed on each side.
9. Cut the roll with a sharp knife into 24 one-in. (2 cm) slices.
10. Lay the slices on a buttered baking sheet. Brush with remainder of cream. Bake for 20 minutes or until golden brown.

Saratoga Potato Chips

		U.S.		Metric	
Portions:		8	50	8	50
Potatoes, peeled		8	50	8	50
Virgin olive oil, as needed, for frying					
Salt					

1. Slice potatoes as thinly as possible. Place slices in a large bowl of ice water. Let stand for several hours.
2. Drain potatoes well and pat dry.
3. Place 1¼ in. (3 cm) olive oil in large skillet.
4. Add the potatoes and fry until crispy and golden.
5. Drain on paper towels. Season with salt to taste.

Note: Everyone loves potato chips, but how did they come into being? They were the brainchild of George Crum, chef at the Moon's Lake Lodge in Saratoga, New York, developed as a result of a customer's demand for thinner potatoes.

DESSERTS

Dutch Honey Cake

		U.S.		Metric	
Portions:		*8*	*50*	*8*	*50*
Active dry yeast, envelope		1	6	1	6
Warm milk		2½ tsp	5 Tbsp	12 ml	75 ml
Sugar, to taste					
Eggs, separated		6	37	6	37
Honey		1⅓ cups	2 qt	320 ml	1.9 l
Strong coffee, cool		⅓ cup	2 cups	80 ml	480 ml
Vanilla		½ tsp	1 Tbsp	3 ml	15 ml
Flour, sifted		2 cups	12½ cups	225 g	1.4 kg
Cinnamon		1 tsp	2 Tbsp	2 g	12 g
Mace		1 tsp	2 Tbsp	8 g	48 g
Ginger, ground		¼ tsp	1½ tsp	2 g	15 g
Salt		¼ tsp	1½ tsp	1 g	7 g
Almonds, toasted, ground		¾ cup	4½ cups	80 g	500 g
Confectioner's sugar, as needed					

1. Combine the yeast, milk, and sugar in a mixing bowl. Let rest for several minutes.
2. In a separate bowl, combine the egg yolks with the honey, coffee, and vanilla. Mix well.
3. Slowly add the sifted flour, cinnamon, mace, ginger, and salt.
4. Add the yeast mixture and almonds. Mix thoroughly.
5. Preheat oven to 350°F (180°C).
6. Beat egg whites until stiff peaks form. Fold ¼ of the egg whites into the cake mixture. Gently fold in remaining whites until no egg whites are evident.
7. Butter 8 in. (20 cm) cake pan and pour in batter. Let rise for 45 to 50 minutes.
8. Bake for 30 to 32 minutes. Remove and let cool in cake pan for 8 minutes.
9. Remove cake and transfer to rack. Let cool.
10. Wrap tightly in plastic wrap and store in a cool area for several days to allow the flavors to blend.
11. Serve garnished with confectioner's sugar.

Apricot Torte

	U.S.	Metric
	For 10–12 servings	For 10–12 servings
Apricots, dried	1 cup	240 g
Sugar	½ cup	120 g
Egg, beaten	1	1
Lemon juice	1 tsp	5 ml
Lemon rind, grated	¼ tsp	1 g
Puff pastry	1½ lb	700 g
Butter, as needed to grease baking sheet		
Almonds, toasted, chopped	½ cup	120 g
Egg, beaten, for glaze	1	1

For Puff Pastry: Yields 3 lb (1.4 kg)

Flour, unbleached	3 cups	338 g
Cake flour	1 cup	113 g
Salt	1 tsp	5 g
Butter	2 cups	480 g
Lemon juice	1 tsp	5 ml
Cold water	1 cup	240 ml

For Puff Pastry:

1. In a food processor, combine the unbleached flour, cake flour, salt, and butter. Blend slightly.
2. Add the lemon juice and water; blend until dough starts to collect on sides.
3. Transfer dough to mixing bowl and work by hand. Chill, for 30 minutes if necessary, to form solid mass.
4. On a lightly floured surface, roll out dough into 12 × 6 in. (30 × 15 cm) rectangle. Fold into thirds.
5. Again roll dough out in 12 × 6 in. (30 × 15 cm) rectangle and fold in thirds.
6. Repeat folding procedure for a total of 3 times.
7. Wrap dough in plastic wrap and chill for 8 hours.
   Note: Allow dough to rest for at least 20 minutes before use. Leftover dough can be frozen.

For Torte:

8. Cover apricots with water in a medium pan. Bring to a boil.
9. Lower heat and simmer for 20 to 25 minutes or until soft.
10. Drain and puree apricots, using a food processor. Transfer to a mixing bowl.
11. Add sugar, egg, lemon juice, lemon rind, and mix well. Cool.

12. Use ½ the puff pastry recipe [approximately 1½ lb (700 g)]. Divide the pastry in two equal parts. Roll out a 10 to 12 in. (25 to 30 cm) circle on a floured surface.
13. Butter a baking sheet and lay the puff pastry on the sheet.
14. Roll out the second half of the puff pastry into a second circle 10 to 12 in. (25 to 30 cm) in diameter and ⅛ in. (3 mm) thick.
15. Sprinkle the first circle with toasted almonds, spread with apricot filling, leaving a 2 in. (5 cm) perimeter.
16. Cover with the second circle of puff pastry, pressing and crimping the edges.
17. Cut a small circle in the center of the torte and remove the circle.
18. Chill for 1 hour.
19. Preheat oven to 400°F (200°C).
20. Brush torte with egg glaze and bake for 30 to 35 minutes.
21. Reduce heat to 350°F (180° C) and bake for an additional 20 to 22 minutes, or until golden brown.

Raspberry Soufflé

	U.S.	Metric
	For 8–12 servings	*For 8–12 servings*
For Almond Paste:		
Egg whites	5	5
Sugar	1 cup	225 g
Almond flour	1½ cups	170 g
For Filling:		
Sugar	1 lb	450 g
Water	1 cup	240 ml
Egg whites	10	10
Raspberries, fresh, pureed	1½ pt	680 g
Lemon juice	2 lemons	2 lemons
Whipped cream	1 pt	480 ml

For Almond Paste:

1. Preheat oven to 200°F (93°C).
2. Line soufflé dish with wax paper.
3. Make paste by beating the egg whites until soft peaks form; add sugar and almond flour and blend until smooth.
4. Bake ¼ in. (6 mm) thick paste for 1 hour and 20 minutes, in 8 oz greased soufflé cups. Remove and transfer to rack and cool.

For Filling:

5. Combine sugar and water in a saucepan. Bring to a slow boil and cook for several minutes to make syrup.
6. Beat the egg whites until stiff peaks form.
7. Pour syrup into the eggs, beating until cold.
8. Add about ⅔ of the raspberries and the lemon juice to syrup mixture.
9. Fold in the whipped cream. Reserve.
10. Line soufflé dish with wax paper. Cut almond paste into circles to fit soufflé dish. Fit first circle in dish. Cover with raspberry mixture.
11. Alternate almond circle with raspberry mixture, ending with almond circle on top.
12. Freeze for 4 hours.
13. To serve, unmold, remove wax paper. Cut and serve with reserved fresh raspberry puree.

CHAPTER 7

Deep South

According to Emeril LaGasse of Emeril's Restaurant in New Orleans, "The trend is toward healthier living. This is no longer a craze or a fad, it has become a way of life." Southern food is very much part of a way of life. The slow cooking and leisurely meals of the South reflect its Spanish, French, English, African, and Native American heritages. The French left a legacy of roux used in Creole cooking. Today, at Emeril's and throughout the South, chefs are meeting the call for lower fat dishes by eliminating roux and are thickening sauces, soups, and gumbos with pureed vegetables, legumes, fruits, and a variety of starches from arrowroot to rice.

Traditional southern dishes were high in fat, particularly in saturated animal fat. Grits were drenched with butter or high-fat gravies. Many dishes were flavored with ham hocks or salt pork. Lard was the fat of choice and frying the preferred method of cooking. Vegetables that were not fried were cooked slowly for hours, destroying many of the vitamins. Things have begun to change. The cooking time for vegetables is generally shorter. Deep-fried foods are making way for lower fat cooking methods, such as blackened, broiled, or pan sautéed with minimum fat. Rice, corn, seafood, legumes, vegetables, fruits, and buttermilk, the nutritional strengths of the South, are replacing fatty meats as the focus of the meal.

Game meats, used in rural southern cooking, are usually lean and need only be prepared in a low-fat way. Today's pork is bred to be leaner. This makes it easier to prepare lower fat versions of old favorites like ham and barbecued pork. Lean ham and Canadian bacon are being used in place of salt pork or lard for flavor. Lard is being replaced by mono- and polyunsaturated oils in many dishes. The broad spectrum of flavors used in Cajun cooking makes it relatively easy to reduce fat and salt.

Rural southern cooking, on the other hand, continues to rely on animal fat and the ingredients themselves for flavor. It is essential to use the freshest ingredients in these dishes. The nuts abundant in the South are good sources of protein, vitamins, and fiber, but should be used in moderation because of their high-fat content. There

123

are, of course, dishes that cannot be made low in fat, such as the rich, mayonnaise-based sauces of New Orleans, fried hush puppies, biscuits, and pie pastry of the rural South. It is not realistic to expect a region so steeped in tradition to abandon these dishes, but such high-fat foods should be balanced by those lower in fat.

APPETIZERS

Shrimp Soufflé

	U.S.		Metric	
Portions:	8	50	8	50
Butter, unsalted	1/4 cup	1 1/2 cups	60 g	360 g
Pepper, green, minced	1/4 cup	1 1/2 cups	60 g	340 g
Celery, minced	1/4 cup	1 1/2 cups	60 g	340 g
Onion, finely chopped	1/4 cup	1 1/2 cups	60 g	340 g
Scallions, finely chopped	1/4 cup	1 1/2 cups	60 g	340 g
Shallots, chopped	2 Tbsp	3/4 cup	30 g	170 g
Shrimp, small	2 1/2 cups	15 1/2 cups	575 g	3.5 kg
Salt				
White pepper, fresh ground				
Fish stock	4 1/2 cups	7 qt	1.1 l	7 l
Flour	2 1/2 cups	15 1/2 cups	280 g	1.7 kg
Egg yolks	8	50	8	50
Egg whites	12	75	12	75
For Sauce:				
Butter, unsalted	7 Tbsp	2 3/4 cups	105 g	650 g
Flour	1/4 cup	1 1/2 cups	30 g	170 g
Scallions, chopped	1/4 cup	1 1/2 cups	60 g	340 g
Shrimp, small, peeled and deveined	2 cups	12 1/2 cups	454 g	2.8 kg
Seafood stock	3 cups	4 1/2 qt	720 ml	4.4 l
Thyme, dry	1 tsp	2 Tbsp	1 g	6 g
Garlic, minced	1 tsp	2 Tbsp	3 g	20 g
Heavy cream	2 cups	3 qt	480 ml	2.9 l
Salt				
White pepper, fresh ground				

1. Preheat oven to 350°F (180°C).
2. In a skillet, melt the butter and sauté the peppers, celery, onion, scallions, shallots, and shrimp. Season with salt and pepper and cook for 3 to 4 minutes or until vegetables are tender.
3. Add the fish stock and bring to a boil over high heat. Reduce heat and simmer for 10 to 12 minutes.
4. Add the flour, a little at a time, stirring constantly until thick. Cook for an additional 5 minutes.
5. Beat in egg yolks one at a time, using a wooden spoon. Set aside to cool.
6. In a separate bowl, whip egg whites to a stiff peak.
7. Fold 1/4 of the egg whites into the cooled soufflé. Smooth the whites.
8. Slowly fold soufflé base into remaining beaten egg whites.
9. Put mixture into buttered soufflé dishes. Bake for 12 to 17 minutes and serve immediately.

For Sauce:

10. Melt ½ of the butter in a saucepan. Make roux by adding flour to butter, cooking and stirring until smooth. Set aside.

11. In a separate saucepan, sauté the scallions in the remaining butter until soft.

12. Add the shrimp, stock, thyme, and garlic. Cook for 1 minute, gradually stir in ½ of the reserved roux. Stir until smooth.

13. Stir in the remaining roux, then stir in cream. Season with salt and pepper. Keep warm until ready to serve.

SOUPS

Shrimp Bisque

		U.S.		Metric	
Portions:		8	50	8	50
Shrimp, small, peeled, uncooked		⅔ lb	4 lb	300 g	1.8 kg
Butter		2⅔ Tbsp	1 cup	40 g	240 g
Brandy		1¼ Tbsp	½ cup	20 ml	120 ml
Shallots, chopped		¼ cup	1½ cups	60 g	340 g
White wine		⅓ cup	2 cups	80 ml	480 ml
Carrots, shredded		⅓ cup	2 cups	40 g	225 g
Onions, chopped		⅓ cup	2 cups	40 g	225 g
Leeks, chopped		½ cup	3 cups	115 g	680 g
Celery, chopped		⅔ cup	4 cups	150 g	900 g
Parsley, finely chopped		1¼ Tbsp	½ cup	3 g	18 g
Basil, dry		Pinch	To taste	Pinch	To taste
Tarragon, dry		Pinch	To taste	Pinch	To taste
Bay leaves		1	6	1	6
Oregano, dry		Pinch	½ tsp	To taste	335 mg
Thyme, dry, whole		2 pinches	1 tsp	To taste	1 g
Black peppercorns		2	12	2	12
Fish stock		1 qt	6 qt	1 l	6 l
Water		1 qt	6 qt	1 l	6 l
Tomato puree		½ cup	3 cups	115 g	680 g
Rice, raw		¼ cup	1½ cups	60 g	360 g
Salt					
Black pepper, fresh ground					
Heavy cream		⅓ cup	2 cups	80 ml	480 ml

1. In a heavy stockpot, sauté the shrimp in butter for 2 or 3 minutes, or until pink.
2. Flame with brandy, then stir in the shallots and cook for 20 or 30 seconds.
3. Add the white wine and the carrots, onions, leeks, celery, parsley, basil, tarragon, bay leaf, oregano, thyme, and peppercorns, stirring constantly. Cook for about 40 seconds.
4. Add the fish stock and water and cook for 5 to 6 minutes.
5. Add the tomato puree and rice. Season with salt and pepper and cook for 8 to 10 minutes.
6. Transfer the mixture to a food processor and puree for 1 minute.
7. Return mixture to pot and bring to a boil.
8. Reduce heat and add the cream, stirring briskly until thick.
9. Serve hot.

Turtle Soup

	Portions:	U.S.		Metric	
		8	50	8	50
Water					
Salt		1/3 cup	2 cups	75 g	454 g
Turtle meat, fresh or frozen		1 cup	6 cups	230 g	1.3 kg
Veal shank meat, ground		1 cup	6 cups	230 g	1.3 kg
Veal stock		2 qt	3 gal	2 l	12 l
Garlic cloves, chopped		3	18	3	18
Bay leaves		3	18	3	18
Thyme, whole, dry		2 pinches	1/2 Tbsp	2 pinches	2 g
Tomato puree		1/4 cup	1 1/2 cups	60 g	340 g
Celery, chopped		2/3 cup	4 cups	150 g	900 g
Onions, chopped		1 1/4 cups	7 1/2 cups	285 g	1.7 kg
Parsley, fresh		2 tsp	1/4 cup	2 g	9 g
Lemons, halved		3 lemons	18 lemons	3 lemons	18 lemons
Sherry		1/4 cup	1 1/2 cups	60 ml	360 ml
Eggs, boiled, chopped		3	18	3	18
Salt					
Black pepper, fresh ground					
Butter, as needed					
Flour, as needed					

For Veal Stock: Yields 1 qt (1 l) for 8

Veal bones		2 lb		900 g	
Salt, rock		1 oz		30 g	
Water		2 gal		8 l	
Onions, sliced		2 2/3 cups		600 g	
Carrots, sliced		2 cups		454 g	
Leeks, sliced		1 cup		230 g	
Celery, sliced		1 1/3 cups		300 g	
Parsley		1 cup		40 g	
Thyme		1 tsp		1 g	
Bay leaves		2		2	
Garlic head, peeled		1/2		1/2	
Tomato puree		1/2 cup		115 g	
Black peppercorns		6		6	

For Veal Stock:

1. Preheat oven to 425°F (220°C).
2. Brown veal bones in roasting pan with salt for about 30 to 40 minutes.
3. In a stockpot, combine the bones with the water to cover and add onions, carrots, leeks, celery, parsley, thyme, bay leaves, garlic, tomato puree, and black peppercorns. Bring to a rapid boil over high heat.
4. Reduce heat and simmer for 2 1/2 to 3 1/2 hours, stirring as necessary.
5. Strain, then return the stock to the stockpot, reduce by 2/3 its volume. Stock will hold for 1 week in refrigerator.

For Turtle Soup:

6. In a large pot, combine enough water to cover turtle meat and ½ the salt and bring to a boil. Reduce heat, add turtle meat, and simmer for 30 to 45 minutes.
7. In another large pot, combine enough water to cover shank meat and the remainder of the salt and bring to a boil. Reduce heat, add veal, and simmer for 30 to 45 minutes.
8. Remove meat from both pots and chop, using a food processor. Reserve, keeping warm. Discard any liquid.
9. In a stockpot, boil the veal stock with garlic, bay leaves, and thyme.
10. Add the tomato puree, celery, onions, parsley, and lemon juice. Bring to a boil, reduce heat, and simmer for 8 to 12 minutes.
11. Add both reserved meats and the sherry. Bring to a boil, reduce heat and simmer for 5 minutes.
12. Add eggs, salt, and pepper. Thicken with a small amount of roux or butter as needed.

Conch Chowder

	U.S.		Metric	
Portions:	8	50	8	50
Salt pork, finely chopped	4 oz	1½ lb	115 g	700 g
Onions, finely chopped	3	18	3	18
Peppers, green, chopped	1½	9	1½	9
Red chili peppers	1	6	1	6
Plum tomatoes, canned, chopped	28 oz	5½ qt	1 l	5.5 l
Tomato puree	8 oz	1½ qt	227 g	1.5 l
Conch meat, minced	¾ lb	4½ lb	340 g	2 kg
Bay leaves	2	12	2	12
Thyme, fresh, chopped	2½ tsp	5 Tbsp	3 g	15 g
Salt				
Black pepper, fresh ground				
Potatoes, peeled, cubed	4	25	4	25

1. In a large skillet, sauté salt pork for 8 to 10 minutes.
2. Add the onions, green pepper, and chili peppers, and cook over medium heat for 10 minutes.
3. Add the tomatoes, tomato puree, conch meat, bay leaves, thyme, salt, and pepper.
4. Bring to a boil and reduce heat. Cover and simmer for 30 minutes.
5. Add the potatoes and continue to simmer for an additional 20 to 25 minutes. Discard bay leaves before serving.

ENTRÉES

Almond Trout

👒 AMERICAN WINE SUGGESTION
Mirrasou Pinot Blanc

		U.S.		Metric	
Portions:		8	50	8	50
Trout filets, fresh, 8 oz. (225 g) each		8	50	8	50
Flour, as needed					
Butter		1¼ cups	7½ cups	300 g	1.8 kg
Lemon juice		1 lemon	6 lemons	1 lemon	6 lemons
Almonds, sliced, roasted under low heat of broiler for 1 minute		2 cups	12½ cups	454 g	2.8 kg
Lemon slices, as needed					
Parsley, fresh, chopped, as needed					

1. Dredge trout in flour.
2. Heat ½ the butter and sauté the filets over high heat for about 4 to 6 minutes per side.
3. In a separate pan, heat the remaining butter over low heat. Add the lemon juice, stirring constantly.
4. To serve, pour lemon sauce over the trout filets and cover with browned almonds.
5. Garnish with lemon slices and chopped parsley. Serve hot.

Cajun Pan-Fried Bass

❧ AMERICAN WINE SUGGESTION
Beringer Vineyards Chenin Blanc

	U.S.		Metric	
Portions:	8	50	8	50
Flour	1 cup	6 cups	115 g	675 g
Cornmeal, yellow or white, stone-ground	1 cup	6 cups	230 g	1.3 kg
Cayenne	2 tsp	4 Tbsp	2 g	12 g
Black pepper, fresh ground				
Salt				
Bass, small, whole, 1 lb (450 g) each, cleaned	8	50	8	50
Virgin olive oil, as needed for frying				
Lemons, sliced, as needed				

1. In a bowl, combine the flour, cornmeal, cayenne, black pepper, and salt. Dredge fish in flour mixture.
2. In a heavy skillet, heat enough olive oil to fry the fish.
3. When the oil is hot, fry bass, making sure not to crowd, until golden brown on both sides, or until bass becomes flaky.
4. When done, remove from pan, drain on paper towels, and serve with lemon slices.

Chicken with Orange Sauce

🦐 AMERICAN WINE SUGGESTION
Martin Brothers Moscato Frizzanté

		U.S.		Metric	
Portions:		8	50	8	50
Chicken, whole, 4–4½ lb (1.8–2.0 kg) each		2	13	2	13
Garlic cloves, minced		2	12	2	12
Salt					
White pepper, fresh ground					
Oranges, small, halved		4	25	4	25
Bread, cubed		2 cups	12½ cups	454 g	2.8 kg
Celery stalks, finely chopped		2	12	2	12
Butter, unsalted		½ cup	3 cups	120 g	720 g
Tarragon, dry		½ tsp	1 Tbsp	375 mg	2 g
Rosemary, dry		½ tsp	1 Tbsp	500 mg	3 g
Chicken stock		1 qt	6 qt	1 l	6 l
Vinegar, white wine		½ cup	3 cups	120 ml	720 ml
Sugar		6 Tbsp	2⅓ cups	90 g	560 g
Cornstarch		2 Tbsp	¾ cup	20 g	100 g

1. Preheat oven to 375°F (190°C).
2. Wash chicken thoroughly and season with salt, pepper, and minced garlic.
3. In a bowl, squeeze out the orange juice from half the oranges. Remove orange peel and cut into slivers. Set aside. Cut the remaining oranges into sections.
4. Combine the bread cubes, celery, butter, salt, pepper, and half of the tarragon and rosemary.
5. Add the orange segments and a small amount of the stock to moisten. Spoon mixture into cavity of the chickens. Tie closed.
6. Roast chickens, basting occasionally with stock and oven juices, for about 1½ hours.
7. While roasting, in a heavy saucepan combine the vinegar, sugar, and ¾ of the stock. Bring to a boil and then simmer until reduced by half.
8. Add the orange juice and the remaining tarragon and rosemary. Simmer over low to moderate heat for 8 to 10 minutes.
9. Remove roasted chicken and transfer cooking juices to a bowl with the cornstarch. Whisk cornstarch mixture into orange sauce, cooking over low heat, stirring constantly.
10. Season with salt and pepper. Serve the sauce with sliced chicken.

Coquilles St. Jacques

❧ AMERICAN WINE SUGGESTION
Jekel Johannesberg Riesling

		U.S.		Metric	
Portions:		8	50	8	50
Scallops, medium-sized, without shell		3½ lb	22 lb	1.6 kg	10 kg
Salt					
White pepper, fresh ground					
Flour		⅔ cup	4 cups	75 g	450 g
Butter		¼ lb	1½ lb	120 g	750 g
Herbsaint liqueur		⅓ cup	2 cups	80 ml	480 ml
Scallions, chopped		2⅔ cups	16½ cups	600 g	3.75 kg
Tomatoes, diced		1 cup	6 cups	225 g	1.4 kg
Garlic, finely chopped		⅓ cup	2 cups	50 g	320 g

1. Season scallops with salt and pepper and dredge in flour.
2. In a sauté pan, melt the butter and sear the scallops.
3. Remove excess butter, add Herbsaint liqueur, and flambé.
4. Add the scallions, tomato, and garlic, stirring constantly for 2 to 3 minutes.
5. Divide mixtures into individual casserole dishes, and finish under broiler to a light brown.
6. Serve immediately.

Eggs Sardou

	U.S.		Metric	
Portions:	8	50	8	50
Butter	¼ cup	1½ cups	60 g	360 g
Artichoke bottoms, large, cooked	8	50	8	50
Anchovy filets	16	100	16	100
Ham, finely diced	½ cup	3 cups	115 g	680 g
Eggs	8	50	8	50
Creamed spinach	2 lb	12½ lb	900 g	5.6 kg
Hollandaise sauce, as needed				
Lemon juice, as needed				

For Creamed Spinach:

Butter	¼ cup	1½ cups	60 g	360 g
Spinach, frozen, chopped, well drained	20 oz	7½ lb	575 g	3.4 kg
Flour	4 tsp	¼ cup	5 g	30 g
Heavy cream	1 cup	6 cups	240 ml	1.4 l
Salt				
White pepper, fresh ground				
Nutmeg, ground, to taste				
Herbsaint liqueur, to taste				

For Creamed Spinach:

1. In a skillet, melt the butter. Add the spinach and toss until all excess liquid has evaporated.
2. Add flour and stir well.
3. Add cream and stir well until thick.
4. Season with salt, pepper, and nutmeg. Add Herbsaint liqueur to taste.
5. Remove from heat and keep warm.

For Eggs:

6. Preheat oven to 300°F (150°C).
7. Place butter in baking dish and heat until melted.
8. Add artichoke bottoms and turn to coat with butter.
9. Place anchovies and ham in the dish, keeping them separate. Cover and heat through.
10. Poach the eggs until whites are set but yolks are still runny.
11. Spoon creamed spinach onto hot plates, place artichoke bottoms on top with ham and anchovy.
12. Place poached eggs on top of anchovy.
13. Spoon hollandaise sauce over eggs and sprinkle with lemon juice.

Georgian Veal Stew with Fresh Mushrooms and Snow Peas   COLOR PLATE 17

🦋 AMERICAN WINE SUGGESTION
Monterey Vineyards Chardonnay

	U.S.		Metric	
Portions:	8	50	8	50
Butter, unsalted	7 Tbsp	2¾ cups	100 g	660 g
Stewing veal, cubed	4½ lb	28 lb	2 kg	12.6 kg
Flour	3 Tbsp	1⅛ cups	20 g	130 g
Onions, small, finely chopped	2	12	2	12
Chicken stock	1 cup	1½ qt	240 ml	1.5 l
Wine, dry, white	1 cup	1½ qt	240 ml	1.5 l
Bouquet garni: 2 sprigs fresh thyme, 6 sprigs fresh parsley, 2 bay leaves, 2 scallions, 2 crushed garlic cloves	1	6	1	6
Virgin olive oil	2½ tsp	5 Tbsp	12 ml	75 ml
Mushroom caps	1 lb	6 lb	450 g	2.7 kg
Snow peas, shelled	1 cup	6 cups	225 g	1.4 kg
Egg yolks	3	18	3	18
Cream, heavy	¾ cup	4½ cups	180 ml	1.1 l
Nutmeg, fresh, grated	¼ tsp	1½ tsp	500 mg	3 g
Tabasco	Dash	To taste	Dash	To taste
Lemon juice	1½ Tbsp	9 Tbsp	22 ml	135 ml
Salt				
White pepper, fresh ground				

1. Melt ⅔ of the butter in a heavy saucepan. Sauté the veal over medium heat for 3 to 6 minutes, or until golden. Stir.
2. Add flour and cook for 1½ minutes, stirring constantly.
3. Continue stirring and add onions. Cook for an additional 2 minutes.
4. Add the stock and wine, stirring briskly. Bring to a boil, reduce heat.
5. Add the bouquet garni. Cover and cook until meat is done, about 40 to 45 minutes. Stir as needed.
6. In another skillet, heat the remainder of the butter with the oil and sauté the mushrooms until golden. Remove and reserve.
7. When meat is done, remove bouquet garni and add mushrooms and snow peas. Cook for 5 minutes. Reduce heat to low.
8. In a small bowl, combine the egg yolk with cream, and whip.
9. Slowly whip 4 Tbsp (60 ml) of the hot liquid from the saucepan into the egg yolk mixture. Add the mixture to the veal stew. Cook for 3 minutes over low heat to thicken slightly. Do not allow stew to boil.
10. Add the nutmeg, Tabasco, lemon juice, salt, and pepper.

Gumbo

🐝 AMERICAN WINE SUGGESTION
Charles Krug Sauvignon Blanc

		U.S.		Metric	
Portions:	8	50	8	50
Bacon strips	4	25	4	25
Flour	1/3 cup	2 cups	40 g	225 g
Onions, chopped	2/3 cup	4 cups	150 g	900 g
Scallions	2/3 cup	4 cups	150 g	900 g
Peppers, green, chopped	1/3 cup	2 cups	40 g	225 g
Celery, chopped	2/3 cup	4 cups	150 g	900 g
Garlic, chopped	1 1/4 tsp	2 1/2 Tbsp	4 g	25 g
Thyme, whole	Pinch	To taste	Pinch	To taste
Bay leaves	1	6	1	6
Parsley, chopped	2 2/3 Tbsp	1 cup	6 g	40 g
Shrimp, small	10 oz	4 lb	300 g	1.8 kg
Crabmeat, quartered	10 oz	4 lb	300 g	1.8 kg
Tomatoes, chopped	2/3 cup	4 cups	150 g	900 g
Shrimp stock	2 2/3 cups	1 gal	640 ml	3.9 l
Okra, sliced, quartered	2 2/3 cups	16 1/2 cups	600 g	3.7 kg
Salt				
Black pepper, fresh ground				
Cayenne, to taste				

For Shrimp Stock: Yields 2 qt (1.9 l)

Carrot, sliced	1		1	
Celery stalks, sliced	3		3	
Onion, small, white, sliced	1/2		1/2	
Bay leaves	3		3	
Cloves	3		3	
Black peppercorn, whole	60		60	
Salt	1/8 cup		30 g	
Water	3 qt		3 l	
Shrimp, raw, with shells	1 1/4 lb		560 g	

For Shrimp Stock:

1. Combine carrot, celery, onion, bay leaves, cloves, peppercorns, and salt with water. Bring to a boil over high heat. Boil for 6 minutes.
2. Add the shrimp and cook for 3 to 4 minutes. Remove from heat and strain, reserving shrimp for future use.

For Gumbo:

3. Heat the bacon strips until the fat is cooked.
4. Remove bacon, add the flour to the bacon fat, stirring constantly. Do not brown.
5. Reduce heat and add the onions, scallions, green pepper, celery, and garlic.

6. Add the thyme, bay leaf, and parsley. Cook for 6 to 8 minutes over low heat.
7. Add the shrimp, crabmeat, tomatoes, and shrimp stock. Bring to a boil over high heat. Remove any foam, as necessary.
8. Reduce heat and simmer for 20 to 25 minutes.
9. Add the okra and simmer for an additional 25 minutes, skimming as necessary.
10. Season with salt, pepper, and cayenne.

Ham with Redeye Gravy

 AMERICAN WINE SUGGESTION
Quail Ridge Merlot

		U.S.		Metric	
Portions:		8	50	8	50
Ham steaks, ¼ in. (1 cm) thick, approximately 8 oz (225 g) each		8	50	8	50
Clarified butter		¼ cup	1½ cups	60 ml	360 ml
Water		1 cup	1½ qt	240 ml	1.4 l
Coffee, brewed		1 cup	1½ qt	240 ml	1.4 l
Cream, heavy		¼ cup	1½ cups	60 ml	360 ml

1. Trim any fat from ham steaks and sauté in clarified butter until edges turn golden. Discard any excess fat as steaks cook. Remove from pan and keep warm.
2. In same pan, combine water, coffee, and cream. Heat quickly, bringing liquid to a boil. Scrape pan as necessary. Cook until thick.
3. Serve sauce with ham steaks.

Grillades Grits

🦃 AMERICAN WINE SUGGESTION
La Crema Vineyards Pinot Noir

		U.S.		Metric	
Portions:	8	50	8	50
Veal or beef round, 1½ lb (675 g) each, no fat, cubed	2	12½	2	12½
Salt				
Black pepper, fresh ground				
White pepper, fresh ground				
Corn oil	1 cup	6 cups	240 ml	1.4 l
Flour	½ cup	3 cups	55 g	350 g
Onions, chopped	2 cups	12½ cups	454 g	2.8 kg
Peppers, green, chopped	2 cups	12½ cups	454 g	2.8 kg
Celery, chopped	1 cup	6 cups	230 g	1.3 kg
Garlic cloves, minced	4	25	4	25
Beef stock	3 cups	4½ qt	720 ml	4.3 l
Tomatoes, 16 oz (454 g) cans	2	12½	2	12½
Parsley, chopped	¼ cup	1½ cups	9 g	60 g
Thyme, dry	1 tsp	2 Tbsp	1 g	6 g
Lemon juice	2 Tbsp	¾ cup	30 ml	180 ml
For Grits:				
Water	7 cups	2 ¾ gallons	1.7 l	10.4 l
Grits	½ cup	3 cups	115 g	680 g
Salt				
Butter				

1. Pound meat and season on both sides with salt, black pepper, and white pepper.
2. Heat ⅓ of the oil in a deep skillet. Add meat and brown on both sides. Brown meat in batches if necessary.
3. When all meat has been browned, remove from skillet, add the remaining oil to the skillet. Add flour to oil in skillet. Cook, stirring constantly, until hazelnut in color.
4. Remove from heat, add onion, green pepper, celery, and garlic. Return to heat and cook until vegetables are wilted. Stir.
5. Add the stock, tomatoes, parsley, thyme, and lemon juice. Bring to a boil. Lower heat, return meat to skillet, and simmer for 45 minutes, partly covered.

For Grits:

6. Prepare grits about 30 minutes before meat is done. In a heavy saucepan, boil the water. Sprinkle the grits into the boiling water, stirring constantly.
7. Salt grits to taste. Let boil. Reduce heat and cook for 15 to 20 minutes.
8. Remove grits from heat and cook, covered, until desired consistency is reached. Add pats of butter to taste.
9. To serve, pile grits on plate and serve with grillades.

North Carolina Fish Stew

🦃 AMERICAN WINE SUGGESTION
Domaine St. George Reserve Chardonnay

	U.S.		Metric	
Portions:	8	50	8	50
Salt pork, diced	½ cup	3 cups	115 g	680 g
Green onions, small, chopped	12	75	12	75
Green peppers, chopped	1	6	1	6
Carrots, chopped	2	12	2	12
Potatoes (baking), cooked, peeled, and diced	4	25	4	25
Fish stock	1 qt	6 qt	1 l	6 l
Scallops	1 lb	6 lb	450 g	2.7 kg
Haddock filets, cut in small pieces	1 lb	6 lb	450 g	2.7 kg
Nutmeg	¼ tsp	1½ tsp	500 mg	3 g
Salt				
Black pepper, fresh ground				
Tabasco	Dash	To taste	Dash	To taste
Parsley, chopped, as needed for garnish				
Lemon slices, as needed for garnish				

1. In a heavy skillet, sauté the salt pork over medium heat until golden, stirring occasionally.
2. Add the green onions, peppers, carrots, and ½ the potatoes. Cover and cook for about 12 to 15 minutes, stirring occasionally.
3. Mash the remaining potatoes, and add them and the fish stock to the sautéed vegetables. Bring to a boil, reduce heat, cover, and simmer for 8 to 10 minutes.
4. Add the scallops, haddock, and nutmeg. Cook, covered, until fish is cooked, approximately 5 minutes. If stew becomes too thick, add fish stock until desired consistency is achieved.
5. Season with salt, pepper, and Tabasco. Garnish with chopped parsley and lemon slices.

Oysters and Crabmeat

🐝 AMERICAN WINE SUGGESTION
Vendange Gamay Beaujolais

		U.S.		Metric	
Portions:		8	50	8	50
Oyster liquid		2 qt	3 gal	2 l	12 l
Wine, a cabernet sauvignon		1 qt	1½ gal	1 l	6 l
Garlic cloves, chopped		6	38	6	38
Scallions, sliced		2 cups	12½ cups	454 g	2.8 kg
Mushrooms, sliced		1 lb	6 lb	454 g	2.8 kg
Demi-glace		2 cups	3 qt	480 ml	2.9 l
Crabmeat		2 lb	12½ lb	900 g	5.7 kg
Flour		1½ cups	9 cups	170 g	1 kg
Seafood seasoning		2 Tbsp	¾ cup	18 g	115 g
Oysters, freshly shucked		48	300	48	300
Oil, as needed					

For Seafood Seasoning: Makes 2 cups (220 g)

Salt		⅓ cup		80 g
Garlic, granulated		¼ cup		20 g
Black pepper, fresh ground		¼ cup		28 g
Cayenne		2 Tbsp		14 g
Thyme, dry		2 Tbsp		6 g
Oregano, dry		2 Tbsp		4 g
Paprika		⅓ cup		40 g
Onion, powdered		3 Tbsp		20 g

For Seafood Seasoning:

1. Combine salt, garlic, black pepper, cayenne, thyme, oregano, paprika, and onion powder thoroughly. Reserve.

For Oysters and Crabmeat:

2. In a saucepan, reduce oyster liquid to ¼ volume. Add the wine, garlic, scallions, mushrooms, and demi-glace. Reduce until thick.
3. Add crabmeat and simmer over low heat for 2 to 3 minutes. Remove and reserve.
4. Combine flour with seafood seasoning.
5. Heat oil to 350°F (180°C). Dust oysters with seasoned flour and fry in oil until golden, 2 to 3 minutes. Drain excess oil.
6. Serve 6 oysters per plate with reserved sauce.

Redfish with Shrimp

❧ AMERICAN WINE SUGGESTION
Napa Ridge Chardonnay

		U.S.		Metric	
Portions:		8	50	8	50
Shrimp, medium, peeled and deveined		32	200	32	200
Butter		10 Tbsp	3 ¾ cups	150 g	900 g
Flour		2 Tbsp	¾ cup	14 g	85 g
Seafood stock		2 cups	3 qt	480 ml	3 l
Seafood seasoning		4 tsp	½ cup	12 g	75 g
Heavy cream		2 cups	3 qt	480 ml	3 l
Redfish filets		8	50	8	50
Butter, melted		¼ cup	1 ½ cups	60 ml	360 ml

1. Sauté shrimp in ⅘ of the butter until pink.
2. Add flour, stirring well until smooth.
3. Add stock and seafood seasoning. Bring to a simmer, stirring constantly. Simmer until reduced by ⅔.
4. Add cream and return to simmer, stirring constantly.
5. Add the remaining butter to glaze the sauce.
6. Brush melted butter on redfish and season with additional seafood seasoning to taste. Broil until done.
7. Serve redfish with sauce.

Sautéed Louisiana Crawfish

❧ AMERICAN WINE SUGGESTION
Silverado Chardonnay

	U.S.		Metric	
Portions:	8	50	8	50
For Crawfish Rice:				
Unsalted butter	½ cup	3 cups	120 g	720 g
Onions, medium, chopped	2	12	2	12
Celery stalks, finely chopped	4	25	4	25
Green peppers, finely chopped	2	12	2	12
Crawfish tails, cooked, peeled, deveined, chopped	1 lb	6 lb	450 g	2.7 kg
Rice, uncooked	2 cups	12 cups	454 g	2.8 kg
Fish stock, boiling	3 cups	4½ qt	720 ml	4.4 l
For Crawfish:				
Unsalted butter	1¼ lb	7 ¾ lb	570 g	3.5 kg
Crawfish tails, peeled and deveined	2 lb	12½ lb	900 g	5.6 kg
Scallions, chopped	2 cups	12½ cups	454 g	2.8 kg
Seafood seasoning	2 Tbsp	¾ cup	20 g	115 g
Worcestershire sauce	2 Tbsp	¾ cup	30 ml	180 ml

For Crawfish Rice:

1. Over low heat, sauté the onion, celery, green pepper, and crawfish in butter for approximately 2 minutes.
2. Add rice and mix well.
3. Add boiling stock, return to a boil, and cover. Lower heat and simmer for 20 minutes or until all liquid has been absorbed. Remove from heat and keep warm.

For Crawfish:

4. In a skillet, melt half the butter. Sauté the crawfish tails with the scallions.
5. Add the seafood seasoning and Worcestershire sauce. Stir until hot. Do not overcook crawfish, which are more delicate than shrimp. Remove from heat.
6. Add remaining butter a little at a time, stirring gently until smooth and creamy.
7. Serve immediately with crawfish rice.

Shrimp Creole   COLOR PLATE 18

🦃 AMERICAN WINE SUGGESTION
Chateau Ste. Michelle Gewürztraminer

		U.S.		Metric	
Portions:	8	50	8	50
Virgin olive oil	6 Tbsp	2⅓ cups	90 ml	540 ml
Onions, chopped	4	25	4	25
Garlic cloves, minced	4	25	4	25
Green peppers, seeded and chopped	2	12	2	12
Celery stalks, chopped	4	25	4	25
Tomatoes, large, ripe, peeled, seeded, and chopped	6	38	6	38
Sugar, to taste				
Bay leaves	2	12	2	12
Thyme, dry	1 tsp	2 Tbsp	1 g	6 g
Shrimp, peeled and deveined	4 lb	25 lb	1.8 kg	11.3 kg
Cayenne	1 tsp	2 Tbsp	2 g	12 g
Salt				
Black pepper, fresh ground				
Sassafras leaves, ground, dry	2 tsp	4 Tbsp	1 g	8 g
Rice servings, hot, cooked	8	50	8	50

1. Sauté the onions for 1 minute in a heavy skillet in the olive oil.
2. Add the garlic, stirring constantly, and cook for 3 to 4 minutes.
3. Add the green peppers, celery, tomatoes, sugar, bay leaves, and thyme. Cover and cook for 8 to 10 minutes.
4. Add the shrimp and cayenne. Cover and cook for 3 to 5 minutes, until shrimp is pink.
5. Season with salt and pepper. Remove from heat.
6. Once away from heat, stir in the sassafras leaves and serve over rice.

ACCOMPANIMENTS

Cajun Dirty Rice

		U.S.		Metric
Portions:	8	50	8	50
Chicken livers	½ lb	3 lb	225 g	1.4 kg
Turkey gizzards	¼ lb	1½ lb	115 g	700 g
Chicken fat, rendered, or bacon drippings	¼ cup	1½ cups	60 ml	360 ml
Pork, ground	½ lb	3 lb	225 g	1.4 kg
Onions, chopped	½ cup	3 cups	115 g	680 g
Celery, chopped	½ cup	3 cups	115 g	680 g
Green peppers, chopped	½ cup	3 cups	115 g	680 g
Garlic cloves, minced	2	12	2	12
Chicken stock	2 cups	3 qt	480 ml	2.9 l
Salt				
Black pepper, fresh ground				
Cayenne	¼ tsp	1½ tsp	600 mg	4 g
Paprika	½ tsp	1 Tbsp	1 g	7 g
Rice, long grain	1½ cups	9 cups	340 g	2 kg
Scallions, green only, chopped	½ cup	3 cups	115 g	700 g

1. Trim discoloration from liver and remove tough skin from gizzards.
2. In a food processor, process liver and gizzards to coarse pieces.
3. In a skillet, heat chicken fat and add liver, gizzards, and ground pork. Fry for 8 to 10 minutes or until golden.
4. Add onion, celery, peppers, and garlic, and fry until vegetables are wilted, stirring occasionally.
5. Add the stock, salt, pepper, cayenne, and paprika. Bring to a boil.
6. Cover and simmer, stirring occasionally, for 20 to 25 minutes or until liquid has evaporated.
7. Cook rice in boiling salted water until tender, adding water as needed. Drain well.
8. Add hot rice to the vegetable mixture. Add some chopped scallions. Mix well and serve hot.

South Carolina Black-Eyed Peas

		U.S.		Metric	
Portions:		8	50	8	50
Black-eyed peas, dry		1 cup	6 cups	225 g	1.4 kg
Bacon strips		4	25	4	25
Onions, small, chopped		2	12	2	12
Garlic cloves, minced		2	12	2	12
Rice, cooked		2 cups	12 cups	454 g	2.8 kg
Vinegar, red wine		1/4 cup	1 1/2 cups	60 ml	360 ml
Salt					
Black pepper, fresh ground					
Chives, fresh, chopped		1/4 cup	1 1/2 cups	40 g	240 g

1. Cover peas with water and soak overnight.
2. Drain peas, cover with water in a pan, and bring to a boil. Reduce heat and simmer for 1 hour.
3. Drain peas, reserving the liquid.
4. In a heavy skillet, sauté the bacon until crisp. Remove bacon and pat dry. Crumble bacon and reserve.
5. In the same skillet, sauté the onion for 1 to 1 1/2 minutes.
6. Add the garlic and cook for several minutes.
7. Add the peas and rice. Cook, stirring constantly.
8. Add the vinegar and some of the reserved liquid from the peas to moisten the mixture. Cook for 5 to 6 minutes. Season with salt and pepper.
9. Sprinkle with bacon bits and chives. Serve.

DESSERTS

Bread Pudding with Bourbon Sauce

		U.S.		Metric	
Portions:		8	50	8	50
Milk		1 cup	1½ qt	240 ml	1.4 l
Light cream		1 cup	1½ qt	240 ml	1.4 l
Unsalted butter		6 Tbsp	2⅓ cups	90 g	565 g
Sugar		¾ cup	4½ cups	165 g	1 kg
Eggs, beaten		3	18	3	18
Lemon zest		½ lemon	3 lemons	½ lemon	3 lemons
Vanilla extract		1 tsp	2 Tbsp	5 ml	30 ml
Bread crumbs, coarsely chopped fresh bread		5 cups	31 cups	1.1 kg	7 kg
Raisins, golden		⅓ cup	2 cups	75 g	450 g
Pecans, toasted, chopped		⅓ cup	2 cups	75 g	450 g
For Sauce:					
Brown sugar, finely packed		1 cup	6 cups	225 g	1.4 kg
Unsalted butter		¼ lb	1½ lb	115 g	680 g
Egg yolks		1	6	1	6
Bourbon or dark rum		¼ cup	1½ cups	60 ml	360 ml

For Sauce:

1. Combine brown sugar and butter and heat until butter has melted and sugar has dissolved. Stir frequently.
2. Add egg yolk and bourbon and cook over low heat, stirring constantly, until sauce thickens. Do not boil. Remove and reserve.

For Bread Pudding:

3. In a separate saucepan, combine the milk, cream, and ⅔ of the butter, and scald.
4. Remove from heat and pour mixture into a large bowl. Add the sugar and stir until it dissolves.
5. Mix eggs, lemon zest, and vanilla into milk mixture.
6. Add bread crumbs and raisins, and mix well. Allow mixture to soak for at least 5 minutes. Stir in pecans.
7. Pour the mixture into a shallow, buttered baking dish, spreading evenly.
8. Place baking dish in a roasting pan and surround with water. Bake in a preheated 350°F (180°C) oven for 40 minutes, or until pudding is set and golden on top.
9. Remove from baking dish and cut into squares. Spoon sauce over pudding and serve warm.

Strawberry Shortcake

		U.S.		Metric	
	Portions:	8	50	8	50
Flour		2½ cups	15½ cups	280 g	1.7 kg
Sugar		½ cup	3 cups	120 g	720 g
Baking powder		4 tsp	½ cup	11 g	70 g
Salt		½ tsp	1 Tbsp	2 g	15 g
Cream cheese		3 oz	2⅓ cups	85 g	525 g
Unsalted butter, cold		3 Tbsp	1⅛ cups	45 g	280 g
Eggs, slightly beaten		1	6	1	6
Sour cream		2 Tbsp	¾ cup	30 ml	180 ml
Heavy cream		1¾ cups	2 ¾ qt	420 ml	2.6 l
Butter, melted		2 Tbsp	¾ cup	30 ml	180 ml
Strawberries, fresh,		1 qt	6 qt	1 l	6 l
Grand Marnier		2 Tbsp	¾ cup	30 ml	180 ml
Confectioner's sugar		1 Tbsp	6 Tbsp	9 g	55 g

1. Preheat oven to 450°F (235°C).
2. In a large bowl, combine the flour, half of the sugar, baking powder, and salt.
3. Add the cream cheese and cold butter and mix to a coarse texture.
4. In a separate bowl, combine egg, sour cream, and half the cream.
5. Add cream mixture to the flour mixture and mix to a soft dough.
6. Divide the dough in half. Press out dough on a lightly floured surface to a 8 in. to 10 in. (25 cm) circle.
7. Place dough in a buttered cake pan, smoothing with your hands.
8. Press out second half of dough and place second circle on dough in pan.
9. Drizzle dough with melted butter and bake for 20 minutes.
10. With heat off, open oven and let dough finish for about 35 to 40 minutes. Transfer to rack, split, and cool.
11. Crush half the strawberries and combine with remaining whole strawberries, sugar, and Grand Marnier. Refrigerate for 35 minutes.
12. To serve, whip remaining cream with confectioner's sugar to a stiff peak.
13. Spoon half of the strawberry mixture over the bottom shortcake layer, cover with second shortcake layer, spoon remaining strawberry mixture over second layer, and top with whipped cream.

CHAPTER 8

Texas
and the
Southwest

Regional cooking in Texas and the Southwest reflects local life-styles and ingredients. The region, its people, and its cooking are unique. It is a melting pot of Spanish, Portuguese, Mexican, German, and Native American cultures and foods. Corn, fresh vegetables, legumes, tomatoes, and a host of tropical fruits form the foundation of this potentially nutritious diet. Legumes, prepared with little fat, add protein, complex carbohydrates, vitamins, and minerals to a meal. Legumes, or dried beans, can be used in a variety of ways to add interest and nutrients to a meal. They work well in salsa, soups, as side dishes, or as fillings for burritos and tacos. While the purist's chili contains no beans, vegetarian chili made with no meat is becoming more and more popular. The modern version of this classic dish contains little or no saturated fat. A little olive oil can be used in place of some or all the pork fat traditionally used in preparing dishes of this region. The zest of a variety of hot peppers and chilis used here makes it easy to reduce fat and salt without sacrificing flavor.

The abundance of fish in Texas and the Southwest is often overshadowed by the variety of meat dishes unique to this region. Everything barbecued is popular here. There is some concern that frequently eating barbecued foods increases the risk of cancer. The occasional barbecue is not considered a problem, particularly if the food is cooked for a short period of time and is not charred. Barbecuing is, after all, a low-fat method of cooking. The crisp skin and succulent flesh of fish grilled over aromatic wood, served with a medley of local vegetables and corn products, and accented with cilantro and lime, is too delightful a meal to be missed.

There are some traditional dishes of the Southwest that are fried or made with added bacon or pork fat and are high in fat. Sausages and cheeses brought by Europeans have found their way into regional cooking and, of course, beef is king in some areas of the region. These are not difficult obstacles to overcome. Modern beef is leaner and lean cuts and grades can be used. Lean meats can be marinated to tenderize before barbecuing, baking, or roasting. Low-fat sauces, so popular in the region, can be added to boost flavor and moisture. Reduced-fat sausages or cheeses can replace high-fat varieties, or small amounts can be used when desired for flavor. Corn products and legumes can replace some of the meat and complement smaller meat portions. Frying should be minimized. Desserts that utilize the abundant fruits of the region are generally low in fat and excellent sources of nutrients. William Nassikas, owner of The Bolders in Carefree, Arizona, as well as several other restaurants in the region, has seen a dramatic change in customer expectations: "There is a quiet revolution going on. People are demanding more variety and healthier dishes." Chef Nassikas sees a definite return to Native American cuisine—a cuisine high in complex carbohydrates, low in fat, and with moderate amounts of meat. This is a healthier cuisine for all Americans.

APPETIZERS

Smoked Rainbow Trout

		U.S.		Metric	
Portions:		8	50	8	50
Tomatoes, whole		8	50	8	50
Vinegar, red wine		¼ cup	1½ cups	60 ml	360 ml
Virgin olive oil		¾ cup	4½ cups	180 ml	1.1 l
Salt					
White pepper, fresh ground					
Sorrel, fresh, large bunches, cleaned and stemmed		2	12	2	12
Rainbow trout filets, skinless, boneless, smoked		8	50	8	50

1. Roast the tomatoes over a grill or under a broiler until skin is charred on all sides. Remove tomatoes from heat, but do not peel.
2. In a food processor, puree the tomatoes. Remove to a saucepan.
3. Over medium heat, simmer tomatoes for about 15 minutes or until liquid has reduced by half. Strain.
4. Add the vinegar and olive oil to the tomato puree and blend well. Season with salt and pepper. Set aside to cool.
5. Cut sorrel into thin strips.
6. Ladle sauce onto plates. Make a bed of sorrel in center of each plate.
7. Place the trout on sorrel and serve.

SOUPS

Shrimp and Rice Soup (Sopa de Arroz)

	U.S.		Metric	
Portions:	8	50	8	50
Virgin olive oil	¼ cup	1½ cups	60 ml	360 ml
Rice, long grain	2 cups	12½ cups	450 g	2.8 kg
Tomatoes, chopped and seeded	2 cups	12½ cups	450 g	2.8 kg
Shrimp, cooked, peeled, and deveined	2 cups	12½ cups	450 g	2.8 kg
Water, hot	1½ qt	2⅓ gal	1.4 l	9 l
Salt				
Tabasco	2 tsp	¼ cup	10 ml	60 ml

1. In a heavy skillet, heat olive oil.
2. When oil is very hot, add rice and cook, stirring constantly, until golden.
3. Add tomatoes, shrimp, water, salt, and Tabasco. Cover and cook for 15 to 18 minutes or until most of the liquid has evaporated.

SALADS

Spinach Salad with Smoked Duck

		U.S.		Metric	
Portions:		8	50	8	50
Hot chili oil		2 Tbsp	¾ cup	30 ml	180 ml
Virgin olive oil		¼ cup	1½ cups	60 ml	360 ml
Bacon fat, melted		¼ cup	1½ cups	60 ml	360 ml
Balsamic vinegar		½ cup	3 cups	120 ml	720 ml
Malt vinegar		2 Tbsp	¾ cup	30 ml	180 ml
Garlic cloves, minced		6	38	6	38
Shallots, chopped		6	38	6	38
Thyme, fresh, finely chopped		¼ cup	1½ cups	12 g	70 g
Chives, chopped		2 Tbsp	¾ cup	20 g	120 g
Salt					
White pepper, fresh ground					
Lemon juice		2 lemons	12 lemons	2 lemons	12 lemons
Spinach, fresh, stemmed and cleaned		2 lb	12½ lb	900 g	5.6 kg
Smoked duck breasts, 7–8 oz (200–225 g) per breast, cubed		4–5	25–30	4–5	25–30
Red bell peppers, roasted, julienne		2	12	2	12
Yellow peppers, roasted, julienne		2	12	2	12

1. In a mixing bowl, combine the hot chili oil, olive oil, bacon fat, vinegars, garlic, shallots, thyme, chives, salt, pepper, and lemon juice. Mix well and set aside.
2. Heat a sauté pan over medium heat. Add the spinach and sauté lightly.
3. Slowly add half of the reserved dressing.
4. Remove spinach to a salad bowl.
5. Add the duck and julienne peppers to the salad bowl and mix well.
6. Divide the salad into equal portions.
7. Deglaze the pan with the remaining dressing, add to salad. Serve immediately.

ENTRÉES

Pork Loin with Baked Beans   COLOR PLATE 19

🍒 AMERICAN WINE SUGGESTION
Jundlach Bundshu Gewürztraminer

		U.S.		Metric	
Portions:	8	50	8	50
White beans	1 lb	6¼ lb	450 g	2.8 kg
Virgin olive oil	½ cup	3 cups	120 ml	720 ml
Onions, diced	1	6¼	1	6¼
Garlic cloves, crushed	3–4	22	3–4	22
Salt				
White pepper, fresh ground				
Celery ribs, chopped	1	6¼	1	6¼
Italian parsley sprigs	1	6¼	1	6¼
Carrots, chopped	1	6¼	1	6¼
Tomatoes, diced	4	25	4	25
Tomato paste	1 Tbsp	6 Tbsp	15 ml	90 ml
Pork loins, small, 7–8 oz (200–226 g) each	8	50	8	50
Dry mustard	2 Tbsp	¾ cup	30 ml	180 ml
Butter	3 Tbsp	1⅛ cups	45 g	280 g

1. Bring the beans to a boil in salted water. Boil for 10 minutes. Strain.
2. In a skillet, add oil and sauté the onions and garlic. Add to beans.
3. Place the beans in a baking dish. Combine the salt, pepper, celery, parsley, carrot, and tomatoes, and add to the beans.
4. Dilute the tomato paste in water and add to the beans. Add enough water to cover the beans.
5. Bake in a 375°F (190°C) preheated oven for 2 hours or until beans are cooked. Check occasionally, adding water as necessary.
6. Season the pork with salt, pepper, and dry mustard. Drizzle with butter.
7. Bake or grill the pork until pink. Remove from heat and thinly slice.
8. Arrange the pork in a circle on a bed of beans and serve.

Basque Lamb

🐌 AMERICAN WINE SUGGESTION
Llano Estraeado Cabernet Sauvignon

	U.S.		Metric	
Portions:	8	50	8	50
Legs of lamb, boned, approximately 5 lb (2.3 kg) each	2	13	2	13
Rosemary, dry	1¼ tsp	2½ Tbsp	1 g	6 g
Garlic cloves, minced	8	50	8	50
Salt				
White pepper, fresh ground				
Pork tenderloins, cut in strips to fit into bone cavity	2	13	2	13
Lemon juice	1 cup	1½ qt	240 ml	1.4 l

1. Rub lamb with rosemary, some of the garlic, salt, and pepper.
2. Place pork in bone cavity of the leg of lamb, roll, and tie in place.
3. Rub the lamb with lemon juice and remaining garlic.
4. Place lamb on spit and roast 5 in. to 6 in. (12 to 15 cm) above hot coals, turning every 30 to 35 minutes. Roast for about 2½ hours, or until done.

Chili con Carne

🦐 BEVERAGE SUGGESTION: BEER

	U.S.		Metric	
Portions:	8	50	8	50
Kidney beans, dry	2 lb	12½ lb	900 g	5.4 kg
Unsalted butter	¾ cup	4½ cups	180 g	1.1 kg
Virgin olive oil	2 Tbsp	¾ cup	30 ml	180 ml
Chuck steak, cut into strips	3 lb	18½ lb	1.4 kg	8.3 kg
Beef, ground, lean	3 lb	18½ lb	1.4 kg	8.3 kg
Onions, large, chopped	4	25	4	25
Garlic cloves, minced	4	25	4	25
Chili powder	½ cup	3 cups	60 g	350 g
Tomatoes, large, seeded and chopped	4	25	4	25
Tomatoes and green chilies, canned	20 oz	7 ¾ lb	600 g	3.75 kg
Brown sugar	2 tsp	4 Tbsp	10 g	60 g
Bay leaves	2	12	2	12
Thyme, dry, to taste				
Cayenne	2 tsp	4 Tbsp	5 g	30 g
Worcestershire sauce	2 Tbsp	¾ cup	30 ml	180 ml
Beef stock	3 cups	4½ qt	720 ml	4.4 l
Salt				
Black pepper, fresh ground				

1. Soak beans overnight in cold water.
2. Preheat oven to 300°F (150°C).
3. In a heavy skillet, heat ½ the butter with the oil and sauté the beef strips in batches until brown. Remove beef from skillet, pat dry and transfer to a pot.
4. Brown ground beef in the same skillet, stirring as needed. Transfer browned ground beef to pot with beef strips.
5. Discard all fat from skillet. Add butter and onions. Cook over moderate heat for 2 to 3 minutes.
6. Add garlic and cook for 1 to 2 minutes.
7. Transfer onions and garlic to pot with beef.
8. Add chili powder to beef, stir, then add fresh tomatoes, canned tomatoes and green chilies, brown sugar, bay leaves, thyme, cayenne, Worcestershire sauce, beef stock, salt, and pepper. Bring to a boil, cover, and place in oven. Cook for 1½ to 2 hours.
9. In a heavy saucepan, cover beans with water, bring to a boil, reduce heat and simmer. Skim as needed. Simmer for about 45 minutes or until beans are tender. Drain and reserve.
10. Add beans to meat mixture and bake for an additional 20 to 25 minutes. Add beef stock as needed if it becomes too dry.

Chilied Pork

🐾 BEVERAGE SUGGESTION: BEER

	U.S.		Metric	
Portions:	8	50	8	50
Green peppers, large	4	25	4	25
Pork shoulder, boneless, cubed	3 lb	18½ lb	1.4 kg	8.3 kg
Bacon drippings	¼ cup	1½ cups	60 ml	360 ml
Onions, large, chopped	2½	15½	2½	15½
Garlic cloves, chopped	4	25	4	25
Flour	2½ Tbsp	1 cup	20 g	115 g
Chicken stock	5 cups	2 gal	1.2 l	7.7 l
Green chilies, canned, drained and chopped	20 oz	9½ lb	565 g	4.3 kg
Salt				
White pepper, fresh ground				
Rice servings, cooked	8	50	8	50

1. Char the peppers over a grill or under a broiler.
2. Let peppers cool and remove the skins. Seed, chop, and set aside.
3. In a heavy skillet, sauté the pork in bacon drippings until golden. Remove from skillet and set aside.
4. Add the onions to the bacon drippings and sauté for 1 minute.
5. Add the garlic and cook for an additional 2 minutes.
6. Add the reserved pork and reduce heat.
7. Add flour, stirring constantly.
8. Add the chicken stock, roasted peppers, and chilies. Bring to a boil. Reduce heat and simmer until pork is tender, about 1 hour. Season with salt and pepper and serve with rice.

Chimichangas

🐝 BEVERAGE SUGGESTION: BEER

		U.S.		Metric	
Portions:	8	50		8	50
Beef, coarsely chopped	2½ lb	15½ lb		1.1 kg	7 kg
Potatoes, peeled and diced	3	18		3	18
Green chili peppers, small, seeded and chopped	8	50		8	50
Onions, chopped	1½	9		1½	9
Garlic cloves, chopped	4	25		4	25
Oregano	1½ tsp	3 Tbsp		1 g	6 g
Salt					
Black pepper, fresh ground					
Tortillas (p. 166)	16	100		16	100
Oil, as needed for frying					

1. Combine beef with potatoes, chili peppers, onion, garlic, oregano, salt, and pepper.
2. Add enough cold water to cover and cook, simmering for about 40 to 50 minutes, or until meat is done.
3. Place some of the mixture in the center of each tortilla and fold.
4. Heat about 1¼ in. (3 cm) of oil in a skillet.
5. Add chimichangas to skillet and fry until golden on all sides.

Enchiladas

❦ BEVERAGE SUGGESTION: BEER

		U.S.		Metric	
Portions:		8	50	8	50
Tomatoes, canned		1 qt	6 qt	1 l	6 l
Hot red chili peppers, seeded		3	18	3	18
Salt					
Black pepper, fresh ground					
Sour cream		1¼ cups	7½ cups	300 ml	1.8 l
Chicken, cooked and diced		1¼ lb	8 lb	575 g	3.6 kg
Cheddar cheese, grated		1½ cups	9 cups	340 g	2 kg
Tortillas (p. 166)		16	100	16	100
Oil, as needed for frying					

1. Preheat oven to 350°F (180°C).
2. In a food processor, puree tomatoes and chili peppers. Season with salt and pepper.
3. Add sour cream to tomato mixture, stir, and set aside.
4. In a bowl, combine the chicken with ½ of the cheddar cheese. Reserve.
5. Heat oil and sauté tortillas briefly until golden. Remove.
6. Divide the chicken mixture evenly among the tortillas. Roll.
7. Arrange tortillas in a greased baking dish. Pour tomato mixture over tortillas, cover with aluminum foil, and bake for 20 to 25 minutes.
8. Remove from oven, sprinkle with remaining cheddar cheese, and broil until cheese is melted.

Great American Hamburger   COLOR PLATE 20

🐚 BEVERAGE SUGGESTION: BEER

		U.S.		Metric	
Portions:		8	50	8	50
Onion, chopped, to taste					
Salt					
White pepper, fresh ground					
Black Angus sirloin		4 lb	25 lb	1.8 kg	11.3 kg
Lettuce, as needed					
Tomatoes, sliced, as needed					
Green peppers, sliced, as needed					
Red onions, sliced, as needed					

1. Combine the onion, salt, pepper, and sirloin. Mix well. Form into 8 oz (225 g) patties.
2. Char grill to liking and serve with lettuce, sliced tomatoes, peppers, and red onion. Add mustard and ketchup if desired. Serve with Saratoga chips (p. 118).

Grilled Red Snapper with Two Sauces

🐌 AMERICAN WINE SUGGESTION
Henry Estate Pinot Noir

		U.S.		Metric	
Portions:		8	50	8	50
Red snapper filets, 8 oz (225 g) each		8	50	8	50
Salt					
White pepper, fresh ground					
Virgin olive oil		6 Tbsp	2⅓ cups	90 ml	560 ml
For Black Bean Sauce:					
Black beans, cooked and drained		2 cups	12½ cups	450 g	2.8 kg
Serrano chilies, chopped		2	12	2	12
Shallots, chopped		2	12	2	12
Garlic cloves, chopped		2	12	2	12
Cilantro, fresh, chopped		2 Tbsp	¾ cup	5 g	30 g
Chicken stock		1 cup	1½ qt	240 ml	1.4 l
For Red Chili Sauce:					
Red bell peppers, seeded, peeled, and chopped		4	25	4	25
Shallots, chopped		2	12	2	12
Garlic cloves, chopped		2	12	2	12
Red chilies, chopped		2	12	2	12
Cilantro, chopped		½ cup	3 cups	40 g	240 g
Chicken stock		½ cup	3 cups	120 ml	720 ml
Salt					
White pepper, fresh ground					
Lime juice, fresh, to taste					

For Black Bean Sauce:

1. Combine beans, chilies, shallots, garlic, cilantro, and stock. Cook over high heat for 10 minutes.
2. Remove from heat and puree in a food processor. Set aside.

For Red Chili Sauce:

3. Combine peppers, shallots, garlic, chilies, cilantro, stock, salt, and pepper. Cook over high heat for 10 minutes.
4. Remove from heat and puree in food processor.
5. Add the lime juice and set aside.

For Red Snapper:

6. Season snapper with salt, pepper, and oil.
7. Cook on a hot grill for 4 to 5 minutes per side. Keep moist; do not overcook.
8. Serve the grilled snapper with black bean sauce and red chili sauce.

Halibut with Orange and Horseradish Crust

🐝 AMERICAN WINE SUGGESTION
Robert Mondavi Johannesberg Riesling

		U.S.		Metric	
Portions:		8	50	8	50
Bread crumbs, dry		2 cups	12 cups	450 g	2.8 kg
Horseradish, finely grated		¼ cup	1½ cups	60 g	350 g
Orange peel, grated		3 Tbsp	1⅛ cups	45 g	280 g
Salt					
Garlic cloves, minced		2	12	2	12
Halibut filets, 7–8 oz (200–225 g) each, trimmed and boned		8	50	8	50
Peanut oil		6 Tbsp	2⅓ cups	90 ml	560 ml
Sesame oil		2 tsp	¼ cup	10 ml	60 ml

1. Preheat oven to 375°F (190°C).
2. Combine bread crumbs, horseradish, orange peel, salt, and garlic in a bowl.
3. Press bread crumb mixture firmly into halibut, on both sides.
4. Combine the peanut oil and sesame oil and heat over medium heat.
5. Sauté filets until brown on both sides (1 to 2 minutes; do not burn).
6. Transfer filets to casserole and bake for 5 minutes or until cooked but firm in middle.
7. Remove and serve with oven juices.

Huevos Rancheros

	U.S.		Metric	
Portions:	8	50	8	50
Butter	6 Tbsp	2⅓ cups	90 g	560 g
Garlic cloves	2	12	2	12
Onions, large, chopped	4	25	4	25
Hot red pepper flakes	1 Tbsp	6 Tbsp	3 g	18 g
Whole tomatoes, 16 oz (454 g) cans	2	12	2	12
Salt				
White pepper, fresh ground				
Eggs	16	100	16	100

1. Melt ⅔ of the butter and sauté the garlic and onions for 5 minutes or until soft and golden.
2. Add pepper flakes and tomatoes. Cover and simmer for 40 minutes or until thick. Season with salt and pepper. Remove from heat.
3. Beat eggs lightly.
4. Heat remaining butter and add eggs. Cook until bottom has browned lightly. Then flip omelette over and cook until done.
5. Remove omelette, cut into equal portions, and serve with sauce.

Medallions of Beef in Chili Sauce   COLOR PLATE 21

🦃 AMERICAN WINE SUGGESTION
Shafer Vineyards Merlot

		U.S.		Metric	
Portions:		*8*	*50*	*8*	*50*
Beef medallions, 3 oz (85 g) each		*16*	*100*	*16*	*100*
Salt					
Pepper mixture (mix well):					
Black pepper		*2 tsp*	*4 Tbsp*	*5 g*	*28 g*
White pepper		*1 tsp*	*2 Tbsp*	*2 g*	*12 g*
Cayenne		*1½ tsp*	*3 Tbsp*	*3 g*	*18 g*
Virgin olive oil		*6 Tbsp*	*2⅓ cups*	*90 ml*	*560 ml*
Chili sauce, to taste					
Mixed beans, boiled, as needed for garnish					
Cilantro leaves, fresh, washed and drained, as needed for garnish					

1. Season medallions with salt and pepper mixture.
2. Heat sauté pan, add oil, and sauté medallions of beef for 2½ to 3 minutes per side. Remove beef from pan and keep warm.
3. Add chili sauce to sauté pan. Warm, place on warm plates, place medallions of beef in center, and garnish with beans and cilantro.

Pan-Fried Swordfish with Tomato Vinaigrette

❧ AMERICAN WINE SUGGESTION
Simi Sauvignon Blanc

		U.S.		Metric	
Portions:		*8*	*50*	*8*	*50*
Swordfish steaks, 8 oz (225 g) each		8	50	8	50
Salt					
White pepper, fresh ground					
Virgin olive oil		½ cup	3 cups	120 ml	720 ml
For Vinaigrette:					
Vinegar, white wine		¼ cup	1½ cups	60 ml	360 ml
Virgin olive oil		⅓ cup	2 cups	80 ml	480 ml
Shallots, minced		2	12	2	12
Garlic cloves, minced		2	12	2	12
Tomatoes, peeled, seeded, and diced		2	12	2	12
Tomatillos, dried		½ cup	3 cups	90 g	540 g
Cilantro, chopped		3 Tbsp	1⅛ cups	7 g	45 g
Salt					
White pepper, fresh ground					

For Vinaigrette:

1. Combine the vinegar, oil, shallots, garlic, tomatoes, tomatillos, and cilantro. Season with salt and pepper. Set aside.

For Swordfish:

2. Season swordfish with salt and pepper.
3. Heat olive oil in heavy skillet and sauté swordfish for 4 minutes per side or until done. If the swordfish is thick, it will take longer to cook.
4. Serve with the vinaigrette.

Pork Tostadas

🌶 AMERICAN WINE SUGGESTION
Jundlach Bundshu Gewürztraminer

		U.S.		Metric	
Portions:		8	50	8	50
Pork, ground		2 lb	12½ lb	1 kg	5.6 kg
Onions, medium, chopped		2	12	2	12
Chili powder		1 Tbsp	6 Tbsp	7 g	40 g
Salt					
Cumin		½ tsp	1 Tbsp	1 g	6 g
Garlic cloves, chopped		2	12	2	12
Kidney beans, cooked, drained, and mashed		2 lb	12½ lb	1 kg	5.6 kg
Cooking liquid, reserved from beans		½ cup	3 cups	120 ml	720 ml
Water		1 cup	1½ qt	240 ml	1.4 l
Tortillas		16	100	16	100
Lettuce heads, shredded		½	3	½	3
Cheese, mild, shredded		1 cup	6 cups	230 g	1.3 kg
Tomatoes, chopped		2	12	2	12
For Tortillas:					
Salt		1½ Tbsp	9 Tbsp	22 g	135 g
Corn flour, fine		2 cups	12½ cups	225 g	1.4 kg
Water		1¼ cups	7½ cups	300 ml	1.8 l
Lard, as needed					

For Tortillas:

1. Combine the salt and corn flour in a bowl. Gradually add ½ the water. Knead dough until a ball can be formed.
2. Divide dough into small pieces and flatten with a rolling pin. Shape into thin round disks.
3. Over a low heat, grease a skillet with lard, and cook the tortillas for 30 to 40 seconds on one side. Turn and cook for 10 to 15 seconds on the second side.
4. Remove and stack on wax paper.

For Tostadas:

5. In a skillet, brown pork with onion. Pour off excess fat.
6. Add chili powder, salt, cumin, and garlic.
7. Add mashed beans, bean liquid, and water. Simmer for 15 minutes, stirring occasionally.
8. Spread some of the pork mixture over each tortilla. Add lettuce. Cover with another tortilla, spread with more pork mixture, top with cheese and tomatoes.

Texas Short Ribs

🍷 AMERICAN WINE SUGGESTION
Rodney Strong Zinfandel

		U.S.		Metric	
Portions:		8	50	8	50
Flour		1 cup	6 cups	115 g	675 g
Salt					
White pepper, fresh ground					
Allspice, ground		½ tsp	1 Tbsp	420 mg	2.5 g
Beef short ribs		6–7 lb	40–42 lb	2.7–3.1 kg	18–19 kg
Virgin olive oil		2 Tbsp	¾ cup	30 ml	180 ml
Unsalted butter		½ lb	3 lb	240 g	1.4 kg
Onions, large, chopped		4	25	4	25
Garlic cloves, minced		4	25	4	25
Green chili peppers, small, hot, seeded and chopped		2	12	2	12
Green peppers, small, seeded and chopped		2	12	2	12
Celery stalks, chopped		2	12	2	12
Brown sugar		¼ cup	1½ cups	60 g	360 g
Paprika, sweet		1 tsp	2 Tbsp	3 g	20 g
Chili powder		¼ cup	1½ cups	30 g	175 g
Dry mustard		1 tsp	2 Tbsp	2 g	12 g
Lemon juice		1 cup	1½ qt	240 ml	1.4 l
Chili sauce		1 cup	1½ qt	240 ml	1.4 l
Ale, dark		1 cup	1½ qt	240 ml	1.4 l
Plum tomatoes, chopped, 16 oz cans		2	12	2	12

1. Preheat oven to 350°F (180°C).
2. Combine the flour with salt, pepper, and allspice.
3. Dredge ribs in seasoned flour.
4. Heat oil in skillet and brown ribs on all sides. Brown in batches. Remove ribs from skillet and set aside.
5. Reduce heat and add butter. Sauté the onions, garlic, chili peppers, and green peppers for 3 to 5 minutes, stirring occasionally.
6. Add some flour, scraping pan well. Cook for 1 to 2 minutes.
7. Add the celery, brown sugar, paprika, chili powder, mustard, lemon juice, chili sauce, and ale. Stir well. Add tomatoes.
8. Return short ribs to skillet and boil. Cover and transfer to oven. Bake for 1½ hours, turning meat once.
9. Uncover and bake an additional 15 minutes.
10. Skim any fat before serving.

Roast Duck with Sweet Potato Puree and Cabernet Sauvignon Sauce

🐚 AMERICAN WINE SUGGESTION
Inglenook Cabernet Sauvignon

	U.S.		Metric	
Portions:	8	50	8	50
Duck breasts, 2.5 lb (1.1 kg) each	4	25	4	25
Salt				
White pepper, fresh ground				
Sweet potato puree				
Orange rind, cut into long strips	4 tsp	½ cup	20 g	120 g
Chives, cut to match orange rind strips	4 tsp	½ cup	20 g	120 g
For Sweet Potato Puree:				
Sweet potatoes	4 lb	25 lb	1.8 kg	11.3 kg
Cinnamon sticks	4	25	4	25
Ginger, fresh, grated	1 Tbsp	6 Tbsp	30 g	180 g
Apple juice	1 qt	6 qt	1 l	6 l
Lemon juice, to taste				
Salt				
White pepper, fresh ground				
For Duck Demi-Glace:	2½ cups	1 gallon	600 ml	4 l
Peanut oil	2 Tbsp	¾ cup	30 ml	180 ml
Duck carcasses, uncooked, chopped, fat removed	4	25	4	25
Onions, peeled and diced	2	12	2	12
Carrots, peeled and diced	1	6	1	6
Celery stalks, sliced	1	6	1	6
Black pepper, cracked	4 tsp	½ cup	9 g	60 g
Shallots, peeled and chopped	4	25	4	25
White mushrooms, large, thinly sliced	6	38	6	38
Thyme, fresh bunches	2	12	2	12
Veal demi-glace	2 cups	3 qt	480 ml	2.9 l
Chicken stock	2 cups	3 qt	480 ml	2.9 l
For Cabernet Sauvignon Sauce:				
Cabernet sauvignon, 750 ml bottles	1	6	1	6
Ginger, fresh, grated	2 tsp	¼ cup	20 g	120 g
Orange juice, fresh squeezed	2 oranges	12 oranges	2 oranges	12 oranges
Shallots, chopped	4	25	4	25
Serrano chilies, chopped	2	12	2	12
Ancho chilies, large, dry, seeded	2	12	2	12
Duck demi-glace	2 cups	3 qt	480 ml	2.9 l
Maple syrup, to taste				
Lemon juice, to taste				
Salt				
White pepper, fresh ground				

For Sweet Potato Puree:

1. Place potatoes in salted water and boil until soft, about 30 minutes. Drain and remove skins.
2. Puree sweet potatoes in food processor until smooth.
3. In a saucepan, combine the cinnamon, ginger, apple juice, and lemon juice. Bring to a boil over high heat, reduce heat, and simmer for 12 to 15 minutes, or until almost all of the liquid evaporates.
4. Remove cinnamon sticks and add mixture to sweet potatoes.
5. Season with salt and pepper to taste.

For Duck Demi-Glace:

6. Wash ducks. Remove and reserve breasts. Use carcasses for demi-glace.
7. Heat oil over medium heat, add duck carcasses and brown for 12 to 15 minutes, stirring as needed to prevent burning.
8. Add the onion, carrots, celery, and cook for 8 minutes.
9. Add pepper, shallots, and mushroom, sautéing for 2 minutes. Do not brown.
10. Add thyme, veal demi-glace, and chicken stock. Bring to a boil, lower heat, and simmer for 45 minutes to 1 hour. Reduce by half, skimming as necessary. Strain and reserve.

For Cabernet Sauvignon Sauce:

11. Combine the wine, ginger, orange juice, shallots, and chilies. Bring to a boil, reduce heat, and simmer for 15 minutes.
12. Add duck demi-glace and simmer for 10 additional minutes.
13. Season with maple syrup, lemon juice, salt, and pepper.

For Duck:

14. Preheat oven to 375°F (190°C).
15. Season reserved duck breasts with salt and pepper. Sauté over medium heat for 2 to 4 minutes per side. Remove from heat.
16. Place duck in oven and roast to medium rare, 5 to 8 minutes, depending on the size of the duck.

To Serve:

17. Spoon a mound of sweet potato puree at center of warm dinner plate.
18. Thinly slice the duck breast and arrange in a circle, leaning on potatoes.
19. Pour sauce around plate, garnish with orange rinds and chives.

Note: Sweet potato puree, duck demi-glace, and cabernet sauvignon sauce can be made in advance.

Venison with Spicy Pear Sauce

🦃 AMERICAN WINE SUGGESTION
Meridian Vineyards Syrah

	U.S.		Metric	
Portions:	8	50	8	50
Venison medallions 2½–3 oz (70–85 g) each	16	100	16	100
Salt				
Pepper mixture: (mix well)				
Black pepper	2 tsp	¼ cup	5 g	30 g
White pepper	1 tsp	2 Tbsp	2 g	12 g
Cayenne	1½ tsp	3 Tbsp	3 g	18 g
Vegetable oil	½ cup	3 cups	120 ml	720 ml
Wild rice servings	8	50	8	50
For Spicy Pear Sauce:				
Wild mushrooms, sliced	5	30	5	30
Vegetable oil	2 Tbsp	¾ cup	30 ml	180 ml
Shallots, minced	5	30	5	30
Golden pears, cored and sliced	8	50	8	50
Thyme sprigs, fresh,	5	30	5	30
Black peppercorns, crushed	1½ Tbsp	½ cup	8 g	50 g
Green peppercorns, crushed	1 Tbsp	6 Tbsp	6 g	35 g
Serrano chilies	2	12	2	12
White port wine	1½ cups	9 cups	360 ml	2.1 l
Veal demi-glace	3 cups	4½ qt	720 ml	4.4 l
Salt				
White pepper, fresh ground				
Lemon juice	1½ lemons	9 lemons	1½ lemons	9 lemons

For Spicy Pear Sauce:

1. Sauté mushrooms in oil for 2 minutes.
2. Add the shallots and sauté for an additional minute.
3. Add pears, thyme, black and green peppercorns, serrano chilies, and wine. Bring to a boil, reduce heat, and simmer for 10 minutes, or until reduced by half.
4. Add the demi-glace. Bring to a boil. Remove from heat and skim.
5. Season the sauce with salt, pepper, and lemon juice.

For Venison:

6. Season medallions of venison with salt and pepper mixture.
7. Heat oil in sauté pan and sauté venison over medium heat for 1 to 2 minutes to sear. Cook to medium rare.
8. Serve with spicy pear sauce and wild rice.

ACCOMPANIMENTS

Green Chili Salsa

	U.S.	Metric
Makes 2 cups (480 ml)	8	8
Chili peppers, fresh, green, chopped, with seeds	3	3
Green tomatoes, medium, chopped	4	4
Onions, medium, chopped	2	2
Water, boiling	1 cup	240 ml
Garlic clove, chopped	1	1
Oregano, dry	1 tsp	600 mg
Salt		

1. Cover chili peppers with water, bring to a boil, reduce heat, and cook for 8 to 10 minutes. Remove and drain.
2. Return peppers to saucepan. Add tomatoes, onion, and boiling water. Simmer for 20 minutes. Remove from heat and press through sieve.
3. Discard solids.
4. Add garlic, oregano, salt, and mix well. Mixture should be thick. Refrigerate tightly covered with plastic wrap.

Refried Beans

	U.S.		Metric	
Portions:	8	50	8	50
Kidney beans, dry, rinsed under cold water	4 cups	25 cups	900 g	5.7 kg
Water	3 qt	4½ gal	2.9 l	17 l
Onions, chopped	4	24	4	24
Tomatoes, medium, peeled, seeded, and chopped	2	12	2	12
Garlic cloves, chopped	6	36	6	36
Bacon drippings	1 cup	1½ qt	240 ml	1.4 l
Salt				

1. In a heavy skillet, combine the beans, water, half the onions, half the tomatoes, garlic, and some of the bacon drippings. Bring to a boil; boil for 10 minutes. Reduce heat and simmer for 1½ hours.
2. Season with salt, and continue to simmer, partly covered, for an additional 25 to 30 minutes, until beans are slightly mushy.
3. Stir occasionally, adding additional water, ¼ cup (60 ml) at a time, as needed.
4. Drain beans, reserving liquid.
5. Melt some of the bacon drippings in a pan. Sauté remaining onions for about 5 minutes or until soft and golden.
6. Add remaining tomatoes and sauté for 2 to 3 minutes. Reduce heat.
7. Add ¼ of the beans to skillet, mash, and stir in some bacon drippings.
8. Repeat step 7, until all bacon drippings and all beans are mashed together.
9. Mixture should be crisp on top and creamy on the bottom. If too dry, add some of the reserved bean liquid.

**Georgian Veal Stew with Fresh Mushrooms
and Snow Peas**   *p. 135*

Shrimp Creole *p. 143*

Pork Loin with Baked Beans   *p. 154*

Great American Hamburger *p. 160*

Medallions of Beef in Chili Sauce   *p. 164*

Filet Mignon in a Mild Garlic Sauce   *p. 187*

Lamb Chops with Leeks   *p. 194*

Cream Puffs with Ice Cream and Vanilla Sauce   *p. 206*

Napoleon of Alaskan King Crab   *p. 222*

Salmon with Endive and Lime   *p. 223*

**Salmon Medallions with
Fresh Hot Tomato Sauce** *p. 224*

**Muscat Greens and Wild Flowers
with Champagne Dressing** *p. 238*

California Cioppino   *p. 241*

Pacific Fruit Soup *p. 242*

Lobster California   *p. 254*

Fresh Fruit Tart   *p. 274*

DESSERTS

Pecan and Sweet Potato Pie

	U.S.	Metric
	Makes 1 Pie, 10" (25 cm)	Makes 1 Pie, 10" (25 cm)
Eggs, large	3	3
Egg yolks	1	1
Light brown sugar, packed	½ cup	115 g
Unsalted butter	2 Tbsp	30 g
Pure vanilla	1 tsp	5 ml
Pure maple syrup	4½ tsp	23 ml
Pastry, all-purpose, as needed for 1 crust		
Pecans	1½ cups	340 g
Sweet potatoes, peeled and cubed	2½ cups	565 g
Ginger, ground	¼ tsp	800 mg
Cinnamon, ground, to taste		
Cloves, ground, to taste		
Egg whites	2	2
Sugar	⅓ cup	75 g
Heavy cream, unsweetened, whipped	1 cup	240 ml

1. Preheat oven to 350°F (180°C).
2. Combine the eggs with the egg yolks.
3. Stir in sugar and blend until smooth.
4. Add butter, vanilla, and maple syrup. Stir until well incorporated.
5. Line a 10 in. (25 cm) flan pan with the all-purpose pastry.
6. Sprinkle pastry with pecans and add filling.
7. Bake for 30 minutes or until golden. Remove and let cool.
8. While pie is baking, boil sweet potatoes in salted water. Cook for 12 minutes or until tender. Drain.
9. Combine potatoes with ginger, cinnamon, and cloves until smooth. Cool in the refrigerator for at least 20 minutes.
10. In a separate bowl, beat the egg whites. Add sugar and continue to beat to a stiff peak.
11. Add the sweet potato mixture to the beaten egg whites. Mix well. Place the sweet potato mixture into pie shell over the pecan mixture.
12. Bake for an additional 20 minutes or until firm. Remove from oven and cool.
13. Serve with whipped cream.

Soft Tacos with Glazed Bananas in Grand Marnier Glaze

	U.S.		Metric	
Portions:	*8*	*50*	*8*	*50*
Flour	2 cups	12½ cups	225 g	1.4 kg
Flour, bread	2 cups	12½ cups	225 g	1.4 kg
Sugar	¼ cup	1½ cups	60 g	360 g
Salt				
Milk	1 qt	1½ gal	1 l	5.8 l
Eggs, large, beaten	8	50	8	50
Egg yolks, large, beaten	8	50	8	50
Unsalted butter, melted and still hot	½ lb	3 lb	240 g	1.4 kg
Cognac	½ cup	3 cups	120 ml	720 ml
Butter, as needed for tacos				
Glazed bananas				
Grand Marnier glaze				

For Grand Marnier Glaze:

Egg yolks, large	10	62	10	62
Sugar	½ cup	3 cups	120 g	720 g
Grand Marnier	6 Tbsp	2⅓ cups	90 ml	560 ml

For Glazed Bananas:

Unsalted butter	½ lb	3 lb	240 g	1.4 kg
Light brown sugar, packed	1 lb	6 lb	450 g	2.8 kg
Orange juice, fresh squeezed	¼ cup	1½ cups	60 ml	360 ml
Grand Marnier	¼ cup	1½ cups	60 ml	360 ml
Bananas, peeled and sliced	12	75	12	75

For Grand Marnier Glaze:

1. Beat egg yolks and sugar in a double boiler over simmering water for 10 minutes.
2. Remove from heat and cool slightly. Whisk in Grand Marnier. Reserve.

For Glazed Bananas:

3. Combine butter and brown sugar in a saucepan over medium heat.
4. Cook until liquified. Add orange juice and Grand Marnier. Cook for 5 minutes. Remove from heat and add sliced bananas. Keep warm.

For Tacos

5. In a bowl, combine flour, bread flour, sugar, and salt.
6. Slowly add milk, egg, and egg yolks, beating constantly.
7. Whisk in butter and cognac. Mix well. Let set for at least 15 minutes.
8. Butter pan. Over medium heat, add enough batter to cover pan.
9. Cook for 2 to 3 minutes or until lightly browned.
10. Turn taco and cook for 2 to 3 minutes on second side.
11. Repeat steps 8, 9, and 10 until all batter is used.
12. Stuff tacos with bananas, roll, and coat with Grand Marnier glaze.
13. Place under broiler for 1 to 2 minutes, or until lightly browned.

CHAPTER 9

Midwest and Mountain States

Culinary experts generally agree that there is a trend toward American food and a straightforward kind of cooking based on local ingredients.

The cooking of the Midwest and mountain states is considered by many to typify *real* American cooking. The Midwest is, after all, the birthplace of the hamburger and the hot dog. The cuisine of this vast region reflects the abundance of America. Meat forms the basis of most meals. "Stick-to-your-ribs" ingredients include pork, beef, and dairy products. There is not the same use of fruits and vegetables as found in other regional cuisines. Desserts emphasize cakes, pies, and cookies. The food here tends to be sparsely seasoned except for salt and sugar. While rich sauces are not popular, consumption of saturated fat, particularly animal fat, is high. The movement towards reducing fat in the diet is more obvious in the cities than in rural areas, but it is growing.

The strengths of this region's cooking lie in the simple methods used, the abundance of grains, wild game, and the freshwater fish found in some areas. Grains provide complex carbohydrates, vitamins, and minerals. Newer methods of raising cattle and hogs are producing lower fat meat. Settlers from northern and eastern Europe brought their traditional high-fat sausages with them to this region, but lower fat varieties of sausages are now available. Wild game tends to be lean, as is fish. Varieties of trout, bass, perch, and char are plentiful in some regions. Those varieties of fish that are higher in fat can be prepared in a low-fat way to reduce total fat and calories. Seasonal local produce is preferred by the people of this region. This is a positive factor, because locally produced food tends to be fresher and of higher nutritional value.

To improve the nutritional value of traditional high-fat American foods, chefs are using leaner cuts and grades of meat, skimming the fat from the pan drippings before preparing the gravy, and thickening with starches other than roux. Home-style meat loaf is being made with extra-lean ground beef. By offering a choice of portion size, the chef enables the patron to choose lower fat meals. Smaller portions of meat or fish are balanced with larger portions of potato, grains, and vegetables.

In many ways the simplicity of the food eaten here makes it more difficult to adapt nutritionally. Extra-lean ground beef and lean cuts of meat can easily become dry when baked or broiled. To compensate, hamburger can be mixed with carbohydrates such as bread crumbs to retain moisture, lean cuts should be cooked carefully to avoid drying. Game meats such as venison and wild birds can provide interesting meals low in fat. Stews and dumplings are popular in some parts of this region. Limiting fat in cooking and skimming fat from the stew make these wonderful, nutritious dishes. Desserts are more problematic. Pastry dough is high in fat. Phyllo dough can be used to make strudel-like desserts with less fat. Cobblers can be made lower in fat, as can cakes. These can be complemented with a dollop of low-fat cream, ice milk, or frozen yogurt.

APPETIZERS

Apple and Ham Pâté

	U.S.		Metric	
Portions:	8	50	8	50
Smoked ham, sliced, cut into strips	1/4 lb	1 1/2 lb	115 g	680 g
Water	1 qt	1 1/2 gal	1 l	5.8 l
Ruby port wine	3/4 cup	1 qt	180 ml	1 l
Currants, dried	1/4 cup	1 1/2 cups	60 g	360 g
Pork shoulder, lean, ground	1 3/4 lb	11 lb	800 g	5 kg
Beef suet	1/4 lb	1 1/2 lb	115 g	680 g
Fatback, chopped	1/4 lb	1 1/2 lb	115 g	680 g
Heavy cream	1/2 cup	3 cups	120 ml	720 ml
Brandy	1/4 cup	1 1/2 cups	60 ml	360 ml
Eggs, lightly beaten	2	12	2	12
Apples, cored, peeled, and sliced	2	12	2	12
White wine	1/2 cup	3 cups	120 ml	720 ml
Garlic, minced	1 1/2 tsp	3 Tbsp	5 g	30 g
Nutmeg, ground	1/4 tsp	1 1/2 tsp	500 mg	3 g
Allspice, ground	1/2 tsp	1 Tbsp	500 mg	3 g
Salt				
Black pepper, fresh ground				
Bacon, sliced	3/4 lb	4 1/2 lb	340 g	2 kg

1. Soak ham for 1 hour in cold water. In a separate pot, soak the currants in port wine for 1 hour. Drain both, reserving port wine.
2. Using a food processor, puree the pork shoulder, suet, and fatback. Puree in batches if necessary. Add cream and port as necessary to each batch to maintain consistency. Process each batch for at least 25 seconds, or until smooth and pastelike.
3. In a large bowl, combine the batches of meat mixture.
4. In a sauté pan, warm the brandy to ignite it. Burn off alcohol and add it to the meat mixture.
5. Add the eggs, apples, white wine, garlic, nutmeg, allspice, and season with salt and pepper to taste. Mix well until blended.
6. Line a pâté mold with bacon strips to form an even layer.
7. Add 2 cups (480 g) of pâté mixture and smooth evenly. Cover with bacon strips.
8. Repeat step 7, ending with bacon layer. Cover with foil.
9. Place pâté in a deep baking dish and surround with water.
10. Preheat oven to 300°F (150°C).
11. Bake the pâté for 2 hours. Remove foil and bake for an additional 30 minutes.
12. Remove from oven. Cool on a rack for at least 50 minutes. Refrigerate overnight before serving.

Celery Root Pancakes with Smoked Salmon

	Portions:	U.S.		Metric	
		8	50	8	50
Red bell pepper		1	6	1	6
Corn kernels, fresh		⅔ cup	4 cups	145 g	900 g
Celery root, shredded, in vinegar, 12¼ oz. (350 g) cans		1	6½	1	6½
Eggs		1	6	1	6
Salt					
White pepper, fresh ground					
Flour		5 Tbsp	2 cups	35 g	225 g
Unsalted butter		3 Tbsp	1⅛ lb	45 g	285 g
Smoked salmon, 2 oz (60 g) slices		8	50	8	50
Sour cream, as needed					

1. Using an open flame grill, char the outside of the peppers on all sides. Then steam peppers until skin begins to peel.
2. Peel and seed the pepper. Cut julienne and reserve.
3. In a small saucepan, boil the corn for about 2 minutes. Drain and reserve.
4. Combine the bell pepper, corn, celery root, egg, salt, and pepper.
5. Add flour and mix well.
6. To make pancakes, cook ⅓ of the celery root mixture for 2 to 3 minutes, until golden, in ⅓ of the butter. Repeat this process in batches, adding butter as needed.
7. Cover with smoked salmon and serve with sour cream.

Snails with Mushrooms

		U.S.		Metric	
Portions:		*8*	*50*	*8*	*50*
Garlic, minced		2²/₃ Tbsp	16½ Tbsp	30 g	170 g
Shallots, finely chopped		2²/₃ Tbsp	16½ Tbsp	30 g	170 g
Butter		5¹/₃ Tbsp	2 cups	80 g	480 g
Snails, canned		32	200	32	200
Red wine		1 cup	1½ qt	240 ml	1.5 l
Salt					
White pepper, fresh ground					
Mushrooms, large, stemmed		32	200	32	200
Parsley, chopped, as needed for garnish					

1. Sauté garlic and shallots in ½ of the butter for 1 to 2 minutes.
2. Add the snails and cook for 1½ minutes.
3. Add wine and cook for 3 minutes. Season with salt and pepper.
4. In a separate pan, sauté the mushrooms in remaining butter for about 3 to 4 minutes.
5. Stuff each mushroom with a snail and garnish with parsley. Serve hot.

SOUPS

Oyster Bisque

	U.S.		Metric	
Portions:	8	50	8	50
Chicken stock	3 cups	1 gal	720 ml	3.8 l
Oysters, fresh, shucked, reserve liquid	2 qt	3 gal	1.8 kg	11.3 kg
Onion, small, chopped	1/2	3	1/2	3
Celery, finely sliced	2 cups	12 1/2 cups	450 g	2.8 kg
Cloves, whole	8	50	8	50
Salt				
White pepper, fresh ground				
Sherry	1/4 cup	1 1/2 cups	60 ml	360 ml
Milk, scalded	2 qt	3 gal	1.9 l	11.5 l
Butter	1/4 cup	1 1/2 lb	60 g	360 g

1. Combine the chicken stock and the reserved oyster liquid.
2. Add the onion, celery, and cloves and simmer over moderate heat for 20 to 25 minutes.
3. Strain through a sieve.
4. Add oysters. Heat, and season with salt and pepper. Add sherry.
5. Prior to serving, add the milk and butter, stirring well.

Sausage and Corn Chowder

		U.S.		Metric	
Portions:		*8*	*50*	*8*	*50*
Corn ears, fresh		4	25	4	25
Whipping cream		5⅓ cups	2 gal	1.3 l	8 l
Chicken stock		2⅔ cups	1 gal	640 ml	3.9 l
Garlic cloves, minced		5⅓	33½	5⅓	33½
Thyme sprigs, fresh		13	82	13	82
Bay leaves		1	6	1	6
Onions, finely chopped		2	12	2	12
Italian sausage, hot		⅔ lb	4 lb	300 g	1.8 kg
Unsalted butter		2⅔ Tbsp	1 cup	40 g	240 g
Jalapeño chilies, minced, with seeds		2⅔ tsp	⅓ cup	15 g	90 g
Cumin, ground		⅔ tsp	4 tsp	1 g	6 g
Flour		2⅔ Tbsp	1 cup	20 g	115 g
Potatoes, baked, peeled, and cubed		3	19	3	19
Salt					
White pepper, fresh ground					
Chives, fresh, chopped		2 tsp	¼ cup	6 g	40 g

1. Cut corn from cob and place cob in a saucepan, reserving kernels.
2. Add the cream, stock, garlic, thyme, bay leaf, and ⅔ of the onion. Simmer over moderate heat for 40 to 55 minutes. Remove from heat.
3. Strain through a sieve and reserve corn stock.
4. In a heavy skillet, cook the sausage, turning occasionally. Remove, let cool, and cut into pieces.
5. In a separate pan, sauté the remaining onions, chilies, and cumin in butter for about 4 to 5 minutes.
6. Add flour and cook, stirring constantly for several minutes.
7. Gradually whisk in the corn stock.
8. Add the sausage and potatoes. Cover and cook for about 20 minutes, or until potatoes are tender.
9. Add corn and cook for an additional 4 minutes. Season with salt and pepper.
10. Garnish with fresh chives.

Wisconsin Cheddar Cheese Soup

	U.S.		Metric	
Portions:	8	50	8	50
Butter	¼ cup	1½ cups	60 g	360 g
Flour	4½ Tbsp	1¾ cups	32 g	200 g
Chicken stock	5½ cups	2⅛ gal	1.3 l	8.1 l
Milk	2½ cups	1 gal	600 ml	3.8 l
Onion, chopped	½	3	½	3
Cheddar cheese, grated	⅔ lb	4 lb	300 g	1.8 kg
Half and half	1⅓ cups	2 qt	320 ml	2 l
Salt				
White pepper, fresh ground				
Cayenne	Dash	To taste	Dash	To taste

1. Make a roux by cooking the butter with the flour, blending until smooth.
2. Slowly add chicken stock. Stir until well blended.
3. Add milk and stir.
4. Add onion and cook over low heat for 4 minutes.
5. Add cheese, stirring. Cook until cheese is melted.
6. Remove from heat and stir in half and half. Season with salt, pepper, and cayenne. Serve hot.

ENTRÉES

Breast of Capon

🐦 AMERICAN WINE SUGGESTION
Robert Mondavi Chardonnay

		U.S.		Metric	
Portions:		8	50	8	50
Bay leaves		16	100	16	100
Rosemary		Pinch		To taste	
Black peppercorns		4 tsp	½ cup	8 g	50 g
Celery, chopped		2 cups	12 cups	450 g	2.8 kg
Onions, chopped		2 cups	12 cups	450 g	2.8 kg
Capons, 3 lb (1.4 kg) each		4	25	4	25
Chablis wine		2 cups	3 qt	480 ml	2.9 l
Chicken stock		2 cups	3 qt	480 ml	2.9 l
Bread, white, slices		8	50	8	50
Butter, as needed					
Ham, cooked, 2 oz (60 g) each slice		8	50	8	50
Mushroom caps, large, cooked		8	50	8	50
Hollandaise sauce		2 cups	3 qt	480 ml	2.9 l
Cream, whipped		3 cups	4½ qt	720 ml	4.5 l
Parmesan cheese, grated		2 cups	12½ cups	450 g	2.8 kg

1. Combine bay leaves, rosemary, and peppercorns in cheesecloth.
2. Place wrapped spices in a pan and add celery and onion.
3. Remove legs and wings from capons and place capons in pan with spices.
4. Add wine and chicken stock. Cover and cook at a gentle boil for about 20 minutes.
5. Fry the bread slices in a separate pan in a little butter. Remove from pan.
6. Top each bread slice with a slice of ham and half of a breast of capon. Cover with a mushroom cap.
7. Combine the hollandaise and whipped cream. Spoon over each serving.
8. Sprinkle with Parmesan cheese, and brown under a broiler. Serve immediately.

Buffalo Stew

🐚 AMERICAN WINE SUGGESTION
Cuvaison Zinfandel

		U.S.		Metric	
Portions:	8	50	8	50
Buffalo meat, trimmed and cut into 1½ in. (3 cm) cubes	4 lb	25 lb	1.8 kg	11.3 kg
Salt				
Black pepper, fresh ground				
Flour	¼ cup	1½ cups	30 g	170 g
Oil	¼ cup	1½ cups	60 ml	360 ml
Carrots, medium, cut into 1 in. (2 cm) pieces	3	18	3	18
Onions, large, cut into 1 in. (2 cm) pieces	3	18	3	18
Mushrooms, whole	¾ lb	6¼ lb	340 g	2.8 kg
Beef stock	1½ cups	2⅓ qt	360 ml	2.3 l
Beer, dark	1½ cups	2⅓ qt	360 ml	2.3 l
Bay leaves	2	12	2	12
Marjoram	⅔ tsp	4 tsp	3 g	16 g
Savory (sage)	⅔ tsp	4 tsp	650 mg	4 g

1. Season meat with salt and pepper and dust with flour.
2. In a heavy skillet, combine the oil and meat. Brown meat on all sides for about 6 to 8 minutes.
3. Add carrots, onion, mushrooms, and sauté for an additional 4 minutes.
4. Add stock, beer, bay leaves, marjoram, and savory. Bring to a boil, reduce heat, and simmer, covered, for about 2½ hours, or until meat is tender.

Note: If sauce is too thin, strain and reduce until thick.

Chicken-Fried Steak

❦ AMERICAN WINE SUGGESTION
Conn Creek Cabernet Sauvignon

		U.S.		Metric	
Portions:		8	50	8	50
Steaks, each approximately 8 oz (225 g), ½" (1.5 cm) thick		8	50	8	50
Salt					
White pepper, fresh ground					
Flour, as needed for dredging					
Milk, as needed					
Oil, as needed					
For Gravy:					
Milk		3½ cups	1⅓ gal	840 ml	5.3 l
Pan drippings, from pan in which steaks were fried					
Butter		7 Tbsp	2¾ cups	100 g	660 g
Cayenne		⅓ tsp	2 tsp	800 mg	5 g
Tabasco		Dash		To taste	
Salt					
Flour		⅔ cup	4 cups	75 g	450 g

1. Pound steaks to tenderize. Season steaks with salt and pepper.
2. Dredge steaks in flour. Dip in milk, and dredge in flour again.
3. Heat oil over medium heat. Add steaks and fry for 2 to 3 minutes per side. Remove from pan and keep warm.

For Gravy:

4. In a skillet, heat milk over low heat. Do not boil.
5. Meanwhile, add butter, cayenne, Tabasco, and salt to pan used for frying steaks. Cook over low heat, stirring constantly, for 2 minutes. Slowly add flour to thicken, making a roux.
6. Add heated milk to roux, stirring constantly to blend evenly. Simmer until thick. Serve with steak.

Cornish Game Hens with Leek Stuffing

🦃 AMERICAN WINE SUGGESTION
Chateau Ste. Michelle Pinot Noir

		U.S.		Metric	
Portions:		8	50	8	50
Peanut oil		2 Tbsp	¾ cup	30 ml	180 ml
Cornish game hens, approximately 1 lb (450 g) each		8	50	8	50
Salt					
White pepper, fresh ground					
Thyme sprigs, fresh		8	50	8	50
White wine		½ cup	3¼ cups	120 ml	780 ml
Chicken stock		1 cup	1½ qt	240 ml	1.5 l
Heavy cream		2 Tbsp	¾ cup	30 ml	180 ml
Butter		½ cup	3 cups	120 g	720 g
For Leek Stuffing:					
Leeks, white only, large, halved vertically		8	50	8	50
Butter		½ cup	3 cups	120 g	720 g
Chicken stock		1½ qt	2⅓ gal	1.4 l	8.9 l
Salt					
White pepper, fresh ground					

For Leek Stuffing:

1. Sauté the leeks in butter over medium heat until soft but not brown.
2. Add the stock and cook until most of liquid evaporates. Season with salt and pepper.

For Cornish Game Hens:

3. Preheat oven to 500°F (260°C).
4. Coat roasting pan with peanut oil.
5. Remove and reserve wings. Fill hens with stuffing and tie. Season outside of the bird with salt and pepper.
6. Place birds breast down in pan and cook for 10 minutes.
7. Reduce oven temperature to 350°F (180°C). Turn birds and cook for 7 minutes. Remove birds.
8. Add wings and thyme to roasting pan. Return birds, breast up, and cook for an additional 20 minutes, or until done. Transfer to platter and keep warm.
9. Degrease pan drippings and bring to a boil.
10. Add white wine and deglaze by scraping.
11. Add chicken stock and reduce by half.
12. Add cream and simmer for 20 to 25 minutes.
13. Strain sauce and thicken by adding butter as needed, whisking constantly. Serve sauce over hens.

Filet Mignon in a Mild Garlic Sauce   COLOR PLATE 22

🦃   AMERICAN WINE SUGGESTION
Mondavi Cabernet Sauvignon

	U.S.		Metric	
Portions:	8	50	8	50
Garlic cloves	16	100	16	100
Dry white wine	2 cups	3 qt	480 ml	3 l
White wine vinegar	1 cup	1½ qt	240 ml	1.5 l
Whipping cream	5 cups	1 gal	1.2 l	3.8 l
Butter	1 lb	6 lb	450 g	2.7 kg
Salt				
White pepper, fresh ground				
Filets mignons, 6–7 oz (170–200 g) each, trimmed	8	50	8	50
Meat glaze, warmed, as needed				
Broccoli, small sprigs	5	31	5	31
Parisienne potatoes, cooked	5	31	5	31

1. Boil the garlic cloves for approximately 2 to 2½ minutes, refresh, then drain.
2. Repeat four times.
3. In a saucepan, reduce the wine and wine vinegar to about 1 Tbsp (15 ml) for 8 servings; 6 Tbsp (90 ml) for 50 servings. Add the whipping cream and simmer for 4 minutes.
4. Add ⅛ of the butter to the garlic cloves. Process in a food processor for 30 seconds. Pass through a fine sieve. Season with salt and pepper. Keep warm but do not let boil.
5. Season the filets with salt and pepper. Cook in a heavy skillet with a small amount of butter for 3 to 4 minutes on each side, keeping filets rare.
6. Remove filets and keep warm.
7. Spoon sauce over warm plates. Arrange the beef on top of the sauce and garnish with the meat glaze, sprigs of broccoli, and Parisienne potatoes.

Fresh Grilled Rabbit

❦ AMERICAN WINE SUGGESTION
Ridge Vineyards Zinfandel

		U.S.		Metric	
Portions:	8	50	8	50
Virgin olive oil	2 cups	3 qt	480 ml	2.9 l
Garlic cloves, minced	4	25	4	25
Shallots, chopped	4	25	4	25
Lemon juice	1 lemon	6 lemons	1 lemon	6 lemons
Sage sprigs, fresh	4	25	4	25
Thyme sprigs, fresh	4	25	4	25
Bay leaves	2	12	2	12
White wine, dry	1 cup	1½ qt	240 ml	1.5 l
Salt				
White pepper, fresh ground				
Rabbits, cut into serving pieces	2	12	2	12

1. Combine olive oil, garlic, shallots, lemon, sage, thyme, bay leaves, dry white wine, salt, and pepper to make marinade.
2. Marinate rabbits in the refrigerator, covered with plastic wrap, for at least 2 days; the longer, the better. Turn rabbits occasionally.
3. Preheat grill or broiler. Mesquite woods are best. Grill for about 7 minutes per side, depending on size. Rabbit is done if juices run clear when flesh is pierced with a fork.

Goose with Wild Rice and Cranberry Stuffing

ह▲ AMERICAN WINE SUGGESTION
Robert Sinsky Vineyards Pinot Noir

		U.S.		Metric	
Portions:		8	50	8	50
Water		3 cups	1⅛ gal	720 ml	4.5 l
Vegetable oil		3 Tbsp	1⅛ cups	45 ml	280 ml
Wild rice		1 cup	6¼ cups	225 g	1.4 kg
Scallions, chopped		8	50	8	50
Dill, fresh		1 tsp	2 Tbsp	830 mg	5 g
Cranberries, fresh		1 cup	6¼ cups	225 g	1.4 kg
Goose, 8–10 lb (3.6–4.5 kg) each		1	6	1	6
Virgin olive oil		¼ cup	1⅓ cups	60 ml	320 ml
Salt					
White pepper, fresh ground					
Allspice, ground		1 tsp	2 Tbsp	830 mg	5 g
Celery ribs		4	25	4	25
White onions, small		6	38	6	38
Maple syrup		⅓ cup	2 cups	80 ml	480 ml

For Stuffing:

1. Combine water with ⅔ of the vegetable oil and bring to a boil.
2. Add the wild rice to the water and oil. Reduce heat to low, stir, cover, and simmer for 35 to 40 minutes.
3. Sauté scallions for 3 minutes in the remaining vegetable oil.
4. Add sautéed scallions, dill, and cranberries to the wild rice. Mix well and allow to simmer, uncovered, for a few minutes. Reserve and keep warm.

For Goose:

5. Preheat oven to 425°F (220°C).
6. Rub goose with olive oil, salt, and pepper, inside and out. Stuff goose with wild rice and cranberry stuffing. Tie. Sprinkle with allspice.
7. Place goose in roasting pan, add water, and surround the goose with celery and white onions. Cover.
8. Place roasting pan in the oven and reduce heat to 330°F (165°C).
9. Add maple syrup to goose drippings and baste goose several times during roasting. Prick the skin of the goose several times during roasting to release fat. Roast for 2 to 2½ hours, removing cover for last ½ hour of cooking.
10. Remove and transfer to serving platter. Serve with oven juice.

Indian-Style Veal Steak

AMERICAN WINE SUGGESTION
Kenwood Zinfandel

	U.S.		Metric	
Portions:	8	50	8	50
Veal steaks, 5–6 oz (140–170 g) each	8	50	8	50
Salt				
White pepper, fresh ground				
Oil	½ cup	3 cups	120 ml	720 ml
Butter, as needed				
Onions, medium, diced	2	12	2	12
Black pepper, fresh ground	2 tsp	¼ cup	5 g	30 g
Vinegar, white wine	½ cup	3 cups	120 ml	720 ml
White wine, dry	1 cup	1½ qt	240 ml	1.5 l
Veal stock	1½ qt	2⅓ gal	1.5 l	9 l
Heavy cream	1 qt	1½ gal	1 l	6 l
Chick peas, cooked and drained	2 cups	12½ cups	450 g	2.8 kg
Red peppers, julienne	2	12	2	12
Green peppers, julienne	2	12	2	12
Beef jerky, julienne	¼ lb	1½ lb	115 g	700 g

1. Preheat oven to 350°F (180°C).
2. Season veal steaks with salt and pepper.
3. Pan-sear steaks: heat oil until hot and brown steaks for approximately 3 minutes per side. Remove, reserving pan, and place steaks on a buttered baking dish.
4. Bake for 4 to 6 minutes.
5. Remove excess grease from pan in which veal was seared. Sauté onion with black pepper for 4 to 5 minutes.
6. Deglaze pan with vinegar and reduce by ⅔.
7. Add white wine and ⅔ of the veal stock. Bring to a boil, boil until the liquid becomes syrupy.
8. Reduce heat, add cream, and simmer to reduce by ¼ to make a creamy veal stock.
9. In another saucepan, simmer the chick peas in the remaining veal stock until thick.
10. Strain creamy veal stock into a pan, add red and green peppers and chick pea mixture. Bring to a boil and simmer for 5 to 6 minutes, skimming as needed.
11. Serve with veal and garnish with julienne beef jerky.

Kansas City Pickled Beef

🦃 AMERICAN WINE SUGGESTION
Inglenook "Reserve" Pinot Noir

		U.S.		Metric	
Portions:		8	50	8	50
Round steak, boned		4 lb	25 lb	1.8 kg	11.3 kg
Onions, thinly sliced		2	12	2	12
Lemons, sliced		1	6	1	6
Black peppercorns, to taste					
Juniper berries		1 tsp	2 Tbsp	5 g	30 g
Bay leaves		1	6	1	6
Cider vinegar		2 cups	3 qt	480 ml	2.9 l
Virgin olive oil		2 Tbsp	¾ cup	30 ml	180 ml
Salt					
Red wine		1 cup	1½ qt	240 ml	1.5 l

1. Combine the steak, onions, lemon slices, peppercorns, juniper berries, and bay leaf with the vinegar.
2. Cover bowl and marinate in refrigerator for 2 to 3 days, turning daily.
3. Remove the steak from the marinade, reserving the liquid.
4. Heat oil in a heavy skillet. Add the steak and brown on all sides, 2 to 4 minutes per side.
5. Add 1 cup (240 ml) of reserved marinade, salt, and wine. Cover and simmer for 1½ hours, or until steak is tender.
6. Remove from heat, cool, transfer to platter, and thinly slice. Serve with sauce.

Rib-Eye of Beef with Wild Rice

🦃 AMERICAN WINE SUGGESTION
Wild Horse Merlot

	U.S.		Metric	
Portions:	8	50	8	50

For Roast: Prepare one day in advance for best results

Rib-eye, boneless, beef roast, trimmed of fat	5 lb	31 lb	2.3 kg	14 kg
Black pepper, cracked	½ cup	3 cups	50 g	300 g
Cardamom, ground	½ tsp	2 Tbsp	4 g	24 g
Tomato paste	1 Tbsp	6½ Tbsp	15 g	100 g
Garlic powder	½ tsp	1 Tbsp	1 g	6 g
Paprika	1 tsp	2 Tbsp	2 g	15 g
Soy sauce	1 cup	1½ qt	240 ml	1.5 l
Vinegar, red wine	¾ cup	4½ cups	180 ml	1.1 l

For Gravy:

Meat drippings from roast				
Water, as needed				
Cornstarch	1½ Tbsp	9 Tbsp	15 g	90 g

For Wild Rice:

Wild rice, soaked in water overnight	1½ cups	9½ cups	340 g	2.1 kg
Water	1 qt	1½ gal	1 l	5.8 l
Salt				
White onions, small	1	6½	1	6½
Bacon strips, diced	4	25	4	25
Green onions, finely chopped	4	25	4	25
Mushrooms, fresh, thinly sliced	6	38	6	38
White pepper, fresh ground				
Poultry seasoning	1 tsp	2 Tbsp	1 g	6 g

1. Rub roast with pepper and cardamom, pressing spices into meat.
2. Combine the tomato paste, garlic powder, paprika, soy sauce, and vinegar. Pour marinade over meat and marinate in the refrigerator for at least 12 hours.
3. Preheat oven to 300°F (150°C).
4. Remove meat from marinade 3 to 4 hours before cooking. Let stand at room temperature for 1 hour.
5. Wrap meat in foil and roast in a shallow pan for 2 hours.
6. Remove drippings from pan to a saucepan.
7. Increase oven temperature to 350°F (180°C).
8. Return meat to oven and continue to roast until bronzed.

For Gravy:

9. Strain meat drippings and skim fat.

10. Add 1 cup (240 ml) of water for each 1 cup (240 ml) of meat drippings. Add some of the marinade, if desired, for flavor.
11. Dissolve cornstarch in a small amount of cold water and add to gravy to thicken.

For Wild Rice:

12. Drain rice and combine with water, 1 qt (1 l) for 8 servings or 1½ gal (5.8 l) for 50 servings, salt, and whole onion. Cover and simmer for 30 to 35 minutes.
13. Remove onion and drain rice.
14. In a separate pan, fry bacon, green onion, and mushrooms, until tender.
15. Add rice to bacon, stir, and season with salt, pepper, and poultry seasoning.
16. Serve wild rice with roast and gravy.

Lamb Chops with Leeks   COLOR PLATE 23

❧ AMERICAN WINE SUGGESTION
Cabernet Sauvignon

	U.S.		Metric	
Portions:	8	50	8	50
Racks of lamb, trimmed	4	25	4	25
Garlic cloves, crushed	8	50	8	50
Leeks, trimmed, leaving 2 in. (5 cm) of the green	2 lb	12½ lb	0.9 kg	5.6 kg
Butter	1 cup	6¼ cups	240 g	1.5 kg
Chicken stock	¼ cup	1½ cups	60 ml	360 ml
Parsley, finely chopped	4 tsp	½ cup	3 g	20 g
Salt				
White pepper, fresh ground				
Shallots, chopped	7	44	7	44
Garlic cloves, chopped	4	25	4	25
Dry vermouth	1½ cups	9⅓ cups	360 ml	2.2 l
Veal stock	1 qt	6 qt	1 l	6 l
Rosemary, chopped	2 tsp	¼ cup	2 g	12 g
Mint, fresh, as needed for garnish				

1. Preheat oven to 425°F (220°C).
2. Rub lamb with garlic cloves.
3. Cover bones with foil and roast for 25 to 30 minutes, or until pink.
4. Remove lamb from oven and keep warm.
5. Thinly slice the leeks.
6. In a sauté pan, combine the leeks and butter. Sauté and then add chicken stock and parsley. Season with salt and pepper and cook gently until liquid has almost disappeared and leeks are tender. Do not allow them to become discolored.
7. Remove and puree leeks. Keep warm.
8. In a saucepan, combine the shallots and garlic with vermouth and veal stock. Reduce to ⅓.
9. Add the rosemary and simmer gently for 5 minutes. Season to taste and keep warm.
10. Divide the lamb and arrange on plates. Place the leek puree in the center and spoon sauce over the lamb. Garnish with fresh mint.

Roast Tenderloin with Black Walnut and Port Sauce

❧ AMERICAN WINE SUGGESTION
Sterling Vineyards Merlot

		U.S.		Metric	
Portions:		8	50	8	50
Tenderloin, 4 lb (1.8 kg) each		1	6¼	1	6¼
Salt					
White pepper, fresh ground					
Dry mustard, to taste					
Butter, melted		3 Tbsp	1⅛ cups	45 g	280 g
For Sauce:					
Garlic cloves		3	18	3	18
Shallots, minced		3	18	3	18
Butter		2 Tbsp	¾ cup	30 g	180 g
Port wine		½ cup	3 cups	120 ml	720 ml
Salt					
White pepper, fresh ground					
Demi-glace		2 cups	3 qt	480 ml	3 l
Black walnuts		½ cup	3 cups	115 g	680 g
For Garnish:					

Tomatoes, sliced, as needed
Zucchini, lightly poached in salt water, as
   needed
Leeks, julienne, sautéed, as needed

1. Preheat oven to 400°F (200°C).
2. Season tenderloin with salt, pepper, mustard, and melted butter. Cook for 1 hour.
3. Sauté the garlic and shallots in the butter until golden.
4. Add the port. Reduce by half. Season with salt and pepper.
5. Simmer for 5 minutes, then add demi-glace and walnuts.
6. Remove tenderloin and slice.
7. Arrange the sliced tenderloin over a bed of tomato and zucchini. Serve with sauce.
8. Garnish with sautéed julienne leeks.

Smoked Boar

❦ AMERICAN WINE SUGGESTION
Inglenook Charbono

		U.S.		Metric	
Portions:		8	50	8	50
Saddles of boar or porkloin, 8–10 lb (3.6–4.5 kg) each		1	6½	1	6½
Salt					
White pepper, fresh ground					
For Sauce:					
Currants, dry		½ cup	3 cups	115 g	680 g
Cassis liqueur		¾ cup	4½ cups	180 ml	1 l
White wine		¾ cup	4½ cups	180 ml	1 l
Veal stock		2¼ cups	3½ qt	540 ml	3.4 l
Shallots, chopped		4	25	4	25
Lemon juice		2 tsp	¼ cup	10 ml	60 ml
Unsalted butter		2 Tbsp	¾ cup	30 g	180 g
Salt					
White pepper, fresh ground					

1. Season boar or porkloin with salt and pepper.
2. Smoke in a smoker for 1½ to 2 hours, or until meat is cooked through. Hickory chips are suggested.

For Sauce:

3. Soak currants in liqueur and wine for at least 1 hour. Strain and reserve.
4. Reduce veal stock by ⅔ over high heat. Add currants, shallots, lemon juice, unsalted butter, salt, and pepper. Simmer for 5 minutes or until flavors have blended.
5. Serve with smoked boar or porkloin.

Steak in a Mild Garlic Sauce

AMERICAN WINE SUGGESTION
Villa Mt. Eden Cabernet Sauvignon

		U.S.		Metric	
Portions:	8	50	8	50
Sirloin steaks	8	50	8	50
Salt				
Black pepper, fresh ground				
Garlic cloves, unpeeled	10²/₃	66½	10²/₃	66½
Heavy cream	1²/₃ cups	10½ cups	400 ml	2.5 l
Potatoes, boiled, peeled, and sliced	2²/₃ lb	16½ lb	1.2 kg	7.4 kg
Milk	1⅓ cups	2 qt	320 ml	2 l
Garlic cloves, minced	1⅓	8½	1⅓	8½
Unsalted butter	½ cup	3 cups	120 g	720 g
Gruyère cheese, grated	1⅓ lb	8½ lb	600 g	3.8 kg
Cognac	2²/₃ Tbsp	1 cup	40 ml	240 ml
White wine, dry	1⅓ cups	2 qt	320 ml	2 l
Veal stock	2 cups	3 qt	480 ml	2.9 l

1. Season sirloin with salt and pepper. Set aside.
2. Preheat oven to 350°F (180°C). Bake garlic cloves for 8 to 10 minutes.
3. Remove garlic from oven and skin. Puree with ⅔ of the cream, using a food processor. Set aside.
4. Cook potato slices in milk, minced garlic, remainder of cream, and butter. Place in a gratiné dish, add grated cheese and broil until golden.
5. In a heavy skillet, pan-sear sirloin to taste. Remove from pan.
6. Deglaze pan with cognac and wine.
7. Add veal stock and reduce by half over moderate heat.
8. Add garlic cream and simmer for 4 to 6 minutes. Season to taste and serve with sirloin and potatoes.

Stuffed Trout

🦃 AMERICAN WINE SUGGESTION
Chateau Ste. Michelle Reserve Semillon

		U.S.		Metric	
Portions:		8	50	8	50
Trout, boned, approximately 10 oz (300 g) each		8	50	8	50
Butter		2 lb	12½ lb	1 kg	5.6 kg
Mushrooms, chopped		2 cups	3 qt	450 g	2.8 kg
Crabmeat		2 lb	12½ lb	900 g	5.6 kg
Shallots, chopped		2 tsp	¼ cup	9 g	50 g
Chives, chopped		2 tsp	¼ cup	7 g	40 g
Béchamel sauce		2 qt	3 gal	2 l	12 l
White wine, dry		1 qt	1½ gal	1 l	6 l
Salt					
White pepper, fresh ground					
Lemons		8	50	8	50
Parsley, as needed for garnish					
For Béchamel Sauce:					
Butter		¼ cup	1½ cups	60 g	360 g
Flour		¼ cup	1½ cups	30 g	170 g
Milk		2 cups	3 qt	480 ml	2.9 l
Salt					
White pepper, fresh ground					

For Béchamel Sauce:

1. Heat butter over moderate heat.
2. Add flour and whisk briskly, so as not to brown.
3. Add milk and whisk vigorously until mixture boils. Continue whisking and cook until sauce becomes thick.
4. Season to taste with salt and pepper.

For Trout:

5. Sauté the trout in ⅔ of the butter until brown on both sides. Remove and keep warm.
6. In the remainder of the butter, sauté the mushrooms and crabmeat.
7. Add the shallots and chives; cook for an additional 5 minutes, stirring occasionally.
8. Add the béchamel and wine. Mix well, season with salt and pepper.
9. Stuff the trout with crabmeat mixture.
10. Sprinkle with lemon and serve immediately.

Sweet and Sour Pork

❦ AMERICAN WINE SUGGESTION
Columbia Crest Johannesberg Riesling

		U.S.		Metric	
Portions:		8	50	8	50
Pork rib roasts, center cut, 1 lb (450 g) each		8	50	8	50
Sugar		4 cups	25 cups	900 g	5.6 kg
Vinegar, white		2 cups	3 qt	480 ml	2.9 l
Green pepper, chopped		1/4 cup	1 1/2 cups	60 g	340 g
Salt					
Water		2 cups	3 qt	480 ml	2.9 l
Cornstarch		8 tsp	1 cup	24 g	150 g
Water		1/4 cup	1 1/2 cups	60 ml	360 ml
Paprika		4 tsp	1/2 cup	9 g	55 g
Parsley, as needed					
Baked apples, small		8	50	8	50

1. Preheat oven to 450°F (230°C).
2. Roast pork for 30 minutes.
3. In a pan, combine the sugar, vinegar, green pepper, salt, and water. Simmer for 5 to 8 minutes.
4. In a bowl, combine the cornstarch with the smaller amount of water.
5. Add cornstarch mixture to sauce in pan and stir over heat until thick.
6. Strain and season with paprika and parsley.
7. Turn pork and add sauce. Reduce oven temperature to 300°F (150°C) and continue to roast, basting occasionally, until done.
8. Garnish with baked apples and serve immediately.

Veal Medallions with Apple Vinaigrette

AMERICAN WINE SUGGESTION
Simi Chardonnay

	U.S.		Metric	
Portions:	8	50	8	50

For Apple Vinaigrette:

Veal and chicken bones	4 lb	25 lb	2 kg	12 kg
Meat scraps, veal and chicken	2 lb	12 lb	1 kg	6 kg
Water	2 qt	3 gal	2 l	12 l
Red wine, dry	1 cup	1½ qt	240 ml	1.5 l
White wine, dry	1 cup	1½ qt	240 ml	1.5 l
Onions, quartered	2	12	2	12
Carrots, diced	2	12	2	12
Celery stalks, diced	2	12	2	12
Parsley sprigs	6	38	6	38
Thyme sprigs, fresh	4	25	4	25
Bay leaves	1	6	1	6
Cloves, whole	2	12	2	12
Apples, cored and sliced	4	25	4	25
Vinegar, cider	2 Tbsp	¾ cup	30 ml	180 ml
Salt				
White pepper, fresh ground				
Butter, as needed for thickening				

For Veal:

Veal rib-eye roasts, 3½–4 lb (1.6–1.8 kg) each	2	12	2	12
Onion, chopped	1	6	1	6
Carrots, chopped	2	12	2	12
Parsley, chopped	½ cup	3 cups	18 g	115 g
Celery and leaves, minced	1 cup	6½ cups	225 g	1.4 kg
Garlic cloves, minced	2	12	2	12
Salt				
White pepper, fresh ground				

For Apple Vinaigrette:

1. In a stockpot, heat the bones, meat scraps, water, wine, onions, carrots, and celery. Bring to a boil. Season with parsley, thyme, bay leaf, and cloves. Skim as needed. Reduce heat and simmer for 3 hours, uncovered.
2. Strain stock through a cheesecloth, extracting all liquid from vegetables. Discard all solids, and return liquid to a boil.
3. Continue to boil, skimming as needed, and reduce to 1 qt (1 l) for 8 servings; 6 qt (6 l) for 50 servings.
4. Add ½ of the apples and vinegar and simmer over moderate heat for 25 to 30 minutes, or until apples are mushy.
5. Puree apple sauce in food processor.

6. Return to heat and simmer until thick. Season to taste with salt and pepper. Add some butter to thicken, if needed.

For Veal:

7. Preheat oven to 350°F (180°C).
8. Season veal with salt and pepper.
9. In a roasting pan, combine the onion, carrots, parsley, celery, and garlic, with the veal.
10. Roast for 45 minutes or until done. Remove from oven and let cool for 15 minutes before slicing veal.
11. Serve veal with vinaigrette and remainder of apples, sliced for garnish.

Venison Sausage

🐌 AMERICAN WINE SUGGESTION
Lytton Springs Zinfandel

	U.S.		Metric	
Portions:	8	50	8	50

For Sausage: Prepare 3 days in advance

Venison	2 lb	12½ lb	900 g	5.6 kg
Lean pork	2 lb	12½ lb	900 g	5.6 kg
Slab bacon	⅔ lb	4 lb	300 g	1.8 kg
Pork fat	1⅓ lb	8½ lb	600 g	3.8 kg
Black pepper, fresh ground	4 tsp	½ cup	9 g	60 g
Shallots, chopped	4	25	4	25
Vinegar, red wine	6 Tbsp	2⅓ cups	90 ml	560 ml
Salt				
Parsley, chopped	⅔ cup	4 cups	25 g	160 g
Coriander leaves, chopped	⅔ cup	4 cups	20 g	130 g
Casings, rinsed well and soaked	8 ft	50 ft	2.4 m	15.2 m

For Mustard Sauce:

Grainy mustard	1 cup	6½ cups	240 g	1.5 kg
Garlic cloves, crushed	2	12	2	12
Horseradish, grated	2 Tbsp	¾ cup	60 g	180 g
Dry vermouth	¼ cup	1½ cups	60 ml	360 ml

For Potatoes:

Baked potatoes, large, cooked and sliced	8	50	8	50
Pork fat	¼ lb	1½ lb	115 g	675 g
Vinegar, cider	¼ cup	1½ cups	60 ml	360 ml
Salt				
White pepper, fresh ground				
Italian parsley, chopped	1 Tbsp	6 Tbsp	2 g	12 g

For Sausage:

1. Cut venison, pork, bacon, and pork fat into chunks and combine. Season with pepper.
2. Add shallots, vinegar, salt, parsley, and coriander. Mix well.
3. Grind mixture, using a grinder.
4. Stuff meat into casing, tie off as desired to make sausages.
5. Arrange sausage on a rack and refrigerate for 3 days. Do not cover.

For Mustard Sauce:

6. Combine the mustard, garlic, horseradish, and vermouth. Mix well and reserve.

For Potatoes:

7. Sauté potato slices in fat until brown, 13 to 15 minutes. Season with vinegar, salt, pepper, and parsley. Reserve.

To Prepare Sausage:

8. Blanch sausage in lightly salted water, just simmering, for 3 to 5 minutes. Remove and dry.
9. Sauté sausage for 4 to 5 minutes per side in a heavy skillet until golden.
10. Serve with mustard sauce and potatoes.

Venison Stew

ᘒ& AMERICAN WINE SUGGESTION
Sebastiani Zinfandel

		U.S.		Metric	
Portions:		8	50	8	50
Venison, cut into chunks		4 lb	25 lb	1.8 kg	11.3 kg
Carrots, cut into thick slices		2	12	2	12
Onions, small, quartered		2	12	2	12
Celery rib, cut into thick slices		1	6	1	6
Thyme, fresh		1½ tsp	3 Tbsp	1.5 g	9 g
Salt					
Black pepper, fresh ground					
Cayenne		¼ tsp	1½ tsp	600 mg	3.5 g
Red wine, dry, full-bodied		1 qt	1½ gal	1 l	6 l
Vinegar, red wine		2 tsp	¼ cup	10 ml	60 ml
Oil		6 Tbsp	2⅓ cups	90 ml	560 ml
Flour		2 Tbsp	¾ cup	15 g	85 g
Water		1 cup	1½ qt	240 ml	1.5 l

1. In a large bowl, marinate the venison with the carrot, onion, celery, thyme, salt, pepper, cayenne, wine, and vinegar. Cover and refrigerate for at least 3 days, stirring daily.
2. Drain the venison and vegetables, reserving the marinade.
3. Set aside the meat and vegetables.
4. In a skillet, heat the oil and sauté the venison until brown, 5 minutes. Brown meat in batches. Add oil as needed. Set meat aside.
5. Sauté the vegetables in batches to brown, about 5 minutes. Set aside.
6. Preheat oven to 300°F (150°C).
7. Add oil, if needed, to pan and add flour. Heat for 3 to 5 minutes over moderate heat , stirring constantly to make a roux.
8. Add the marinade, increase heat, add water, and bring to a boil.
9. Add the meat and vegetables and cover.
10. Cook in oven for 3½ hours, or until meat is tender.
11. Remove meat and vegetables and keep warm.
12. Thicken sauce by reducing. Cook for about 30 minutes, skimming as needed.
13. Return meat and vegetables to sauce, and serve.

ACCOMPANIMENTS

Corn Fritters

		U.S.		Metric	
Portions:	8	50	8	50
Eggs, separated	3	19	3	19
Corn kernels, fresh	2½ cups	15½ cups	570 g	3.5 kg
Whipping cream	3½ Tbsp	1⅓ cups	50 ml	320 ml
Flour	1⅓ cups	8½ cups	150 g	960 g
Baking powder	1⅓ tsp	8½ tsp	4 g	25 g
Salt				
Sugar	1⅓ tsp	8½ tsp	7 g	45 g
Oil , as needed for frying				

1. Beat the egg yolks until light in color. In a separate bowl, beat the egg whites.
2. Stir corn and cream into the egg yolks.
3. Beat until soft peaks form.
4. Combine the flour, baking powder, salt, and sugar. Gradually add to corn mixture.
5. Fold in beaten egg whites.
6. Heat oil in skillet and drop batter by the tablespoonful into oil. Fry until golden, turning once. Remove from oil, drain on paper towels, and serve.

DESSERTS

Indian Doughnuts

	U.S.	Metric
	Makes 36 doughnuts	Makes 36 doughnuts
Scalded milk	1½ cups	360 ml
Yellow cornmeal, stone-ground	2 cups	454 g
Flour	2 cups	225 g
Sugar	1½ cups	360 g
Baking powder	1 Tbsp	8 g
Cinnamon, ground	1 Tbsp	6 g
Butter, melted, blueberry flavored	1 cup	240 g
Eggs, slightly beaten	3	3
Peanut oil, as needed for frying		
Confectioner's sugar, as needed for garnish		

1. Combine the milk with the cornmeal, whisking vigorously until smooth. Let cool.
2. Sift together flour, sugar, baking powder, and cinnamon. Add flour mixture to the cooled cornmeal mixture. Mix well.
3. Add the butter and eggs. If dough is not firm enough, add more flour. Mix well.
4. On a lightly floured surface, knead the dough and roll out ½ in. (1.5 cm) thick.
5. Using a doughnut cutter, cut dough into doughnuts and let set for 20 minutes.
6. In a deep skillet, heat the oil and add the doughnuts in batches. Do not crowd. Fry until golden, turning as necessary.
7. Remove doughnuts from oil, drain on paper towels, and coat with confectioner's sugar.

Cream Puffs with Ice Cream and Vanilla Sauce   COLOR PLATE 24

		U.S.	Metric
	Portions:	8	8
Water		1 cup	240 ml
Salt			
Sugar		1 tsp	5 g
Unsalted butter, cut up		4 oz	115 g
Flour		5 oz	140 g
Eggs, large		5	5
Raspberries, as needed for garnish			
Shaved chocolate, as needed for garnish			
For Sauce:			
Sugar		²/₃ cup	160 g
Egg yolks, room temperature		4	4
Cornstarch		5 tsp	15 g
Salt		¹/₈ tsp	625 mg
Milk, hot		1 qt	1 l
Vanilla extract		1¹/₂ tsp	7 ml

For Sauce:

1. Mix the sugar, egg yolks, cornstarch, and salt in a 3-qt (3 l) heavy saucepan. Do not beat.
2. Pour in the hot milk, stirring constantly.
3. Cook over medium heat, stirring constantly until mixture begins to thicken. Reduce heat to low.
4. Stir mixture rapidly until the sauce is thick enough to coat a spoon.
5. Remove the pan from the heat and stir the sauce rapidly to bring the temperature down. Stir in the vanilla.
6. Set the pan in an ice bath and stir until cool.
7. Cover and refrigerate.
8. Reheat gently over hot water when ready to serve.

For Cream Puffs:

9. Preheat the oven to 400°F (200°C).
10. Line a baking sheet with baking parchment and fit a pastry bag with a ¹/₂ in. (1 cm) plain, round tube.
11. In a heavy saucepan, combine the water, salt, sugar, and butter.
12. Bring to a boil and add the flour all at once.
13. Stir vigorously for 2 minutes over medium heat until the mixture pulls away from the pan.
14. Transfer to a bowl and beat for 3 to 4 minutes to cool mixture.
15. Add eggs one at a time. Ensure each is incorporated before adding the next one.

16. Beat mixture until smooth and shiny.
17. Transfer to a pastry bag and pipe into desired shape.
18. Bake for 20 minutes or until puffed and golden.
19. Remove and let cool. Split in half. Fill with choice of ice cream. Cover.
20. Pour vanilla sauce over cream puffs, garnish with fresh raspberries and shaved chocolate.

CHAPTER 10

Pacific Northwest
and Alaska

M ere mention of the name of this region conjures up visions of rugged coasts and rich, forested land. Chris Canlis of Canlis' Restaurant in Seattle, Washington, gives definition to the region's cuisine: "Natural products define our cuisine. Fresh local, not farmed, fish are our strength. What we do with these ingredients is up to the individual's taste. The people of the Northwest are fiercely independent. They are not willing to follow the crowd."

This tradition of independence and regard for nature is reflected in the food and cooking of the region. Alaskan and northwestern cuisine emphasizes the freshest ingredients, including an abundance of seafood. Boiling, broiling, and steaming are the usual cooking methods. Wild game is popular and generally low in fat. Venison, for example, contains less than one-third the fat of beef. The Northwest is well known for its fresh fruits and vegetables. While much of Alaska imports its fruits, vegetables, and grains, there are areas that support hearty berries, rhubarb, and vegetables. Fiddlehead ferns, introduced by settlers from New England, are popular and thrive in this region. Wild mushrooms, fruits, and sourdough bread are also popular and add to the uniqueness of northwestern cooking.

Traditional Northwest and Alaskan cuisine is based on hunting, fishing, and with the arrival of settlers, farming. This, too, is a region where abundant supplies and a history of strenuous physical labor make large portions an integral part of eating. Moderate portions of even such healthy fare as seafood and wild game are, of course, more prudent from a nutritional standpoint. Occasional feasts of boiled, broiled, baked, smoked, or roasted seafood can, however, be worked into a balanced diet.

The cooking of the Northwest and Alaska has been influenced by the people of New England, Europe, and Asia who settled there. New Englanders brought their rich chowders and use of pork fat, Europeans brought cheese, rich sauces and desserts, and a love for fishing, and Asian settlers brought a preference for only the freshest, highest quality ingredients prepared with traditional herbs and spices and little added fat. Rich chowders, sauces, and desserts can be modified to be lower in fat or balanced with lower fat ingredients. Lower fat varieties of cheese should be used or cheese used in moderation. Once again, lean beef and pork should replace fatty cuts and portions should be moderate. The eclectic nature of this cuisine makes it simple to modify nutritionally. The flavors and low-fat cooking methods of the Orient blend well with simple American cooking such as grilling and the barbecue. The abundance of grains and vegetables easily complement smaller meat portions. Desserts based on wild and cultivated fruits can be low in fat and high in nutrients.

APPETIZERS

Alaskan Crab Soufflé

	Portions:	U.S.		Metric	
		8	*50*	*8*	*50*
Cream sauce		1⅓ cups	2 qt	320 ml	1.9 l
Light cream, as needed					
Egg yolks, beaten		4	25	4	25
Dijon mustard		⅔ tsp	4 tsp	3 g	20 g
Onion, minced		2⅔ tsp	5 Tbsp	11 g	70 g
Lemon juice		1⅓ tsp	8 tsp	7 ml	40 ml
Parsley, fresh, chopped		2⅔ tsp	5 Tbsp	2 g	12 g
Crabmeat, shelled, cleaned, and cooked		1⅓ lb	8 lb	600 g	3.6 kg
Egg whites, stiffly beaten		4	25	4	25
Toasted pecans, as needed for garnish					

1. Preheat oven to 350°F (180°C).
2. Heat cream sauce with some of the cream.
3. Stir a small amount of the sauce into beaten egg yolks, then return mixture to hot sauce. Cook for 2 minutes, stirring constantly.
4. Add mustard, onion, lemon juice, parsley, and crabmeat.
5. Fold the stiffly beaten egg whites into the crabmeat mixture.
6. Pour into a buttered casserole. Place casserole in a pan filled halfway with hot water.
7. Bake for 40 to 50 minutes, or until soufflé is firm in the middle.
8. Remove and serve immediately, sprinkled with toasted pecans.

Alaskan King Crab Loaf

	U.S.		Metric	
Portions:	8	50	8	50
Milk	1⅓ cups	2 qt	320 ml	1.9 l
Bread crumbs, soft	2 cups	12½ cups	450 g	2.8 kg
Butter, melted	1⅓ Tbsp	½ cup	20 ml	120 ml
Crabmeat, cooked	1⅓ lb	8 lb	600 g	3.6 kg
Egg yolks, beaten	4	25	4	25
Lemon juice	2⅔ Tbsp	1 cup	40 ml	240 ml
Onion, minced	2⅔ Tbsp	1 cup	40 g	200 g
Celery stalk, minced	½	3	½	3
Salt				
White pepper, fresh ground				
Egg whites, stiffly beaten	4	25	4	25
Tomato concassé (page 230)	2 cups	3 qt	480 ml	3 l

1. Preheat oven to 350°F (180°C).
2. Scald milk.
3. Add bread crumbs and butter and beat until smooth.
4. Combine mixture with crabmeat, egg yolks, lemon juice, onion, and celery, and season with salt and pepper.
5. Fold in egg whites.
6. Butter a loaf pan and add the mixture.
7. Bake for 20 to 25 minutes or until cooked.
8. Serve hot with tomato concassé.

Marinated Salmon

		U.S.		Metric	
Portions:	8	50	8	50
Salmon filets, approximately 5 oz (140 g) each	8	50	8	50
Dill, fresh, chopped	2/3 cup	4 cups	25 g	150 g
Brown sugar	1/2 cup	3 cups	115 g	680 g
Salt				
White pepper, fresh ground	1 1/2 Tbsp	9 Tbsp	4 g	24 g
Juniper berries, crushed	3/4 Tbsp	4 1/2 Tbsp	11 g	65 g
Toast points, as needed				
Onion, thinly sliced, as needed for garnish				
Capers, as needed for garnish				

1. Place salmon filet in shallow baking dish, skin down.
2. Combine dill, sugar, salt, pepper, and juniper berries. Spread mixture evenly over each filet.
3. Stack the seasoned salmon and wrap in foil.
4. Refrigerate for 4 to 5 days. Unwrap the salmon daily and baste with juices that collect in the foil, then reassemble.
5. To serve, unwrap salmon, cut thinly, and serve on toast points with onion and capers.

SALADS

Crabmeat Salad

	U.S.		Metric	
Portions:	8	50	8	50
Crabmeat, cooked and shelled	2 lb	12½ lb	900 mg	5.6 kg
Apples, cored and coarsely chopped	3	18	3	18
Celery stalks, chopped	3	18	3	18
Almonds, sliced	⅔ cup	4 cups	150 g	900 g
Mayonnaise	1¼ cups	2 qt	300 ml	1.9 l
Lemon juice	3 Tbsp	1⅛ cups	45 ml	270 ml
Tarragon, dry	⅔ Tbsp	4 Tbsp	150 mg	9 g
Sugar	⅔ tsp	4 tsp	3 g	20 g
White pepper, fresh ground	⅔ tsp	4 tsp	1.6 g	10 g
Lettuce leaves	8	50	8	50
Watercress sprigs, as needed for garnish				
Lemon wedges	8	50	8	50

1. Combine the crabmeat, apples, celery, and almonds. Toss together.
2. In a bowl, combine the mayonnaise, lemon juice, tarragon, sugar, and pepper. Add the crabmeat mixture and mix well.
3. Chill for 3 hours.
4. To serve, place a scoop of crabmeat salad on top of lettuce leaf and garnish with watercress and lemon.

ENTRÉES

Alaskan Baked Trout with Fresh Herbs

🦂 AMERICAN WINE SUGGESTION
Columbia Crest Semillon

		U.S.		Metric	
Portions:		8	50	8	50
Trout, 8–10 oz (225–285 g) each		8	50	8	50
Salt					
White pepper, fresh ground					
Butter		3 Tbsp	1¹/₈ cups	45 g	270 g
Onion, medium, chopped fine		1	6	1	6
Parsley, chopped		1¹/₂ Tbsp	9 Tbsp	3.5 g	20 g
Dill, fresh, chopped		1¹/₂ tsp	3 Tbsp	1 g	7 g
Savory, fresh		1¹/₂ tsp	3 Tbsp	1.2 g	7.5 g
Tarragon, fresh		²/₃ tsp	4 tsp	500 mg	3 g
White wine		¹/₄ cup	1¹/₂ cups	60 ml	360 ml
Lemon juice		²/₃ Tbsp	¹/₄ cup	10 ml	60 ml
Sour cream		¹/₂ cup	3 cups	120 ml	720 ml
Bread crumbs		¹/₃ cup	2 cups	75 g	450 g
Parmesan cheese, grated		¹/₃ cup	2 cups	75 g	450 g

1. Preheat oven to 425°F (220°C).
2. Season trout inside and out with salt and pepper.
3. In a skillet, melt ¹/₂ the butter over moderate heat. Add the onion and sauté for 2 to 3 minutes.
4. Add the parsley, dill, savory, and tarragon and sauté for an additional minute.
5. Add the wine and lemon juice.
6. Grease a shallow baking dish with the remaining butter.
7. Place trout side by side in the baking dish and stuff the cavities with the onion/herb mixture.
8. Pour excess sauce over the trout. Cover with foil and bake for 10 to 14 minutes or until fish is firm and flaky.
9. Spread sour cream evenly over the trout. Top with bread crumbs and Parmesan cheese, and bake, uncovered, for an additional 2 to 3 minutes, or until golden.

Barbecue Salmon

🦃 AMERICAN WINE SUGGESTION
Chateau Ste. Michelle Chardonnay

	U.S.		Metric	
Portions:	8	50	8	50
Salmon, cleaned, 6 lb (2.7 kg) each	1	6	1	6
Salt				
White pepper, fresh ground				
Butter	2 Tbsp	¾ cup	30 g	180 g
Onions, thinly sliced	1	6	1	6
Lemon, sliced	1	6	1	6
Oregano, to taste				
Vegetable oil, as needed				
Lemons, as needed for garnish				

1. Season salmon with salt and pepper. Sprinkle with butter.
2. Place onion, lemon slices, and oregano in fish cavity.
3. Brush salmon with oil and wrap in aluminum foil, sealing edges to make it leak proof.
4. Grill over a preheated grill, turning every 6 to 8 minutes. Grill for about 30 minutes or until fish flakes.
5. Remove from heat, fold back foil, and serve with lemon.

Cider Braised Chicken

❧ AMERICAN WINE SUGGESTION
Arterberry Chardonnay

		U.S.		Metric	
Portions:		8	50	8	50
Chicken pieces		4 lb	25 lb	1.8 kg	11.3 kg
Salt					
Black pepper, fresh ground					
Unsalted butter		3 Tbsp	1¹/₈ cups	45 g	280 g
Vegetable oil, as needed					
Flour, as needed					
Dry apple cider		2¹/₂ cups	1 gal	600 ml	3.8 l
Chicken broth		1¹/₂ cups	9 cups	360 ml	2.1 l
Thyme, dry		1¹/₂ tsp	3 Tbsp	1.5 g	9 g
Rosemary, dry		1¹/₂ tsp	3 Tbsp	1.5 g	9 g
Baking apples, large, peeled, cored, sliced		3	18	3	18

1. Preheat oven to 375°F (190°C).
2. Season chicken with salt and pepper.
3. Combine butter and oil in an ovenproof casserole and sauté chicken in batches over moderate heat until evenly browned. Set aside and keep warm.
4. Pour off fat, leaving 2 Tbsp (30 ml) for 8 servings, ³/₄ cup (180 g) for 50 servings. Return pan to the heat and thicken by adding some flour and whisking for 2 to 3 minutes.
5. Add cider and broth and cook over medium heat, stirring vigorously.
6. Bring to a boil, add thyme and rosemary, then return chicken to casserole.
7. Cover casserole and bake for 30 to 35 minutes or until chicken is tender. Add apples for the last 10 to 12 minutes of cooking.

Elk Steak with Herbs

🍷 AMERICAN WINE SUGGESTION
Elk Cove Vineyards Pinot Noir

	Portions:	U.S.		Metric	
		8	50	8	50
Butter, softened		¼ cup	1½ cups	60 g	360 g
Marjoram		1 tsp	2 Tbsp	4 g	24 g
Thyme		1 tsp	2 Tbsp	1 g	6 g
Tarragon		1 tsp	2 Tbsp	750 mg	5 g
Cloves		⅛ tsp	½ tsp	200 mg	1.2 g
Elk steak, cut 1½ in. (4 cm) thick		4½ lb	28 lb	2 kg	12.6 kg
Garlic cloves, sliced		2	12	2	12
Dry mustard		5 Tbsp	2 cups	30 g	180 g
Black pepper, fresh ground					
Red wine		3 Tbsp	1⅛ cups	45 ml	270 ml
Red currant jelly		2 Tbsp	¾ cup	30 ml	180 ml
Parsley, chopped		2 Tbsp	¾ cup	5 g	30 g
Béarnaise sauce, as needed					

1. In a bowl, combine the butter with the marjoram, thyme, tarragon, and cloves. Mix well.
2. Cut several incisions in the elk meat and insert the garlic and some of the herb butter. Reserve remaining herb butter.
3. Combine the mustard, pepper, wine, and jelly. Spread over the steaks.
4. Preheat the broiler. Broil the steaks for 6 to 7 minutes, buttered side up. Turn, broiling for an additional 3 minutes, basting with reserved herb butter. Cook to desired doneness.
5. To serve, slice meat on the bias, garnish with parsley, and serve with béarnaise sauce.

Halibut with Tomato Mousseline

🐛 AMERICAN WINE SUGGESTION
Knudson Erath Johannesberg Riesling

	U.S.		Metric	
Portions:	8	50	8	50
Onions, medium, chopped	1	6	1	6
Virgin olive oil	2 Tbsp	¾ cup	30 ml	180 ml
Tomatoes, fresh, seeded and chopped	2 lb	12½ lb	900 g	5.6 kg
Garlic cloves, minced	3	18	3	18
Basil, fresh, minced	2 Tbsp	¾ cup	4 g	24 g
Sugar	1 tsp	2 Tbsp	5 g	30 g
Salt				
Heavy cream	1 cup	1½ qt	240 ml	1.5 l
Halibut steaks, approx. 5 oz (140 g) each	8	50	8	50

For Milk Court Bouillon:

Water	1 qt	1½ gal	1 l	6 l
Milk	1 cup	1½ qt	240 ml	1.5 l
Salt				
White pepper, fresh ground				

For Milk Court Bouillon:

1. Combine water, milk, salt, and pepper. Reserve for use.

For Entrée

2. Sauté onion in oil until soft. Do not brown.
3. Add the tomatoes, garlic, basil, sugar, and salt. Simmer for 18 minutes, stirring to prevent sticking.
4. Using a food processor, puree mixture in batches until smooth.
5. Press mixture through strainer. Let cool.
6. In a bowl, whip cream until thick and stiff. Season with salt.
7. Blend ⅓ of the whipped cream into the tomato mixture. Blend well.
8. Add the remaining cream to the tomato mixture. Taste for seasoning.
9. Chill.
10. Poach the halibut in milk court bouillon for about 10 to 12 minutes.
11. Remove halibut from court bouillon and pat dry.
12. Serve hot or cold topped with tomato mousseline.

King Crabmeat Flambé

 AMERICAN WINE SUGGESTION
Ste. Chapelle Chardonnay

		U.S.		Metric	
Portions:		8	50	8	50
Butter, melted		5⅓ Tbsp	2 cups	80 ml	480 ml
Green onions, chopped		8	50	8	50
Green peppers, small, chopped		1⅓	8	1⅓	8
Crabmeat, from claws		1⅓ lb	8 lb	600 g	3.6 kg
Salt					
White pepper, fresh ground					
Tarragon		Pinch	To taste	Pinch	To taste
Sherry		⅓ cup	2 cups	80 ml	480 ml
Parsley, chopped		⅓ cup	2 cups	12 g	72 g
Cognac, warmed		½ cup	3 cups	120 ml	720 ml

1. Combine the butter, onions, and peppers, and sauté until tender.
2. Add crabmeat, salt, pepper, and tarragon. Add sherry and toss until mixture is heated.
3. Add the chopped parsley and cognac. Ignite and serve flaming.

Moose Tenderloin Steaks

 AMERICAN WINE SUGGESTION
Columbia Crest Merlot

		U.S.		Metric	
Portions:		8	50	8	50
Butter		2 Tbsp	¾ cup	30 g	180 g
Moose kidney suet, diced chunks		1½	9	1½	9
Moose filet steaks, 1½ in. (4 cm) thick		8	50	8	50
Béarnaise sauce, as needed					

1. Combine the butter and kidney suet. Heat until there is enough fat for sautéing.
2. Sauté moose steaks until brown outside and rare within.
3. Serve with béarnaise sauce.

Moose Stew

ॐ AMERICAN WINE SUGGESTION
Chateau Ste. Michelle Cabernet Sauvignon

		U.S.		Metric	
Portions:	8	50	8	50
Moose stew meat, cubed	6 lb	38 lb	2.7 kg	17 kg
Salt				
White pepper, fresh ground				
Thyme, fresh	1 tsp	2 Tbsp	1 g	6 g
Flour	½ cup	3 cups	60 g	340 g
Bacon fat	⅓ cup	2 cups	80 ml	480 ml
Onions, large, diced	2	12	2	12
Green pepper, diced	1	6	1	6
Carrots, sliced	6	38	6	38
Celery tops, with leaves	4	24	4	24
Marjoram	1 tsp	2 Tbsp	4 g	24 g
Worcestershire sauce	2 tsp	2 Tbsp	10 ml	30 ml
Red wine	1 qt	1½ gallons	1 l	6 l
Garlic cloves, crushed	2	12	2	12
Beef bouillon, powder	4 tsp	½ cup	8 g	50 g

1. Season the moose with salt, pepper, and ½ of the thyme. Coat meat heavily with flour.
2. In a stockpot, melt most of the bacon fat and sauté the meat on all sides, in batches if necessary. Remove meat.
3. Add more bacon fat and sauté the onion, green pepper, carrots, and celery until onions are translucent.
4. Return meat to pan, add marjoram, the remaining thyme, Worcestershire sauce, wine, garlic, and bouillon powder. Cover.
5. Simmer over medium-low heat for 1 to 1½ hours. Add water as liquid absorbs flour from meat.

Napoleon of Alaskan King Crab COLOR PLATE 25

🦐 AMERICAN WINE SUGGESTION
Iron Horse Sauvignon Blanc

		U.S.		Metric	
Portions:		8	50	8	50
Puff pastry, 4 in. (10 cm) diameter round pieces		16	100	16	100
Crab legs		30	188	30	188
Crab claws		64	400	64	400
Broccoli florets		8	50	8	50
For Sauce:					
Shallots, minced		2	12½	2	12½
Mushrooms, chopped		1	6¼	1	6¼
Butter		2 Tbsp	¾ cup	30 g	180 g
White wine		9 Tbsp	3½ cups	135 ml	840 ml
Heavy cream		2½ cups	15 cups	600 ml	3.6 l
Paprika, dusting					
Salt					
White pepper, fresh ground					
Crabmeat, sautéed		½ cup	3 cups	225 g	675 g

1. Bake puff pastry rounds in a preheated 350°F (180°C) oven for 15 minutes.
2. Sauté crabmeat and reserve.

For Sauce:

3. Sauté the shallots and mushrooms in butter.
4. Add the wine and reduce by half.
5. Add the cream, paprika, salt, and pepper.
6. Reduce by half and strain through a fine sieve.
7. Add the sautéed crabmeat.
8. Place sauce on plates, next a round of puff pastry, stuff with crabmeat and crab legs, cover with a round of puff pastry, and garnish with broccoli and crab claws. Serve immediately.

Salmon with Endive and Lime   COLOR PLATE 26

🐛 AMERICAN WINE SUGGESTION
Monterey Chardonnay

		U.S.		Metric	
Portions:		8	50	8	50
Salmon medallions		8	50	8	50
Salt					
White pepper, fresh ground					
Cayenne, to taste					
Butter		¾ cup	4½ cups	180 g	1.1 kg
Endives		2 lb	12½ lb	900 g	5.6 kg
Limes		2	12½	2	12½
Lemon		1	6¼	1	6¼
Sugar		2 tsp	¼ cup	10 g	60 g
Oil, a few drops					
White wine		6 Tbsp	2⅓ cups	90 ml	560 ml
Port wine		6 Tbsp	2⅓ cups	90 ml	560 ml
Heavy cream		2 cups	3 qt	480 ml	3 l
Black caviar, as needed for garnish					
Salmon roe, as needed for garnish					
Carrots, julienne, as needed for garnish					
Zucchini, julienne, as needed for garnish					
Celery, julienne, as needed for garnish					

1. Season salmon with salt and pepper. Gently sauté in ⅓ of the butter for 2 minutes on each side. Reserve.
2. Remove from sauté pan and place salmon on a baking dish. Bake in a preheated 375°F (190°C) oven for 6 to 8 minutes. Reserve.
3. Wash and dry endives. Add lime juice, lemon juice, sugar, salt, and pepper. Mix well.
4. Melt ⅓ of the butter in a saucepan over high heat and cook endives for 2 minutes. Reserve endives and juices for sauce.
5. Using the reserved sauté pan, add the reserved juices, oil, wine, port, and heavy cream. Season with salt, pepper, and cayenne. Let thicken and whisk in remaining butter. Adjust seasoning as necessary.
6. To serve, arrange endives on a plate in a star shape. Place salmon medallion in the center and garnish with julienne vegetables, caviar, and salmon roe.

Salmon Medallions with Fresh Hot Tomato Sauce

COLOR PLATE 27

🐚 AMERICAN WINE SUGGESTION
Meursault

		U.S.		Metric	
Portions:	8	50	8	50
Salmon medallions	24	150	24	150
Salt				
White pepper, fresh ground				
Lemon	½	3⅛	½	3⅛
Oil	¼ cup	1½ cups	60 ml	360 ml
Spinach, sautéed, as needed for garnish				
Julienne vegetables, as needed for garnish				
For Sauce:				
Onions, small, chopped	1	6¼	1	6¼
Unsalted butter	2 Tbsp	¾ cup	30 g	180 g
Garlic cloves, chopped	2	12½	2	12½
Ripe tomatoes, peeled, seeded, and diced	5	31½	5	31½
Bouquet garni, small	1	6	1	6
Tomato juice	½ cup	3 cups	120 ml	720 ml
Salt				
White pepper, fresh ground				
Sugar	½ tsp	1 Tbsp	3 g	15 g

1. Season salmon with salt, pepper, and lemon juice.
2. Place oil in a skillet and preheat.
3. Sauté the salmon for 4 to 5 minutes per side. Remove and keep warm.

For Sauce:

4. In a pan, sauté the onion with butter and garlic for 4 to 5 minutes.
5. Add the tomatoes, bouquet garni, and sauté for 3 to 4 minutes.
6. Add tomato juice, salt, pepper, and sugar. Simmer for 10 minutes. Remove bouquet garni.
7. To serve, place sauce on plates. Place salmon in the center of the plate and surround with sautéed spinach and julienne vegetables. Serve immediately.

Salmon in Orange and Madeira Sauce

❧ AMERICAN WINE SUGGESTION
Oak Knoll Gewürztraminer

		U.S.		Metric	
Portions:		8	50	8	50
Oranges		2	12	2	12
Fish stock		⅔ cup	1 qt	160 ml	1 l
Lemon juice, fresh		¼ cup	1½ cups	60 ml	360 ml
Butter		½ cup	3 cups	120 g	720 g
Dry Madeira wine		¼ cup	1½ cups	60 ml	360 ml
Salmon filets, approximately 6 oz (170 g) each		8	50	8	50
Heavy cream		½ cup	3 cups	120 ml	720 ml
Salt					
White pepper, fresh ground					

1. Peel and clean rind of oranges. Grate 2 tsp (10 g) of the zest for 8 servings, or ¼ cup (60 g) for 50 servings.
2. Slice the remaining orange crosswise for garnish.
3. Combine the fish stock, lemon juice, orange zest, butter, and wine in a skillet. Bring to a boil. Reduce heat, allowing sauce to thicken.
4. Add the salmon to the sauce, cover, and gently simmer for 6 to 9 minutes or until cooked through.
5. Remove salmon and keep warm.
6. Raise the heat under the liquid and reduce by ⅓.
7. Add the cream and continue to reduce until thick. Season with salt and pepper.
8. To serve, spoon sauce over salmon filet and garnish with orange slices.

Salmon with Tarragon Sauce

🦩 AMERICAN WINE SUGGESTION
Adams Vineyards Chardonnay

	U.S.		Metric	
Portions:	8	50	8	50
Fish stock	5 cups	2 gal	1.2 l	7.6 l
Dry white wine	5 Tbsp	2 cups	75 ml	480 ml
Butter, softened	10 Tbsp	4 cups	150 g	1 kg
Salmon filets, 6 oz (170 g) each	8	50	8	50
Heavy cream	1 cup	1½ qt	240 ml	1.5 l
Tarragon, fresh	¼ cup	1½ cups	9 g	55 g

1. In a skillet, combine the fish stock, white wine, and ⅔ of the butter. Bring to a boil.
2. Poach the salmon filets in the fish stock mixture for 7 to 9 minutes or until cooked through. Remove the filets and keep warm.
3. Increase the heat and allow poaching liquid to reduce by ⅓.
4. Add cream and continue to reduce until thick.
5. Add tarragon and slowly whisk in remaining butter over medium heat. Season to taste.
6. Spoon sauce over salmon and serve hot.

Smoked Trout Ravioli

❧ AMERICAN WINE SUGGESTION
Chateau Ste. Michelle Fumé Blanc

	U.S.		Metric	
Portions:	8	50	8	50
Ravioli dough, portions (page 229)	8	50	8	50
Smoked trout, skinned and boned	2	12	2	12
Parsley, fresh, minced	2 Tbsp	¾ cup	5 g	30 g
Salt				
White pepper, fresh ground				
Butter, softened	2 Tbsp	¾ cup	30 g	180 g
Eggs, hard-boiled, peeled, and chopped	2	12	2	12
For Sauce:				
Heavy cream	2 cups	3 qt	480 ml	2.9 l
Salt				
White pepper, fresh ground				
Nutmeg, ground	Pinch	To taste	Pinch	To taste
Horseradish	2 tsp	¼ cup	10 g	60 g

1. Prepare ravioli dough.
2. Cut the fish into small pieces, removing all small bones.
3. Add parsley, salt, and pepper to fish and mix well.
4. Work soft butter and egg into fish mixture. Blend mixture well and season to taste.
5. Fill ravioli with 1 tsp (5 g) of mixture. Seal and boil in salted water.

For Sauce:

6. Combine the heavy cream, salt, pepper, nutmeg, and horseradish in a saucepan. Reduce until thick.
7. Spoon sauce over ravioli and serve.

Trout Stuffed with Scallops

❧ AMERICAN WINE SUGGESTION
Arterberry Chardonnay

		U.S.		Metric	
Portions:		8	50	8	50
Bacon slices		10	62	10	62
Scallops		1 lb	6¼ lb	450 g	2.8 kg
Chives, minced		2 Tbsp	¾ cup	20 g	120 g
Butter, softened		½ cup	3 cups	120 g	720 g
Trout, whole, boned and eviscerated		8	50	8	50
Salt					
White pepper, fresh ground					
Lemon wedges, as needed for garnish					

1. Preheat oven to 400°F (200°C).
2. Chop ⅕ of the bacon slices coarsely. Reserve the remaining bacon.
3. Fry the chopped bacon until almost done. Remove, leaving bacon fat. Add the scallops and sauté for 3 to 4 minutes or until firm and light brown.
4. Remove scallops, reserving bacon fat. Let scallops cool, then chop them.
5. In a mixing bowl, combine the chives, butter, bacon, and scallops. Blend well. Reserve.
6. Brush a baking pan and trout with some of the reserved bacon fat.
7. Season trout with salt and pepper and stuff with scallop mixture.
8. Cut the reserved ⅕ of the bacon into 1 in. (3 cm) pieces, and use them to cover the tail and head of the trout to ensure that they do not burn.
9. Bake trout for 10 to 12 minutes or until done.
10. Remove and serve hot with lemon wedges.

ACCOMPANIMENTS

Ravioli Dough

	U.S.		Metric	
Portions:	8	50	8	50
All-purpose flour	2¼ lb	14 lb	1 kg	6.3 kg
Salt	1 tsp	2 Tbsp	5 g	30 g
Eggs, large, room temperature	12	75	12	75
Water	2 Tbsp	¾ cup	30 ml	180 ml

1. Place flour and salt in a food processor and mix in quick pulses.
2. Add the eggs and process for 15 seconds.
3. Add the water and process in bursts, until dough forms a ball, pulling away from the sides.
4. Divide ravioli dough into sections, flour them, and cover with a kitchen towel.
5. Using a pasta machine or a rolling pin, flatten out the dough on a floured surface into strips 2 in. × 12 to 18 in. (5 cm × 30 to 45 cm).
6. To stuff, place the filling on top of a strip of pasta dough, cover with a second strip, and moisten. Cut with a zigzag wheel.

Tomato Concassé

	U.S. For 2 cups	Metric For 480 ml
Butter	1 Tbsp	15 g
Oil	1 Tbsp	15 ml
Onion, small, chopped	1	1
Plum tomatoes, peeled, seeded, and chopped	2 cups	450 g
Garlic clove, minced	1	1
Bay leaf	1	1
Thyme	½ tsp	500 mg
Salt		
White pepper, fresh ground		

1. Combine butter and oil and sauté the onion for 1 to 2 minutes.
2. Add tomatoes, garlic, bay leaf, and thyme.
3. Cook for 12 to 15 minutes or until thick and moisture has evaporated.
4. Season with salt and pepper.

CHAPTER 11

California and Hawaii

California has become synonymous with healthy life-styles and an abundance of fresh, exciting, and often exotic foods. French, Italian, Asian, Spanish, and Middle Eastern settlers brought with them a love of food, wine, and fine dining. Alain Rondelli, executive chef at Ernie's Restaurant in San Francisco, sees that tradition continuing into the nineties. According to Chef Rondelli: "I believe that people in the nineties will have the benefit of the eighties in that they will seek out a better quality food. . . . If the restaurants in California continue to serve quality food with application, dedication, and perfection, they will have the clientele they deserve. The customers in the nineties will go into restaurants more for a culinary experience oriented to the simple test of flavor and savor."

The culinary experience in California is one of a bold, daring, and inventive cuisine that draws on the vast cultural diversity of the region, its Native American roots, as well as its bountiful farms and vineyards. Californians expect and demand the freshest local ingredients produced in a healthful way. In fact, California is often credited with being the birthplace of the current culinary revolution. Food here is prepared and presented simply, but with creative as well as traditional combinations of taste and texture. The simplicity of preparation coupled with the variety of fresh fruits, vegetables, legumes, fish, and moderate portions of meat make Californian cuisine one of the healthiest in the country. Very little fat is used. The fat that is used is generally a flavorful nut or seed oil, olive oil, or infused canola oil. These are all poly- or monoun-saturated, and little is needed because of their distinctive flavors.

The cooking of Hawaii clings more closely to its native origins. The waves of Asian, particularly Japanese, and Portuguese settlers have, however, left their stamp. Fried foods and high-fat sausages of Portuguese origin have made their way into everyday cooking. Those should, of course, be limited. Japanese and Chinese cooking and foods tend to be low in fat, but may be high in sodium. Pork is preferred over beef throughout Hawaiian cooking. Modern leaner hogs and lean cuts are replacing fattier ones in traditional dishes. Fresh seafood is plentiful. Fish and meats are baked, barbecued, or prepared in the Japanese manner. Poi, the staple of Hawaiian meals, is a good source of complex carbohydrates, vitamins, and minerals. Tropical fruits are plentiful, as are fresh vegetables from Hawaii's fertile farmland. Macadamia nuts are popular, but should be used in moderation because of their fat content. Coconut and coconut milk are also common ingredients in Hawaiian food. These are very high in saturated fats and should be used in moderation. Part of the coconut milk can be replaced with reduced-fat milk in most recipes.

It is not difficult to find healthy local foods in either Hawaii or California. Both offer a cornucopia of bright, vibrant vegetables and delightful tropical fruits.

APPETIZERS

Baked Goat Cheese with Herbs

	U.S.		Metric	
Portions:	8	50	8	50
Goat cheese	6 oz	2⅓ lb	170 g	1 kg
Virgin olive oil	¾ cup	4½ cups	180 ml	1.1 l
Tarragon, fresh	2 tsp	¼ cup	1.5 g	9 g
Oregano, fresh	2 tsp	¼ cup	1.3 g	8 g
Thyme, fresh	2 tsp	¼ cup	2 g	12 g
Basil, fresh	2 tsp	¼ cup	1.3 g	8 g
Parsley, fresh	2 tsp	¼ cup	1.5 g	9 g
Garlic heads	4½	31	4½	31
Chicken stock	⅔ cup	1 qt	300 ml	1 l
Butter, melted	3 Tbsp	1⅛ cups	45 ml	270 ml
French bread, as needed				

1. Cover the goat cheese with olive oil and sprinkle with tarragon, oregano, thyme, basil, and parsley. Marinate, refrigerated, at least overnight.
2. Preheat oven to 325°F (160°C).
3. Cut ¾ in. (2 cm) from the top of each garlic head, leaving the bulb whole.
4. Place garlic in a baking dish and cover with stock and butter.
5. Bake for about 1 hour and 10 minutes, uncovered.
6. During the last 35 minutes of baking, add the container of cheese to the oven and cook until slightly brown and bubbling. Do not overbake.
7. Remove garlic and cheese from the oven and place on a serving platter. Serve with hot French bread.

Crab Canapés

		U.S.		Metric	
	Portions:	8	50	8	50
Egg whites		2	12	2	12
Mayonnaise		1 cup	6¼ cups	240 ml	1.5 l
Onion, grated		3 Tbsp	1⅛ cups	45 g	285 g
Worcestershire sauce		1 Tbsp	6½ Tbsp	15 ml	100 ml
Crabmeat		¾ lb	4½ lb	340 g	2 kg
Salt					
White pepper, fresh ground					
Bread points, 1 in. (3 cm) each, toasted, as needed					

1. Beat egg whites to stiff peaks.
2. Fold in mayonnaise and add onion and Worcestershire sauce. Mix gently.
3. Add crabmeat and season with salt and pepper.
4. Place mixture in center of toast points and broil until golden.

Lomi Lomi Salmon

		U.S.		Metric	
	Portions:	8	50	8	50
Salmon, smoked, shredded		½ lb	3¼ lb	225 g	1.5 kg
Tomatoes, peeled and cubed		4	25	4	25
Green pepper, diced		1	6	1	6
Scallions, chopped		3	18	3	18
Onion, chopped		1	6	1	6
Crushed ice		1 cup	6 cups	240 ml	1.4 l

1. Combine the salmon, tomatoes, green peppers, scallions, and onions. Chill.
2. Fold mixture into crushed ice and serve cold.

Sausage Pâté

	U.S. Makes 2½ cups	Metric Makes 560 g
Butter	1 Tbsp	15 g
Italian sausage, hot, removed from casing	1 lb	450 g
Chicken liver	1 lb	450 g
Onion, minced	1	1
Heavy cream	¼ cup	60 ml
Bourbon	3 Tbsp	45 ml
Salt		
Nutmeg	½ tsp	1 g
Gherkins, fanned	2	2
Toast points, preferably sourdough, as needed		

1. In a heavy skillet, melt the butter over moderate heat.
2. Add the sausage to the butter and sauté. Cook until brown, about 4 to 5 minutes.
3. Remove sausage from pan and set aside.
4. Add the chicken liver to the pan in which the sausage was cooked and sauté for 5 minutes.
5. Add the onions to the liver and cook for an additional 2 minutes. Remove and set aside.
6. In a food processor, blend the sausage, onion, and chicken livers.
7. Add cream, bourbon, salt, and nutmeg. Process until smooth.
8. Place mixture in a deep serving dish and garnish with gherkins.
9. Serve with toasted bread points.

Sautéed Scallops

	U.S.		Metric	
Portions:	8	50	8	50
Butter, clarified	¼ cup	1½ cups	60 ml	360 ml
Bay scallops, fresh	3 lb	19 lb	1.4 kg	8.6 kg
Pine nuts	1 cup	6½ cups	240 g	1.4 kg
Garlic, minced	2 Tbsp	¾ cup	20 g	120 g
Shallots, minced	½ cup	3 cups	110 g	640 g
White wine, dry	2 cups	3 qt	480 ml	2.9 l
Lemon juice	½ cup	3 cups	120 ml	720 ml
Unsalted butter	1 cup	3 lb	240 g	1.4 kg
Salt				
White pepper, fresh ground				

1. Heat the clarified butter and sauté the scallops with the pine nuts, constantly stirring, for 1 minute, or until golden.
2. Remove the scallops and pine nuts. Reserve, keeping the liquid in the pan. Add the garlic and shallots and sauté for 30 seconds.
3. Deglaze pan with wine and lemon juice, and cook until liquid is reduced to ½ cup (120 ml) for 8 servings; or 3 cups (720 ml) for 50 servings.
4. Cooking over low heat, add any liquid from the reserved scallops and some of the unsalted butter to the pan. Do not let sauce boil. Whisk constantly until thick, adding more butter if needed.
5. Once sauce is thick, return scallops and pine nuts to pan and heat. Season with salt and pepper and serve.

Warm Scallop Salad with Roasted Red Peppers

	U.S.		Metric	
Portions:	8	50	8	50
Fish stock	1 cup	1½ qt	240 ml	1.4 l
Shallots, minced	2	12	2	12
Sauvignon blanc	1 cup	1½ qt	240 ml	1.4 l
Vinegar, white wine	¼ cup	1½ cups	60 ml	360 ml
Black pepper, fresh ground	½ tsp	1 Tbsp	1 g	7 g
Ginger root, to taste				
Dijon mustard	1½ tsp	3 Tbsp	7 g	45 g
Butter	½ cup	3 cups	120 g	720 g
Walnut oil	¼ cup	1½ cups	60 ml	360 ml
Butter	2 Tbsp	¾ cup	30 g	180 g
Scallops, cleaned	1½ lb	9 lb	675 g	4.1 kg
Baby red-leaf lettuce, bunches	6	38	6	38
Radicchio heads	1	6	1	6
Avocados, sliced and fanned	3	18	3	18
Red bell peppers, large, roasted, peeled, and sliced	3	18	3	18
Walnut halves, toasted	¼ cup	1½ cups	60 g	340 g
Herbs, various, as needed for garnish				

1. Combine the fish stock, shallots, sauvignon blanc, vinegar, pepper, and ginger. Bring mixture to a vigorous boil.
2. Gradually add the mustard and ½ cup (3 cups for 50 servings) of butter.
3. Gradually add walnut oil to taste until emulsified.
4. In a skillet, heat butter and sauté the scallops for 3 to 4 minutes.
5. Place avocado fans on a bed of lettuce and radicchio with roasted peppers. Top with scallops and garnish with walnut halves and herbs.

SALADS

Muscat Greens and Wild Flowers with Champagne Dressing   COLOR PLATE 28

	U.S.		Metric	
Portions:	8	50	8	50
Watercress bunches, leaves only	2	12	2	12
Bibb lettuce, small heads, separated	2	12	2	12
Radicchio, small heads	3	19	3	19
Belgian endive heads	4	25	4	25
Basil, fresh, chopped	3 Tbsp	1⅛ cups	6 g	36 g
Flowers: nasturtiums, pansies, marigolds, petunias	32	200	32	200
For Dressing:				
Champagne vinegar	¼ cup	1½ cups	60 ml	360 ml
Shallots, chopped	4	25	4	25
Garlic cloves, minced	2	12½	2	12½
Olive oil, extra virgin	⅔ cup	1 qt	160 ml	1 l
Basil, fresh	½ cup	3 cups	16 g	100 g
Nasturtium leaves, medium	4	25	4	25
Salt				
White pepper, fresh ground				

1. Combine the vinegar, shallots, garlic, oil, basil, nasturtium leaves, salt, and pepper in a food processor. Mix well and refrigerate until needed.
2. Wash all greens and pat dry.
3. Tear greens into small pieces. Add basil and toss.
4. Arrange on plates, garnish with flowers, and drizzle with dressing.

Warm Crab Salad

	U.S.		Metric	
Portions:	8	50	8	50
Watercress bunches, chop ½, reserve the other ½ for garnish	1	6	1	6
Bibb lettuce, chopped, large heads	2	12	2	12
Papayas, cubed	2	12	2	12
Tomatoes, cubed	2	12	2	12
Butter	¼ cup	1½ cups	60 g	360 g
Crabmeat, from legs	3 lb	18½ lb	1.4 kg	8.3 kg
White pepper, fresh ground				
Virgin olive oil	⅔ cup	1 qt	160 ml	1 l
Vinegar, red wine	6 Tbsp	2⅓ cups	90 ml	560 ml
Brandy	½ cup	3 cups	120 ml	720 ml
Salt				

1. Combine the chopped watercress, lettuce, papaya, and tomatoes. Set aside.
2. In a skillet, melt the butter and sauté the crab over low heat, turning the crab frequently. Season with fresh ground pepper.
3. Remove crab and reserve juices.
4. Raise heat and add oil, vinegar, and brandy. Season with salt and pepper.
5. Add crabmeat to salad and toss with warm dressing. Garnish with reserved watercress.

SOUPS

Avocado Soup

		U.S.		Metric	
Portions:		8	50	8	50
Onions, chopped		2	12	2	12
Celery stalks, chopped		2	12	2	12
Butter		¼ cup	1½ cups	60 g	360 g
Flour		¼ cup	1½ cups	30 g	170 g
Curry powder		4 tsp	½ cup	8 g	50 g
Green apples, tart, peeled, cored, and chopped		2	12	2	12
Chicken stock		2 qt	3⅛ gal	1.9 l	12 l
Avocados, peeled, pitted, and chopped		6	38	6	38
Light cream		2 cups	3 qt	480 ml	2.9 l
Salt					
Coconut, as needed for garnish					

1. Combine the onion and celery and sauté in a heavy skillet in butter until tender.
2. Add flour and curry and cook for 3 to 5 minutes, stirring constantly.
3. Add apples and ½ of the chicken stock. Blend well and cook over low heat until apples are tender.
4. Transfer the mixture to a food processor, add ⅔ of the avocados, and blend until smooth.
5. Return mixture to pot.
6. Add remaining chicken stock and cream. Blend well.
7. Season with salt and chill for 3 hours.
8. Thinly slice remaining avocado and garnish soup with avocado slices and coconut before serving.

California Cioppino   COLOR PLATE 29

		U.S.		Metric	
Portions:		8	50	8	50
Virgin olive oil		½ cup	3 cups	120 ml	720 ml
Onions, medium, chopped		2	12½	2	12½
Garlic cloves, minced		2	12½	2	12½
Tomatoes, whole, peeled, seeded, and diced		4	25	4	25
Salt					
White pepper, fresh ground					
Basil leaves		2 Tbsp	¾ cup	4 g	24 g
Dry white wine		2 cups	3 qt	480 ml	3 l
Fish filets, any kind, cut into chunks		2 lb	12½ lb	900 g	5.6 kg
Shrimp, shelled and deveined		1 lb	6¼ lb	450 g	2.8 kg

1. In a saucepan, heat the oil and sauté the onion and garlic until tender.
2. Add the tomatoes and juices, salt, pepper, basil, and 2 qt (2 l) of water for 8 servings, 3 gal (11.5 l) of water for 50 servings. Bring to a boil over high heat. Reduce heat, cover, and simmer for 30 minutes, stirring occasionally.
3. Add the wine, fish filets, and more water if necessary.
4. Return to a boil, reduce heat, and simmer, covered, for 5 minutes, stirring occasionally.
5. Add the shrimp, cover, and cook for an additional 4 minutes or until shrimp are done.

Pacific Fruit Soup   COLOR PLATE 30

	U.S.		Metric	
Portions:	8	50	8	50
Sugar syrup	1 cup	1½ qt	240 ml	1.5 l
Lemon juice, fresh	1 lemon	6¼ lemons	1 lemon	6¼ lemons
Orange juice, fresh	1½ oranges	9 oranges	1½ oranges	9 oranges
Bananas	1½	9⅓	1½	9⅓
Pineapple, ripe	¾	4⅔	¾	4⅔
Mangos, skinned and pitted	2	12½	2	12½
Lemon peel	1 piece	6¼ pieces	1 piece	6¼ pieces
Orange peel	1 piece	6¼ pieces	1 piece	6¼ pieces
Cinnamon stick	¾	4⅔	¾	4⅔
Selected seasonal fruits: mango, kiwi, bananas, strawberries, etc.				
Mint leaves, as needed for garnish.				

1. Place syrup, lemon juice, orange juice, bananas, pineapple, mangos, lemon peel, orange peel, and cinnamon stick in a large pan.
2. Bring to a boil and simmer for 5 minutes.
3. Reduce, then remove and chill overnight.
4. Strain and adjust consistency by adding rum if necessary .
5. Add the fresh fruits and garnish each serving with fresh mint before serving.

Spinach-Parsnip Soup

		U.S.		Metric	
Portions:		8	50	8	50
Parsnips, large, sliced		8	50	8	50
Carrots, sliced		4	25	4	25
Onions, large, quartered		2	12	2	12
Celery stalks, sliced		2	12	2	12
Celery tops, chopped		¼ cup	1½ cups	60 g	360 g
Chicken stock		3 qt	4½ gal	2.9 l	18 l
Spinach, washed and torn into pieces		1 lb	6 lb	450 g	2.7 kg
Salt					
White pepper, fresh ground					
Nutmeg		1 tsp	2 Tbsp	2 g	12 g

1. Combine the parsnips, carrots, onions, celery, celery tops, and stock in a large stock pot.
2. Bring to a boil, covered.
3. Reduce heat and simmer for 25 to 30 minutes.
4. Remove vegetables from stock. Place vegetables and a small amount of the cooking liquid in a blender and puree until smooth.
5. Add spinach to vegetable puree and continue to puree an additional 30 to 45 seconds.
6. Return puree to stock.
7. Season with salt, pepper, and nutmeg.
8. Heat gently before serving.

Thai Prawn Soup

	U.S.		Metric	
Portions:	8	50	8	50
Shrimp or prawn, shelled and deveined, reserve shells, tails, and heads	2 lb	12½ lb	900 g	5.6 kg
Virgin olive oil	1 Tbsp	6¼ Tbsp	15 ml	90 ml
Salt				
Lemon grass stalks, cut into 2 in. (5 cm) pieces	3	18	3	18
Lemon peel, chopped	1 tsp	2 Tbsp	5 g	30 g
Lime peel, dried, to taste				
Jalapeño chilies	2	12	2	12
Fish sauce	1 Tbsp	6 Tbsp	15 ml	90 ml
Lemon or lime juice	2–3 Tbsp	¾ cup	30–45 ml	180 ml
Cilantro, chopped	2–3 Tbsp	¾ cup	5–7 g	30 g
Green onions, with tops	4	25	4	25

1. Sauté reserved shrimp shells, tails, and heads in olive oil until pink.
2. Add 1 qt (1 l) of water for every 2 lb (900 g) of shrimp. Add salt, lemon grass, lemon and lime peel, and chilies.
3. Cover and bring to a boil. Reduce heat and simmer for 15 to 20 minutes.
4. Strain the stock, discarding solids.
5. Return liquid to a boil and add the shrimp. Reduce heat and simmer for 3 to 4 minutes.
6. Add the fish sauce and add the lemon or lime juice, to taste, to the soup.
7. Garnish with cilantro and green onions and serve.

Three-Onion Soup

		U.S.		Metric	
Portions:		8	50	8	50
Unsalted butter		¼ cup	1½ cups	60 g	360 g
Oil		2 Tbsp	¾ cup	30 ml	180 ml
Bermuda onions, thinly sliced		4	25	4	25
Yellow onions, thinly sliced		4	25	4	25
Sugar		½ tsp	1 Tbsp	3 g	15 g
Leeks, white only, thinly sliced		4	25	4	25
Veal stock		2½ qt	4 gal	2.4 l	15.4 l
Garlic cloves, minced		3	18	3	18
Bay leaves		1	6	1	6
White wine, dry		1 cup	1½ qt	240 ml	1.5 l
Brandy		¼ cup	1½ cups	60 ml	360 ml
Salt					
White pepper, fresh ground					
Thyme, fresh, chopped		1 tsp	2 Tbsp	1g	6 g
French bread, as needed					
Gruyère cheese, shredded		¼ lb	1½ lb	115 g	675 g

1. Heat the butter and oil and sauté the Bermuda onions and yellow onions over medium heat until wilted.
2. Add sugar and cook, stirring frequently, until light brown.
3. Add the leeks and cook, stirring frequently, until mixture is caramel in color.
4. Add veal stock, garlic, bay leaf, white wine, and brandy.
5. Lower heat, cover partially, and simmer for 30 minutes.
6. Season with salt, pepper, and thyme. Discard the bay leaf.
7. Preheat broiler.
8. Place soup in ovenproof casseroles. Cover with French bread slices, and top with shredded Gruyère cheese.
9. Broil until cheese is brown. Serve hot.

Tomato-Basil Soup

	U.S.		Metric	
Portions:	8	50	8	50
Butter	6 Tbsp	2⅓ cups	90 g	560 g
Virgin olive oil	2 Tbsp	¾ cup	30 ml	180 ml
Onions, chopped	2	6	2	6
Leeks, cleaned and chopped	2	6	2	6
Carrots, chopped	2	6	2	6
Celery stalks, chopped	2	6	2	6
Bouquet garni	1	6	1	6
Basil, fresh, chopped	¼ cup	1½ cups	8 g	50 g
Tomatoes, ripe, chopped	8	50	8	50
Tomato paste	6 Tbsp	2½ cups	12 g	75 g
Flour	¼ cup	1½ cups	30 g	170 g
Chicken stock	5 cups	2 gal	1.2 l	7.7 l
Whipping cream	1 cup	1½ qt	240 ml	1.4 l
Salt				
White pepper, fresh ground				
Basil leaves, fresh, as needed for garnish				

1. Heat butter and oil and sauté the onion, leek, carrot, celery, bouquet garni, and basil for 5 minutes over low heat, stirring occasionally.
2. Add tomatoes and tomato paste and cook for 4 to 6 minutes. Sprinkle flour over tomato mixture and mix well.
3. Add chicken stock, cover, and simmer for 15 minutes. Remove bouquet garni.
4. Using a food processor, puree mixture, then pass through a fine sieve.
5. Heat soup in a saucepan and add whipping cream. Bring to a boil, reduce heat, and simmer for 2 minutes.
6. Season with salt and pepper to taste and serve hot, garnished with fresh basil.

ENTRÉES

Baked Avocado with Seafood

 AMERICAN WINE SUGGESTION
Edna Valley Chardonnay

	U.S.		Metric	
Portions:	8	50	8	50
Avocados	4	25	4	25
Lemon juice	1 lemon	6 lemons	1 lemon	6 lemons
Water	6 Tbsp	2⅓ cups	90 ml	560 ml
Mayonnaise	1½ cups	9⅓ cups	360 ml	2.2 l
Curry powder	1 tsp	2 Tbsp	2 g	12 g
Crabmeat, lobster meat, shrimp, cooked	3 cups	9½ lb	680 g	4.3 kg
Capers	2 Tbsp	¾ cup	30 g	180 g
Hard-boiled eggs, quartered	4	25	4	25
Bread crumbs, buttered	1 cup	6¼ cups	230 g	1.4 kg

1. Cut avocados in half and brush with some lemon juice. Reserve.
2. Combine the water, remaining lemon juice, and mayonnaise. Simmer over low heat.
3. Add curry powder, seafood, capers, and eggs. Mix well.
4. Fill avocados with seafood mixture and top with bread crumbs.
5. Bake for 2 to 3 minutes at 350°F (180°C). Serve hot.

Baked Fish in Ti Leaves

🦐 AMERICAN WINE SUGGESTION
Simi Sauvignon Blanc

	U.S.		Metric	
Portions:	8	50	8	50
White fish, approximately 3 lb (1.4 kg) each, scalded and cleaned	1	6	1	6
Salt pork, boiled	¼ lb	1⅔ lb	115 g	750 g
Ti leaves, remove stem fibers	6	38	6	38

1. Preheat oven to 350°F (180°C).
2. Wrap fish and salt pork in ti leaves. Tie the ends.
3. Place fish in a shallow baking pan and bake for 60 to 75 minutes.
4. Remove ti leaves before serving.

Balinese Chicken

❧ AMERICAN WINE SUGGESTION
Firestone Johannesberg Riesling

	U.S.		Metric	
Portions:	8	50	8	50
Virgin olive oil	2 Tbsp	¾ cup	30 ml	180 ml
Onion, minced	1	6	1	6
Garlic cloves, minced	4	25	4	25
Turmeric	½ tsp	1 Tbsp	1 g	6 g
Coriander	1 Tbsp	6 Tbsp	6 g	36 g
Salt				
Chicken fryers, quartered, approximately 4 lb (1.8 kg) each	2	12½	2	12½
Coconut milk	1 cup	6¼ cups	240 ml	1.5 l
Sugar	2 Tbsp	¾ cup	30 g	180 g
Vinegar	2 Tbsp	¾ cup	30 ml	180 ml
Water	1 cup	6¼ cups	240 ml	1.5 l

1. In a skillet, heat the oil and sauté the onions, garlic, turmeric, coriander, and salt. Sauté for 3 to 4 minutes or until the onions are done.
2. Add the chicken and brown on all sides.
3. Add coconut milk, sugar, vinegar, and water. Reduce heat and simmer for 15 to 20 minutes.
4. Preheat broiler.
5. Broil chicken until tender, basting as needed with sauce from frying pan.

Barbecue Grilled Chicken with Mango-Avocado Salsa

ও **AMERICAN WINE SUGGESTION**
Monterey Chardonnay

		U.S.		Metric	
Portions:	8	50	8	50
White wine, dry	1½ cups	9 cups	360 ml	2.3 l
Orange juice, fresh	½ cup	3 cups	120 ml	720 ml
Lemon juice, fresh	¼ cup	1½ cups	60 ml	360 ml
Basil, fresh, chopped	2 Tbsp	¾ cup	4 g	24 g
Virgin olive oil	2 Tbsp	¾ cup	30 ml	180 ml
Rosemary sprigs, fresh	2	12	2	12
Black peppercorns, cracked	2 Tbsp	¾ cup	12 g	70 g
Bay leaves, small	4	25	4	25
Chicken breasts, boneless, halved	4	25	4	25
For Salsa:				
Mangos, large, peeled, pitted, and diced	2	12	2	12
Onion, small, minced	1	6	1	6
Green peppers, diced	1	6	1	6
Red bell peppers, diced	1	6	1	6
Vinegar, white wine	3 Tbsp	1⅛ cups	45 ml	270 ml
Cilantro, fresh	2 Tbsp	¾ cup	5 g	30 g
Virgin olive oil	2 Tbsp	¾ cup	30 ml	180 ml
Chives, fresh, minced	2 tsp	¼ cup	7 g	40 g
Avocado, large, peeled, pitted, and diced	1	6	1	6
Salt				
White pepper, fresh ground				

For Salsa:

1. Combine the mangos, onions, peppers, vinegar, cilantro, olive oil, and chives. Cover and refrigerate for at least 4 hours.
2. Add the avocado to the salsa, season with salt and pepper.

For Chicken:

3. Combine dry wine, orange juice, lemon juice, basil, olive oil, rosemary, cracked peppercorns, and bay leaves in a large bowl.
4. Add the chicken and coat. Cover and refrigerate at least 4 hours.
5. Preheat grill. Grill chicken on hot grill until cooked through, about 6 to 8 minutes.
6. Serve with mango-avocado salsa.

Barbecued Steak (Bul Kogi)

❦ AMERICAN WINE SUGGESTION
Beaulieu Vineyards Rutherford Cabernet Sauvignon

		U.S.		Metric	
Portions:		8	50	8	50
Sirloin steak		5 lb	31 lb	2.3 kg	14 kg
Soy sauce		½ cup	3 cups	120 ml	720 ml
Sugar		¼ cup	1½ cups	60 g	360 g
Garlic clove, minced		1	6	1	6
Sesame oil		2 Tbsp	¾ cup	30 ml	180 ml
Scallions, chopped		4	25	4	25

1. Cut steaks into large filets.
2. In a bowl, combine the soy sauce, sugar, garlic, oil, and scallions. Mix well to create marinade.
3. Marinate steaks for ½ hour.
4. Broil on hot grill to desired doneness.

Chicken Luau

🍃 AMERICAN WINE SUGGESTION
Franciscan Chardonnay

	U.S.		Metric	
Portions:	8	50	8	50
Chicken fryers, approximately 6 lb (2.7 kg) each, cut into pieces	2	12	2	12
Butter	¼ cup	1½ cups	60 g	360 g
Salt				
Water	1½ cups	2½ qt	360 ml	2.3 l
White pepper, fresh ground				
Spinach leaves, washed and broken into pieces	3 lb	19 lb	1.4 kg	8.4 kg
Coconut milk, warm	3 cups	1⅛ gal	720 ml	4.5 l

1. Preheat oven to 350°F (180°C).
2. In a heavy skillet, melt the butter and brown the chicken on all sides.
3. Add salt and water and simmer until chicken is tender.
4. Drain, reserving broth. Season chicken with salt and pepper.
5. Combine spinach with a small amount of water and cover. Cook over low heat until tender.
6. Add ⅔ of the warm coconut milk to the spinach and simmer for 2 to 3 minutes.
7. Arrange the chicken pieces in a deep dish and add the spinach with coconut milk.
8. Heat the remaining coconut milk and the chicken broth and pour the mixture over the chicken and spinach. Bake for 5 to 8 minutes. Remove and serve.

Flank Steak with Fruit Salsa

🐝 AMERICAN WINE SUGGESTION
Rodney Strong "Old Vines" Zinfandel

		U.S.		Metric	
Portions:		8	50	8	50
Flank steak		3 lb	18½ lb	1.4 kg	8.3 kg
Orange juice, fresh		½ cup	3 cups	120 ml	720 ml
Chili sauce		¼ cup	1½ cups	60 ml	360 ml
Chili powder		¼ cup	1½ cups	28 g	170 g
Soy sauce		¼ cup	1½ cups	60 ml	360 ml
Virgin olive oil		¼ cup	1½ cups	60 ml	360 ml
Honey		2 tsp	¼ cup	10 ml	60 ml
Orange peel, grated		2 tsp	¼ cup	10 g	60 g
Lemon peel, grated		1 tsp	2 Tbsp	5 g	30 g
Garlic cloves, minced		4	25	4	25
Salt					
Cayenne, to taste					
Orange slices, as needed for garnish					

For Fresh Fruit Salsa: Makes 3 cups (720 ml)

Pineapple, diced		1 cup		230 g	
Kiwi, sliced		1		1	
Papaya, chopped		1 cup		230 g	
Hot red pepper flakes		½ tsp		335 mg	
Red bell pepper, large, diced		1		1	
Green pepper, small, diced		1		1	
Vinegar, white wine		2½ Tbsp		38 g	
Cilantro, minced		1½ Tbsp		4 g	
Sugar		4 tsp		20 g	

For Fresh Fruit Salsa:

1. Combine pineapple, kiwi, papaya, pepper flakes, peppers, vinegar, cilantro, and sugar in a bowl and mix well. Chill overnight and serve at room temperature.

For Steak:

2. Place flank steak in a baking dish. Cover with orange juice, chili sauce, chili powder, soy sauce, oil, honey, orange peel, lemon peel, garlic, salt, and cayenne. Spread all over the meat.
3. Marinate flank steak overnight, refrigerated.
4. Preheat grill.
5. Remove meat from marinade and grill to desired doneness.
6. Remove and thinly slice.
7. Garnish with orange wedges and surround with fresh fruit salsa.

Fresh Mussel and Little Neck Stew

❦ AMERICAN WINE SUGGESTION
Iron Horse Sauvignon Blanc

	U.S.		Metric	
Portions:	**8**	**50**	**8**	**50**
Mussels, fresh, cleaned	2½ lb	15½ lb	1.1 kg	7 kg
Little necks, cleaned	2½ lb	15½ lb	1.1 kg	7 kg
White sherry	2 cups	3 qt	480 ml	2.9 l
Clam juice	3 cups	1⅛ gal	720 ml	4.4 l
Lemon juice, fresh	1 lemon	6 lemons	1 lemon	6 lemons
Paprika	¼ tsp	1½ tsp	580 mg	3.5 g
Red bell pepper, seeded, julienne	1	6	1	6
Yellow bell pepper, seeded, julienne	1	6	1	6
Green pepper, seeded, julienne	1	6	1	6
Yellow onion, thinly sliced	1	6	1	6
Zucchini, sliced	1	6	1	6
Yellow crookneck squash, sliced	1	6	1	6
Tomato, peeled, seeded, and cubed	1	6	1	6
Smoked sausage, ½ in. (1 cm) slices	½ lb	3 lb	225 g	1.4 kg
Greek olives, pitted and chopped	½ cup	3 cups	115 g	680 g
Cilantro, fresh, chopped	¼ cup	1½ cups	10 g	60 g

1. Thoroughly wash the mussels and little necks and store in the refrigerator while preparing vegetables.
2. Combine the sherry, clam juice, lemon juice, and paprika. Bring to a boil.
3. Add the shellfish, peppers, onions, zucchini, squash, tomato, sausage, and olives to the liquid. Cover and cook until mussels and clams have opened, about 8 to 11 minutes.
4. Remove stew from heat and serve immediately with chopped cilantro.

Lobster California   COLOR PLATE 31

❦&   AMERICAN WINE SUGGESTION
Kenwood Sauvignon Blanc

	U.S.		Metric	
Portions:	8	50	8	50
Grapefruit, pink, sectioned and chopped	8	50	8	50
Serrano chilies, fresh, cut lengthwise, ½ in. (1 cm) strips	4	25	4	25
Purple onion, finely diced	1	6	1	6
Cilantro, fresh, chopped	½ cup	3 cups	20 g	120 g
Salt				
Lobsters, approximately 1½ lb (675 g) each	4	25	4	25
Tortillas, as needed				
Leeks, julienne, white part only, sautéed	3	18	3	18
Basil leaves, fresh	16	100	16	100

1. Combine the grapefruit, chilies, onion, and cilantro. Season with salt and drain through a colander. Reserve.
2. Cut live lobsters in half. Rinse and clean body cavity. Broil or barbecue lobster meat and claw meat.
3. Combine lobster with some of the grapefruit salsa and wrap with tortillas.
4. Place remaining grapefruit salsa on plates and top with tortillas.
5. Garnish with sautéed leeks and basil leaves.

Leek, Tomato, and Pancetta Pizza

AMERICAN WINE SUGGESTION
Sutter Home Red Zinfandel

	Portions:	U.S.		Metric	
		8	50	8	50
Leeks, white and light green part only, julienne		4 lb	25 lb	1.8 kg	11.3 kg
Butter		6 Tbsp	2⅓ cups	90 g	560 g
Salt		½ tsp	1 Tbsp	250 mg	15 g
White pepper, fresh ground					
Pancetta, thinly sliced		½ lb	3 lb	225 g	1.4 kg
Tomatoes, ripe, peeled, seeded, and chopped		2 lb	12½ lb	900 g	5.6 kg
Basil, fresh, chopped		2 Tbsp	¾ cup	4 g	24 g
Virgin olive oil		2 Tbsp	¾ cup	30 ml	180 ml
Pizza dough (see page 268), as needed					

1. In a heavy skillet, sauté the leeks in butter. Season with salt and pepper.
2. Cover and cook over low heat for 15 minutes or until leeks are tender. Uncover and cook until liquid evaporates.
3. In a separate pan, fry pancetta until crisp and golden. Remove and pat dry. Crumble and reserve pancetta. Discard drippings.
4. Using the same pan as for the pancetta, cook the tomatoes for 10 to 12 minutes or until dry, stirring frequently.
5. Add crumbled pancetta and basil to the tomatoes. Taste for seasoning.
6. Knead the pizza dough on a floured surface and divide into equal parts.
7. Knead the pizza dough into 9 in. (25 cm) circles, slightly higher at the rim.
8. Spread half of the leek mixture over the dough.
9. Cover the leeks with the tomato mixture and top with remaining leeks.
10. Brush pizza rims with olive oil.
11. Place pizza on oiled baking sheets; let rise for 20 minutes.
12. Bake in a preheated 400°F (200°C) oven for 25 to 30 minutes or until dough is golden, but not hard. Serve immediately.

Marinated Lamb in Peanut Sauce

🐝 AMERICAN WINE SUGGESTION
Sterling Vineyards Merlot

		U.S.		Metric	
Portions:		8	50	8	50
Racks of lamb		4	25	4	25
For Marinade:					
Garlic cloves, minced		2	12	2	12
Shallots, medium, chopped		2	12	2	12
Dry mustard		2 tsp	¼ cup	4 g	24 g
Red wine		½ cup	3 cups	120 ml	720 ml
Curry powder		4 tsp	½ cup	8 g	50 g
Thyme, fresh, chopped		2 tsp	¼ cup	2 g	12 g
Lemon zest, chopped fine		1 lemon	6 lemons	1 lemon	6 lemons
Honey		2 Tbsp	¾ cup	30 ml	180 ml
Black pepper, cracked		½ tsp	1 Tbsp	1 g	7 g
Bay leaves		2	12	2	12
For Peanut Sauce:					
Soy sauce		¼ cup	1½ cups	60 ml	360 ml
Garlic cloves, minced		4	25	4	25
Peanut butter, crunchy		1 cup	6½ cups	225 g	1.4 kg
Chicken stock		½ cup	3 cups	120 ml	720 ml
Honey		¼ cup	1½ cups	60 ml	360 ml
Cilantro, chopped		2 Tbsp	¾ cup	5 g	30 g
Lemon juice		¼ cup	1½ cups	60 ml	360 ml

For Marinade:

1. Combine garlic, shallots, mustard, wine, curry, thyme, lemon zest, honey, pepper, and bay leaves in a bowl and add the racks of lamb.
2. Refrigerate at least 4 hours, turning occasionally.

For Peanut Sauce:

3. Combine the soy sauce, garlic, peanut butter, chicken stock, honey, cilantro, and lemon juice. Whisk to incorporate.
4. Preheat oven to 400°F (200°C).
5. Place racks of lamb in roasting pans. Cover bones with foil to prevent burning. Roast for 20 minutes or until pink, basting frequently.
6. Remove from oven, slice, and serve with whisked peanut sauce.

Marinated Rib-Eye Roast

❧ AMERICAN WINE SUGGESTION
Robert Sinskey Pinot Noir

	U.S.		Metric	
Portions:	8	50	8	50
Rib-eye roasts, boneless, approximately 5 lb (2.3 kg) each, trimmed	1	6	1	6
Black pepper, cracked	1/3 cup	2 cups	40 g	225 g
Cardamom, ground	1/2 tsp	1 Tbsp	4 g	25 g
Soy sauce	1 cup	1 1/2 qt	240 ml	1.4 l
Vinegar, red wine	3/4 cup	1 qt	180 ml	1 l
Tomato paste	1 Tbsp	6 Tbsp	15 ml	90 ml
Paprika	1 tsp	2 Tbsp	230 mg	15 g
Garlic cloves, minced	4	25	4	25
Parsley, as needed for garnish				
For Jalapeño Jelly:				
Green pepper, chopped	1/2 cup	3 cups	115 g	680 g
Jalapeño peppers, rinsed and seeded	1/4 cup	1 1/2 cups	60 g	340 g
Vinegar, cider	1 1/4 cups	7 1/2 cups	360 ml	1.8 l
Sugar	3 lb	18 1/4 lb	1.4 kg	8.4 kg
Red bell peppers, diced	1/2 cup	3 cups	115 g	680 g
Fruit pectin	1 bottle	6 bottles	1 bottle	6 bottles
Food coloring, green	8 drops	50 drops	8 drops	50 drops

For Jalapeño Jelly:

1. In a food processor, combine the green pepper, jalapeño pepper, and half of the vinegar. Blend.
2. Transfer mixture to a saucepan and add remaining vinegar, sugar, and red pepper. Bring to a boil.
3. Remove mixture from heat and let stand for 5 minutes. Skim off impurities.
4. Add pectin and food coloring. Stir well until blended.
5. Store jelly in jars and cover.

For Roast:

6. Place roast in a baking pan.
7. Rub cracked pepper and cardamom on meat.
8. In a bowl, combine the soy sauce, vinegar, tomato paste, paprika, and garlic. Pour mixture over meat.
9. Cover and marinate for 1 1/2 hours or to taste, in refrigerator, turning occasionally.
10. Preheat oven to 325°F (160°C).
11. Remove meat from marinade and wrap in aluminum foil.
12. Roast for 2 hours or until cooked to desired doneness. Remove from oven and slice.
13. Garnish with parsley and serve with jalapeño jelly.

Melanzanna Pizza

🍒 AMERICAN WINE SUGGESTION
Martin Brothers Nebbiolo

	U.S.		Metric	
Portions:	8	50	8	50
Virgin olive oil	1 cup	1½ qt	240 ml	1.4 l
Eggplant, small, unpeeled, sliced	2 lb	12½ lb	900 g	5.6 kg
Plum tomatoes, ripe, sliced crosswise	1 lb	6 lb	450 g	2.7 kg
Salt				
White pepper, fresh ground				
Thyme, fresh, chopped	1 Tbsp	6 Tbsp	9 g	55 g
Pizza dough, as needed (see page 268)				
Parmesan cheese, freshly grated	6 Tbsp	2⅓ cups	85 g	530 g

1. In a skillet, heat ½ of the olive oil and add one layer of eggplant. Fry for 2 to 3 minutes on each side, until brown and tender. Remove eggplant from pan and repeat until all eggplant has been fried.
2. Return eggplant to skillet, add the tomatoes, salt, pepper, and thyme, and cook, stirring often, for 8 to 10 minutes, or until done.
3. Knead the dough and divide into 4 equal portions. Knead dough into 9 in. (25 cm) circles and place on 2 oiled baking sheets.
4. Spread mixture over dough, leaving a border with no mixture.
5. Top pizza with olive oil and brush rim of pizza with oil.
6. Allow to rise for 20 minutes and bake in preheated 400°F (200°C) oven for 25 to 30 minutes, or until dough is golden but not hard.
7. Garnish with Parmesan cheese.

Roast Pork Stuffed with Fruit

❧ AMERICAN WINE SUGGESTION
Meridian Vineyards Chardonnay

		U.S.		Metric	
Portions:		8	50	8	50
Pork roasts, boneless, approximately 3 lb (1.4 kg) each		2	13	2	13
Light cream		2 cups	3 qt	480 ml	2.9 l
Sour cream		2 cups	3 qt	480 ml	2.9 l
Sugar		4 tsp	½ cup	20 g	120 g
Sherry		2 Tbsp	¾ cup	30 ml	180 ml
Golden raisins		1 cup	6¼ cups	230 g	1.4 kg
Apricots, dried, chopped		1 cup	6¼ cups	230 g	1.4 kg
Orange juice		2 cups	3 qt	480 ml	2.9 l
Stuffing mix, herb-seasoned		2 lb	12½ lb	900 g	5.6 kg
Eggs, beaten		2	12	2	12
Butter, melted		10 Tbsp	2 lb	150 g	900 g
Salt					
White pepper, fresh ground					
Chicken stock		½ cup	3 cups	120 ml	720 ml
Apricot jam, heated		1 cup	1½ qt	240 ml	1.4 l

1. Slice the roasts lengthwise in half about ¾ of the way through. Refrigerate.
2. In one bowl, combine light cream, sour cream, sugar, and sherry. Refrigerate overnight.
3. In another bowl, combine the raisins, apricots, and orange juice. Refrigerate overnight.
4. Preheat oven to 350°F (180°C).
5. Pound the roasts flat, but not too thin.
6. Drain the raisins and apricots.
7. Add raisins and apricots to the stuffing mix. Add the eggs, ⅗ of the butter, salt, and pepper.
8. Add enough stock to the stuffing mixture so that it will hold together.
9. Season the roasts with salt and pepper.
10. Lay roast cut side up and stuff with mixture.
11. Roll sides of roasts over the stuffing, skewer, and tie with string.
12. Place roasts in a baking dish with seams down. Roast for 1 hour and 45 minutes.
13. Combine the apricot jam and the remaining butter. Baste roast with jam mixture at least 3 times during roasting.
14. Warm cream sauce and serve with roast.

Seafood Baja

🦞 AMERICAN WINE SUGGESTION
Souverain Chardonnay

		U.S.		Metric	
Portions:		8	50	8	50
Butter		6 Tbsp	2⅓ cups	90 g	560 g
Virgin olive oil		6 Tbsp	2⅓ cups	90 ml	560 ml
Garlic cloves, minced		6	38	6	38
Red bell pepper, seeded and cubed		1	6	1	6
Green bell pepper, seeded and cubed		1	6	1	6
Green onions, chopped		12	75	12	75
White fish, cubed		1½ lb	9 lb	675 g	4.1 kg
Shrimp, medium, shelled and deveined		1 lb	6¼ lb	450 g	2.8 kg
Green grapes, seedless		1 lb	6¼ lb	450 g	2.8 kg
Lime juice		½ cup	3 cups	120 ml	720 ml
Cilantro, fresh, chopped		2 Tbsp	¾ cup	5 g	30 g
Rice servings, cooked		8	50	8	50
Limes, sliced, as needed for garnish					

1. Combine the butter and oil and heat over medium heat.
2. Add garlic, bell peppers, onions, and seafood. Sauté, stirring constantly, until fish is flaky and shrimp turns pink. Remove from heat.
3. Add grapes, lime juice, and cilantro.
4. Let sit for 4 to 5 minutes.
5. Serve with rice and garnish with lime slices.

Shrimp Shish Kebab

 AMERICAN WINE SUGGESTION
Simi Rosé of Cabernet

	U.S.		Metric	
Portions:	8	50	8	50
Shrimp, fresh, shelled and deveined	4 lb	25 lb	1.8 kg	11.3 kg
Green peppers, seeded and quartered	3	18	3	18
Cherry tomatoes	1 pt	6¼ pt	450 g	2.8 kg
Onions, quartered	1 lb	6¼ lb	450 g	2.8 kg
Mushrooms, stemmed	16	100	16	100
For Marinade:				
Pineapple juice	1 cup	6¼ cups	240 ml	1.5 l
Soy sauce	¼ cup	1⅔ cups	60 ml	400 ml
Honey	1½ Tbsp	10 Tbsp	25 ml	150 ml
Sesame oil	1 tsp	2 Tbsp	5 ml	30 ml
Ginger, minced	1 tsp	2 Tbsp	10 g	60 g
Cornstarch	1 Tbsp	6 Tbsp	9 g	60 g
Toasted sesame seeds	1 Tbsp	6 Tbsp	2 g	15 g

For Marinade:

1. Combine the pineapple juice, soy sauce, honey, sesame oil, ginger, cornstarch, and toasted sesame seeds, and cook until thick.
2. Add shrimp to marinade and marinate for 1 hour.

For Kebabs:

3. Preheat broiler or grill.
4. Arrange shrimp on skewers, alternating with pieces of peppers, tomatoes, onions, and mushrooms.
5. Cook kebabs on hot grill for 5 minutes or until done, turning as needed. When shrimp is pink, kebabs are done.

Soft-Shell Crab with Capers

🍃 AMERICAN WINE SUGGESTION
Robert Mondavi Fumé Blanc

	U.S.		Metric	
Portions:	8	50	8	50
Soft-shell crabs, cleaned and washed	24	150	24	150
Salt				
White pepper, fresh ground				
Flour, as needed for dredging				
Butter	1 cup	6½ cups	240 g	1.5 kg
Virgin olive oil	¼ cup	1½ cups	60 ml	360 ml
Lemon juice, fresh	1 lemon	6 lemons	1 lemon	6 lemons
Butter	2 Tbsp	¾ cup	30 g	180 g
Lemons, peeled and diced	4	25	4	25
Capers	1 cup	6½ cups	225 g	1.4 kg
Parsley, as needed				
Worcestershire sauce	2 Tbsp	¾ cup	30 ml	180 ml

1. Season the crabs with salt and pepper and dredge in flour.
2. Combine the butter and oil, and heat.
3. Sauté crabs, backs down, for 4 to 5 minutes.
4. Turn crabs and sauté for an additional 2 to 3 minutes. Remove from pan, sprinkle with lemon juice, and keep warm.
5. Heat the butter and sauté the lemons with capers, parsley, and Worcestershire sauce. Stir well until hot and pour sauce over crabs.
6. Serve with parsley.

Squid and Shrimp Sauté

❧ AMERICAN WINE SUGGESTION
Silverado Sauvignon Blanc

	Portions:	U.S.		Metric	
		8	50	8	50
Eggplants, peeled, julienne		4	25	4	25
Salt, as needed					
Virgin olive oil		1 cup	6½ cups	240 ml	1.5 l
Red bell pepper, julienne		2	12	2	12
Green pepper, julienne		2	12	2	12
Garlic cloves, minced		6	38	6	38
Squid, small, cleaned and sliced, reserve the tentacles		2	12	2	12
Shrimp, large, cleaned and deveined		32	200	32	200
Chili powder		2 tsp	¼ cup	5 g	30 g
Tomatoes, seeded and coarsely chopped		8	50	8	50
Lemon juice, fresh		2 lemons	12 lemons	2 lemons	12 lemons

1. Salt eggplant and chill for 1 hour.
2. Heat ¼ of the olive oil and brown the eggplant on both sides. Do not overcook. Remove from heat and keep warm. Reduce heat.
3. Add more oil to skillet, if needed, and sauté the pepper strips and garlic for 1 minute.
4. Add squid bodies, tentacles, shrimp, and eggplant strips. Cook until shrimp are pink.
5. Add chili powder and tomatoes. Simmer gently until slightly thickened.
6. Season with salt and lemon juice to taste.
7. Remove from heat and serve immediately.

Tuna with Tangerine Butter

❧ AMERICAN WINE SUGGESTION
William Hill Reserve Chardonnay

		U.S.		Metric	
Portions:		*8*	*50*	*8*	*50*
Basil, fresh, chopped		8 tsp	1 cup	5 g	32 g
Fennel leaves, chopped		8 tsp	1 cup	5 g	32 g
Tarragon, fresh, chopped		8 tsp	1 cup	6 g	50 g
Italian parsley, chopped		½ cup	3 cups	20 g	115 g
Virgin olive oil		1 cup	6¼ cups	240 ml	1.5 l
Tuna steaks, fresh, approximately 6 oz (170 g) each		8	50	8	50
Tangerine juice		2 cups	3 qt	480 ml	2.9 l
Butter		1 cup	6¼ cups	240 g	1.5 kg
Fresh herbs, as needed for garnish					

1. Preheat the grill.
2. Combine the basil, fennel, tarragon, parsley, and olive oil.
3. Grill the tuna steaks, basting with herb mixture, until pink on inside.
4. Bring tangerine juice to a boil.
5. Add the butter to the juice a small amount at a time, whisking constantly until thick.
6. Arrange herbs for garnish on plates. Place the tuna steaks on the bed of herbs, and spoon tangerine butter over them.

Veal Medallions with Lime and Ginger

🦃 AMERICAN WINE SUGGESTION
Mirrasou Pinot Blanc

		U.S.		Metric	
Portions:		8	50	8	50
Butter		¾ cup	4½ cups	180 g	1.1 kg
Veal medallions, 1 in. (3 cm) thick		8	50	8	50
Ginger, fresh, julienne		2 Tbsp	¾ cup	30 g	180 g
Lime juice		6 Tbsp	2⅓ cups	90 ml	560 ml
Veal stock		2 cups	3 qt	480 ml	2.9 l
Salt					
White pepper, fresh ground					
Lime wedges, as needed for garnish					

1. Melt some of the butter over a medium heat and sauté the veal medallions until brown, 4 to 5 minutes on each side.
2. Remove veal and keep warm. Discard butter.
3. Add ginger to sauté pan, and deglaze the pan over high heat with lime juice, and veal stock, stirring constantly.
4. Bring mixture to a boil and reduce by half, about 2 to 3 minutes. Remove from heat, strain liquid, and return to pan.
5. Reduce heat, and add remaining butter while whisking.
6. Season with salt and pepper.
7. Return medallions to pan to warm. Serve garnished with lime wedges.

Vegetable Chili

🦃 BEVERAGE SUGGESTION: BEER

	U.S.		Metric	
Portions:	8	50	8	50
Kidney beans, dry, soak overnight	¾ cup	4½ cups	170 g	1 kg
Water	3 cups	1⅛ gal	720 ml	4.3 l
Bulgur	½ cup	3 cups	115 g	680 g
Virgin olive oil	¾ cup	4½ cups	180 ml	1.1 l
Red onion, chopped	1	6	1	6
White onion, chopped	1	6	1	6
Garlic, minced	1¾ Tbsp	10½ Tbsp	17 g	105 g
Celery, chopped	½ cup	3 cups	115 g	680 g
Carrots, chopped	½ cup	3 cups	115 g	680 g
Chili powder	3 Tbsp	1⅛ cups	7 g	45 g
Cumin	2½ Tbsp	1 cup	15 g	90 g
Cayenne	½ tsp	1 Tbsp	1 g	6 g
Basil, fresh, chopped	1½ Tbsp	9 Tbsp	3 g	18 g
Oregano, chopped	1¼ Tbsp	½ cup	225 mg	15 g
Summer squash, cubed	1	6	1	6
Zucchini, cubed	1	6	1	6
Green pepper, diced	1	6	1	6
Red pepper, diced	1	6	1	6
Mushrooms, sliced	1 cup	6 cups	230 g	1.4 kg
Tomatoes, large, cubed	1	6	1	6
Tomato paste	¾ cup	4½ cups	180 ml	1.1 l
White wine	1 cup	1½ qt	240 ml	1.5 l
Salt				
White pepper, fresh ground				

1. Drain water from beans.
2. Place beans in a pot with fresh water to cover. Cook for 30 to 45 minutes.
3. Drain beans, reserving water.
4. Bring ⅙ of the water to a boil and pour over bulgur in a bowl. Let rest for 30 minutes.
5. In a skillet, heat the oil and sauté the onions.
6. Add the garlic, celery, and carrots. Cook until glazed.
7. Add chili powder, cumin, cayenne, basil, and oregano.
8. Cook over low heat for 3 to 5 minutes.
9. Add the squash, zucchini, peppers, and mushrooms. Cook for 2 to 3 minutes.
10. Add the bulgur, kidney beans, tomatoes, and reserved liquid. Cook until vegetables are tender.
11. Combine the tomato paste with white wine in a bowl, then add to the vegetable mixture. Continue to cook over low heat until mixture is heated through.
12. Season with salt and pepper and serve.

ACCOMPANIMENTS

Green Chili Mayonnaise

	U.S.	Metric
	Yields 4 cups	*Yields 4 cups*
Egg yolks	8	8
Cider vinegar	2 Tbsp	30 ml
Dijon mustard	2 tsp	10 g
Salt		
White pepper, fresh ground		
Virgin olive oil	2 cups	480 ml
Jalapeño peppers, minced	½ cup	120 g

1. Combine the egg yolks, vinegar, mustard, salt, and pepper, and beat until thick.
2. Slowly add the oil and blend well.
3. Stir in the minced jalapeños.
4. Refrigerate until needed.

Pizza Dough

		U.S.		Metric	
Portions:		8	50	8	50
All-purpose flour		3 lb	18 lb	1.3 kg	8.4 kg
Dry yeast, ¼ oz (7 g) envelopes		8	50	8	50
Warm water		1 qt	1½ gal	1 l	5.8 l
Virgin olive oil		½ cup	3 cups	120 ml	720 ml
Salt		2 Tbsp	¾ cup	30 g	180 g

1. Place flour in a large bowl. Make a well in the center.
2. Pour yeast into well and cover with ½ of the warm water. Let sit for 8 to 12 minutes to dissolve, stirring as necessary.
3. Add remaining water, olive oil, and salt. Mix well. Stir the flour in and mix well. If too dry, knead in additional water. If too sticky, add some flour.
4. Thoroughly knead the dough by hand on a floured surface until elastic in texture.
5. Transfer dough to floured sheet pan. Cover the dough with a damp cloth and let it rise until it is double its volume.
6. Remove dough and knead once more on a floured surface.
7. Let the dough rise an additional 45 minutes, or until it doubles its volume again.

Note: Pizza dough can be refrigerated for up to 1 week. Remove from the refrigerator and let rest at room temperature for 30 minutes before use.

Vegetables à la Grecque

		U.S.		Metric	
Portions:		8	50	8	50
Virgin olive oil		2 Tbsp	¾ cup	30 ml	180 ml
Onion, chopped		½ cup	3 cups	115 g	680 g
Garlic cloves, minced		1	6	1	6
Tomato paste		2 Tbsp	¾ cup	30 ml	180 ml
Tomatoes, large, diced		2	12	2	12
White wine, dry		¼ cup	1½ cups	60 ml	360 ml
Coriander, ground		½ tsp	1 Tbsp	1 g	6 g
Salt					
White pepper, fresh ground					
Zucchini, sliced		1	6	1	6
Eggplant, sliced		1	6	1	6
Artichokes, cleaned and trimmed		6	38	6	38
Cauliflower heads, florets only		1	6	1	6

1. In a heavy skillet, heat the oil and sauté the onion with garlic until translucent.
2. Add tomato paste and cook, stirring, for 1 minute.
3. Add the tomatoes, wine, coriander, and season with salt and pepper.
4. Cook for 30 minutes, stirring occasionally.
5. In a food processor, puree the tomato mixture and return to skillet.
6. Add the zucchini, eggplant, artichokes, and cauliflower.
7. Bring to a boil, reduce heat, and simmer until vegetables are tender, about 14 to 16 minutes.

DESSERTS

Apricot Soufflé with Ginger and Nutmeg Sauce

	U.S.		Metric	
Portions:	8	50	8	50
Butter, as needed to grease soufflé molds				
Sugar, as needed				
Apricots, dried, soak overnight	½ lb	3 lb	225 g	1.4 kg
Sugar	¾ cup	4½ cups	180 g	1.1 kg
Salt	Dash	To taste	Dash	To taste
Vanilla	½ tsp	1 Tbsp	2 ml	15 ml
Eggs, separated	4	25	4	25
Grand Marnier	¼ cup	1½ cups	60 ml	360 ml
Egg whites	2	12½	2	12½
Confectioner's sugar, as needed				

For Ginger and Nutmeg Sauce:

	U.S.		Metric	
Ginger, fresh, peeled and thinly sliced	½ cup	3 cups	115 g	680 g
Sugar	½ cup	3 cups	120 g	720 g
Water	¾ cup	4½ cups	180 ml	1.1 l
Nutmeg, whole, cracked	2	12½	2	12½
Light cream, scalded	2 cups	3 qt	480 ml	2.9 l
Egg yolks	8	50	8	50
Salt				
Vanilla	¼ tsp	1½ tsp	1 ml	7 ml

For Ginger and Nutmeg Sauce:

1. Cook ginger in sugar and water for 12 to 15 minutes or until ginger is tender.
2. Puree ginger in a food processor and strain through a fine sieve. Reserve.
3. Add the nutmeg to the cream and simmer.
4. In another saucepan, heat egg yolks, salt, and vanilla.
5. Strain the cream to remove the nutmeg. Slowly add the cream to the egg yolk mixture.
6. Cook the mixture over low heat until thick, stirring constantly. Do not boil. Remove from heat.
7. Add the ginger sauce to the cream mixture.

For Apricot Soufflé:

8. Preheat oven to 400°F (200°C).
9. Butter individual soufflé molds and add sugar to coat.
10. In a food processor, puree the drained apricots. Strain through a sieve to remove skins.
11. Add sugar, salt, vanilla, and egg yolks, and whip until pale in color.
12. Add the liqueur and whip again.
13. In another bowl, beat egg whites until soft peaks form.

14. Beat ⅓ of the whites into apricot mixture; then slowly fold in remaining whites. Mix well and pour into soufflé dishes.
15. Reduce oven temperature to 375°F (190°C).
16. Bake soufflés for 30 to 32 minutes or until risen and golden in hue.
17. Remove from oven and dust with confectioner's sugar. Serve immediately, with ginger and nutmeg sauce.

California Fruit Terrine

	Portions:	U.S. 8	U.S. 50	Metric 8	Metric 50
Unflavored gelatin, envelopes		4	25	4	25
White grape juice		1 qt	1½ gal	1 l	6 l
Strawberries, sliced		3 cups	4½ qt	680 g	4 kg
Kiwi, peeled and sliced		2	12	2	12
Mango, peeled and thinly sliced		1	6	1	6
For Dressing:					
Honey		¼ cup	1½ cups	60 ml	360 ml
Mayonnaise		½ cup	3 cups	120 ml	720 ml
Heavy cream		½ cup	3 cups	120 ml	720 ml
Raspberry puree		2 Tbsp	¾ cup	30 ml	180 ml

For Dressing:

1. Combine the honey, mayonnaise, and cream. Blend well.
2. Add the raspberry puree and mix.

For Fruit Terrine:

3. Soften gelatin in ½ of the grape juice. Heat to dissolve the gelatin.
4. Add remaining grape juice and let cool until thickened.
5. Fill a pan with ice.
6. Place a 9 in. (25 cm) loaf pan on top of the ice and let it cool.
7. Pour a thin layer of gelatin mixture into the bottom of the loaf pan.
8. Arrange ½ of the strawberry slices and all of the kiwi in a decorative pattern over the layer of gelatin. Allow to set.
9. Arrange a layer of mango on top of the strawberries and kiwi.
10. Cover mango with a layer of the gelatin mixture. Allow to set.
11. Top with the remaining strawberries and cover with additional gelatin mixture, allowing it to set.
12. Chill to completely set.
13. To serve, unmold, slice, and serve with dressing.

Frozen Chocolate Terrine

		U.S.		Metric	
Portions:		*8*	*50*	*8*	*50*
Half and half		1 cup	6¼ cups	240 ml	1.5 l
Whipping cream		1 cup	6¼ cups	240 ml	1.5 l
Vanilla beans, split		2	12	2	12
Egg yolks		8	50	8	50
Sugar		½ cup	3 cups	120 g	720 g
Coffee liqueur		¼ cup	1½ cups	60 ml	360 ml
White chocolate, imported, chopped		1½ oz	9½ oz	45 g	270 g
Semisweet chocolate, chopped		1½ oz	9½ oz	45 g	270 g
Milk chocolate, chopped		1½ oz	9½ oz	45 g	275 g
Whipping cream, chilled		1½ cups	9½ cups	360 ml	2.3 l
Sour cream		⅓ cup	2 cups	80 ml	480 ml

For Coffee Sauce: Yields 2 cups (480 ml) for 8; 3qt (2.9 l) for 50

Water		½ cup	3 cups	120 ml	720 ml
Unsalted butter		½ cup	3 cups	120 g	720 g
Light corn syrup		6 Tbsp	2⅓ cups	90 ml	560 ml
Brandy		2 Tbsp	¾ cup	30 ml	180 ml
Instant coffee powder		1 tsp	2 Tbsp	5 ml	30 ml
Salt					
Semisweet chocolate, chopped		8 oz	3 lb, 2 oz	230 g	1.4 kg

For Ganache: Yields ½ cup (120 ml) for 8; 3 cups (720 ml) for 50

Whipping cream		⅓ cup	2 cups	80 ml	480 ml
Semisweet chocolate, chopped		1 oz	6 oz	30 g	170 g

For Coffee Sauce:

1. Bring water, butter, corn syrup, brandy, coffee, and salt to a boil. Remove from heat.
2. Add chocolate, cover, and let stand for 8 minutes. Stir until smooth.
3. Let cool for about 25 minutes. Reserve until needed.

For Ganache:

4. Bring cream to a boil. Remove from heat, add chopped chocolate, and stir until smooth.
5. Let stand to cool, about 30 minutes. Reserve until needed.

For Terrine:

6. Butter a loaf pan [9 in. × 5 in. × 3 in. (25 cm × 12 cm × 8 cm)].
7. Cut parchment paper to line the pan, allowing paper to hang over the edges.
8. Combine the half and half and the cream. Add vanilla beans and bring to a boil. Remove cream mixture from heat, remove vanilla beans, and let stand for 20 minutes.
9. In a bowl, beat the egg yolks and sugar until thick and pale, about 4 minutes.

10. Bring the cream mixture back to a simmer. Remove from heat and add to the egg yolks, whisking gently.
11. Stir custard over low heat until thick, about 10 minutes.
12. Strain the custard into a bowl and add the coffee liqueur.
13. Place white chocolate, semisweet chocolate, and milk chocolate in separate bowls.
14. Add ⅓ of the custard to each bowl. Stir until chocolate has melted and is smooth.
15. Refrigerate each for 20 to 25 minutes. Do not let set firmly. Remove from refrigerator and bring to room temperature.
16. Chill loaf pan in the freezer.
17. Whip chilled cream in a large bowl until thick. Fold in the sour cream and beat until soft peaks form.
18. Fold ⅓ of the cream into the white chocolate mixture. Mix well and place in bottom of loaf pan to make the first layer. Smooth with a spatula and return to freezer for 2 hours.
19. For the second layer, spread the ganache over the first layer. Return to the freezer for 1 hour.
20. Rewhip the cream and add half to the milk chocolate mixture. Mix well and place over the layer of ganache. Smooth with a spatula and return to the freezer for 2 hours.
21. Repeat step 20, using the semisweet chocolate mixture.
22. Freeze overnight.

To Serve:

23. Dip the loaf pan into hot water to loosen. Remove the terrine from the loaf pan.
24. Heat knife under warm water. Use warm knife to remove parchment paper. Cut terrine into slices and serve with coffee sauce.

Fresh Fruit Tart   COLOR PLATE 32

	U.S.	Metric
	For 1 Tart	For 1 Tart
Pastry, enough for 1 tart		
Milk	2 cups	480 ml
Sugar	½ cup	120 g
Vanilla bean	1	1
Flour	2 Tbsp	15 g
Cornstarch	1 Tbsp	9 g
Egg yolks, large	3	3
Heavy cream, whipped	½ cup	120 ml
Fresh fruit, as desired	2 cups	450 g
Apricot preserves	1 cup	225 g

1. Preheat oven to 350°F (180°C).
2. Line a 10 in. (25 cm) flan ring with pastry, cover with parchment paper, weight center, and bake for 30 minutes or until golden. Flatten crust if bubbles form. Set aside.
3. Combine ¾ of the milk with the sugar and vanilla bean. Slowly bring to a boil and then remove from heat. Remove vanilla bean.
4. Stir together the remaining milk, flour, and cornstarch. Add the egg yolks to the mixture and blend well.
5. Add the egg mixture to the milk and sugar mixture. Return to medium heat and cook until thick, stirring constantly. Remove from heat.
6. Cover custard with wax paper and cool to room temperature using an ice bath.
7. Remove paper and chill for 2½ hours in the refrigerator.
8. When well chilled, fold in whipped cream. Pour mixture into flan.
9. Wash fruit thoroughly, pitting as needed, and slicing evenly.
10. Starting at the outside rim, arrange fruit, alternating colors to contrast.
11. Melt apricot preserves and spread over fruit to glaze.

Hawaiian Pineapple Nut Cake

		U.S.		Metric	
Portions:		*8*	*50*	*8*	*50*
Flour		¾ cup	4 ⅔ cups	85 g	525 g
Baking soda		¼ tsp	1⅔ tsp	750 mg	5 g
Salt		⅛ tsp	¾ tsp	625 mg	3.75 g
Butter, melted		½ cup	3¼ cups	120 ml	780 ml
Sugar		1 cup	6¼ cups	240 g	1.5 kg
Eggs, beaten		2	12	2	12
Pineapple, crushed, 8 oz (227 g) cans, drained		1	6¼	1	6¼
Nuts, chopped		½ cup	3¼ cups	115 g	740 g
Heavy cream, unsweetened, whipped		1 cup	6¼ cups	240 ml	1.5 l

1. Preheat oven to 325°F (160°C).
2. Sift together the flour, baking soda, and salt. Reserve.
3. Combine the butter and sugar, beating constantly.
4. Add the beaten eggs and mix.
5. Add the sifted flour and stir until blended.
6. Add the pineapple and nuts and mix well.
7. Grease 9 in. (25 cm) pan(s) and pour in the mixture. Bake for 45 minutes to 1 hour.
8. Top with fresh whipped cream before serving.

Hazelnut Cheesecake

		U.S.		Metric	
Portions:		8	50	8	50
Hazelnuts		1 cup	6½ cups	230 g	1.4 kg
Cream cheese, softened at room temperature		2 lb	12½ lb	900 g	5.6 kg
Sugar		1¾ cups	5 lb., 1 cup	420 g	2.6 kg
Eggs		4	25	4	25
Lemon rind, grated		½ tsp	1 Tbsp	250 mg	15 g

1. Preheat oven to 350°F (180°C).
2. Cook the hazelnuts in the oven on a baking sheet for 8 to 10 minutes or until brown.
3. Remove skins and coarsely grind nuts in a food processor.
4. Using a mixer, whip the cream cheese until fluffy.
5. Add the sugar and beat.
6. Add the eggs, one at a time.
7. Add hazelnuts and lemon rind. Mix well.
8. Pour batter into a 10 in. (25 cm) flan ring.
9. Place flan in a deep baking dish and surround it with hot water.
10. Bake for 1½ hours or until done.
11. When done, leave cake in oven to cool for 1 hour, with door open and oven off. Top should be golden brown.

Macadamia Pie

	U.S.		Metric	
Portions:	8	50	8	50

For Crust:

Flour, sifted	1 cup	6¼ cups	115 g	700 g
Salt	¼ tsp	1½ tsp	1.25 g	7.5 g
Sugar	1 Tbsp	6 Tbsp	15 g	95 g
Butter	⅓ cup	2 cups	80 g	480 g
Ice water	2 Tbsp	¾ cup	30 ml	180 ml

For Filling:

Butter	½ cup	1⅓ lb	120 g	640 g
Sugar	¾ cup	4 ⅔ cups	180 g	1.1 kg
Eggs, slightly beaten	3	19	3	19
Dark corn syrup	¾ cup	4 ⅔ cups	180 ml	1.1 l
Salt				
Vanilla	1 tsp	2 Tbsp	5 ml	30 ml
Macadamia nuts, chopped	1 cup	6¼ cups	230 g	1.4 kg
Whipped cream, as needed for garnish				

For Crust:

1. Combine the sifted flour, salt, sugar, and butter. Mix well.
2. Add ice water and mix lightly. Knead the dough.
3. Roll out on a flour-dusted surface.
4. Line pie pan with dough and refrigerate until needed.

For Filling:

5. Cream the butter, adding the sugar gradually. Whip until light and creamy in color.
6. Add the beaten eggs.
7. Add the dark corn syrup, salt, vanilla, and nuts. Mix well, then pour into pie shell.
8. Bake for 30 to 40 minutes. Remove from oven and cool on pie rack.
9. Garnish with whipped cream before serving.

White Chocolate and Macadamia Brownies

	U.S. For 24 brownies	Metric For 24 brownies
Butter, as needed		
Flour, unbleached	1 cup	115 g
Salt	¼ tsp	1.25 g
Eggs, large	2	2
Sugar	½ cup	120 g
White chocolate, imported, chopped and melted	7 oz	200 g
Unsalted butter, melted	½ cup	120 ml
Vanilla	1 tsp	5 ml
Macadamia nuts, unsalted, chopped	1 cup	230 g
White chocolate, imported, coarsely chopped	5 oz	140 g

For Hot Fudge Sauce: Yields 1½ cups (360 ml)

Whipping cream	¾ cup	180 ml
Sugar	¼ cup	60 g
Semisweet chocolate, chopped	5 oz	140 g
Unsalted butter	2 Tbsp	30 g
Light corn syrup	2 Tbsp	30 ml

For Hot Fudge Sauce:

1. Cook cream with sugar until sugar dissolves.
2. Add chocolate, stirring until smooth.
3. Add butter and corn syrup, stirring until melted and smooth.

For Brownies:

4. Preheat oven to 350°F (180°C).
5. Butter and flour a 9 in. × 13 in. (25 cm × 32 cm) baking pan.
6. Sift flour and salt into a bowl.
7. In a separate large bowl, beat eggs until frothy.
8. Add the sugar, 1 Tbsp (15 g) at a time, beating until pale yellow.
9. Gently fold in the melted chocolate.
10. Add melted butter and vanilla. Stir well.
11. Add the flour mixture, the nuts, and the chopped chocolate. Mix well.
12. Pour mixture into prepared baking pan. Bake for 20 minutes or until done. Do not overbake.
13. Cool on rack, cut, and serve with hot fudge sauce.

Nutritional Notes

❦ Suggested Daily Servings

Food Group	Suggested Daily Servings	Examples of Servings
Grains, breads, cereals	6–11	1 slice of bread 1 oz (30 g) roll ½ cup (115 g) of cooked rice ½ cup (115 g) of pasta
Fruits	2–4	1 apple, pear, etc. ¾ cup (180 ml) juice
Vegetables	3–5	½ cup (115 g) cooked 1 cup (225 g) raw
Milk, cheese, yogurt	2–3	1 cup (240 ml) of milk or yogurt 2 oz (60 g) of processed cheese 1½ oz (43 g) of natural cheese
Meat, poultry, fish, eggs, legumes, nuts	2–3	Amounts should total 5–6 oz (140–170 g) serving of lean meat or equivalent
Fats, sweets, alcohol	Use in limited amounts	

🍎 Substitutions for Lowering Fat Intake

	Lower Fat Items to Replace	Items Higher in Fat and Cholesterol
Beef	Select or choice grades, round, loin, diet lean ground (drain excess fat after cooking)	Prime grade, lean or regular ground, marbled cuts
Poultry	Skinless, white meat, lean ground	Domestic duck and goose
Veal	Trimmed veal	Veal with visible fat, ground veal with fat added
Lamb	Leg, loin, arm	Any marbled cuts
Pork	Tenderloin, leg, arm, picnic, Canadian bacon	Bacon, ribs
Forcemeat	Should be made in-house with reduced fat ingredients. Commercial chicken or turkey sausage can be as high in fat as pork sausage	
Eggs	Egg whites, cholesterol-free egg substitutes	Egg yolks
Cheese	Low fat with less than 3 g of fat per oz, part skim milk cheese	Whole-milk cheese, cream cheese
Dairy	Skim milk or 1% fat milk, low-fat buttermilk, evaporated skim milk, nonfat yogurt, light or imitation sour cream	Whole milk, whole-milk yogurt, sour cream, full-fat cream, half and half, most nondairy creamers

To reduce the tartness of yogurt, drain it through a filter over a bowl before use. The longer it drains, the thicker it will become. Draining for several hours will produce yogurt cheese, which can be used as a substitute for cream cheese in some recipes. To prevent yogurt from separating during cooking, temper before adding to hot products, add toward the end of the cooking period, and/or add a tsp of cornstarch per cup (240 ml) of yogurt.

Light cream can be used as a substitute for heavy cream. Use 1 cup of light cream with 1 tsp of cornstarch in place of each cup of heavy cream.

	Lower Fat Items to Replace	*Items Higher in Fat and Cholesterol*
Fruits, Vegetables, Legumes	*Fresh, frozen, or dried, without sulfites or sulfates*	*Coconuts, avocados, olives, any items prepared with fat*
Breads	*Most lean dough breads. Whole-grain breads are a better source of fiber and minerals than refined flour breads. Low-fat crackers (2–3 g of fat or less per serving)*	*Rich doughs, sweet rolls, puff pastry, croissants, high-fat crackers*
Grains	*Whole grains or enriched grains such as rice, barley, bulgur, quinoa, pasta*	*Granola cereals, any grains prepared with fat*
Miscellaneous	*Nonfat frozen yogurt, ice milk, fat-free or low-fat cookies, fruit ices, sorbets, poached and baked fruits, phyllo leaves, reduced-fat whipped cream, cocoa, and carob powder*	*Ice cream, cakes and pies, tarts, cookies, frozen tofu, whipped cream, pastry, chocolate, cocoa butter, carob prepared with saturated fat*

Bibliography

Amory, Cleveland, et al. *The American Heritage Cookbook and Illustrated History of American Eating and Drinking*. New York: The New York American Heritage Publishing Company, 1964.

Apicius. *The Roman Cookery Book*. Translated by Barbara Flower and Elizabeth Rosenbaum. London: Harrap, 1958.

Athanaeus, of Naucratis. *The Deipnosophists*. Translated by C.D. Young. London: Henry G. Bohn, 1854.

Bartlett, John. *Familiar Quotations*. 15th ed. Edited by Emily Morison Beck. Boston: Little, Brown and Company, 1980.

Better Homes and Gardens Heritage Cookbook. Des Moines: Meridith Corporation, 1975.

Durant, Will. *The Story of Civilization*. New York: Simon and Schuster, 1935–1975.

Levenstein, Harvey. *Revolution at the Table: The Transformation of the American Diet*. New York: Oxford University Press, 1988.

Meisel, Anthony, and Sehila Rosenzweig. *American Wine*. London: QED Publishing Limited, 1983.

Index

283